Edward Kellogg, Mary Kellogg Putnam

Labor and capital : a new monetary system : the only means of securing the respective rights of labor and property and of protecting the public from financial revulsions

Edward Kellogg, Mary Kellogg Putnam

Labor and capital : a new monetary system : the only means of securing the respective rights of labor and property and of protecting the public from financial revulsions

ISBN/EAN: 9783337229290

Printed in Europe, USA, Canada, Australia, Japan

Cover: Foto ©Suzi / pixelio.de

More available books at **www.hansebooks.com**

LABOR AND CAPITAL;

A

NEW MONETARY SYSTEM:

THE ONLY MEANS OF

SECURING THE RESPECTIVE RIGHTS OF LABOR
AND PROPERTY,

AND OF

PROTECTING THE PUBLIC FROM FINANCIAL REVULSIONS.

BY

EDWARD KELLOGG.

REVISED FROM HIS WORK ON "LABOR AND OTHER CAPITAL,"
WITH NUMEROUS ADDITIONS FROM HIS MANUSCRIPTS.
TO WHICH IS PREFIXED A BIOGRAPHICAL SKETCH OF THE AUTHOR.

EDITED BY HIS DAUGHTER,
MARY KELLOGG PUTNAM.

NEW YORK:
JOHN W. LOVELL COMPANY,
14 AND 16 VESEY STREET,
1883.

TABLE OF CONTENTS.

	PAGE
BIOGRAPHICAL SKETCH OF THE AUTHOR	xi
PREFACE	xxv
INTRODUCTION	17

PART I.

PRINCIPLES OF DISTRIBUTION.

CHAPTER I.

Of Value.. 41

CHAPTER II.

MONEY, THE MEDIUM OF DISTRIBUTION.

SECTION I.

The Nature and Properties of Money.................... 45

SECTION II.

The Power of Money to Represent Value................ 46

SECTION III.

The Power of Money to Measure Value.................. 56

CONTENTS.

SECTION IV.
The Power of Money to Accumulate Value by Interest,   61

SECTION V.
The Power of Money to Exchange Value, ...   68

SECTION VI.
The Material of Money, and the Distinctions between Money and the Material of which it is made, ...   71

CHAPTER III.

THE RATES OF INTEREST THE GOVERNING POWER OF DISTRIBUTION TO LABOR AND CAPITAL.

SECTION I.
The Power of Capital to accumulate Property and Labor, according to the Rate of Interest, ...   79

SECTION II.
The Wealth of Cities, and the Means of its Accumulation, ...   97

SECTION III.
Interest received by the Citizens of New York on Loans to the Country, ...   107

SECTION IV.
The per centage Actual Increase of the Value of the Property of the States of New York and Massachusetts, compared with the per centage Legal Increase on the Property of these States for the same periods, ...   111

CONTENTS.

SECTION V.
Interest on National and State Debts, ... 121

SECTION VI.
No Accumulation of Property by Labor equal to the Accumulation by the Loan of Money at seven per cent. Interest,................................ 126

SECTION VII.
Two Per Cent. per annum too high a Rate of Interest, 135

SECTION VIII.
The Reduction of Interest would be an equal benefit to the Producing Classes, whether Property should Rise or Fall in Price, in consequence of such reduction,. 139

SECTION IX.
Effects upon Producers of High and Fluctuating Rates of Interest, ... 142

SECTION X.
The Oppression of Labor by a Monopoly of Land not so great as the Oppression by High Rates of Interest on money, ... 147

SECTION XI.
The Rate of Interest determines the Price of Property, and a Rise of Interest increases the Power of Money to command property,....................... 153

SECTION XII.
The Rise of the Rate of Interest increases the Liabilities of all Debtors, ... 154

SECTION XIII.

Rents, whether High or Low, bear the same Relative Value to their Principal; but when the Per Centage Interest on money is Increased, not only is its Relative Proportion to the principal Increased, but each Fractional Part has Increased Value, ... 158

SECTION XIV.

To Cheapen Prices by an Unjust Rate of Interest and a Scarcity of Money, is but to Cheapen the Labor of all producers, and Give their Earnings to Capitalists without an equitable equivalent, ... 161

SECTION XV.

Voluntary Agreement no Test of a just Rate of Interest,........................... 164

SECTION XVI.

The Law of Interest on Money an Accumulative not a Producing power,........................ 169

SECTION XVII.

Estimate of a just Rate of Interest,.............. 175

SECTION XVIII.

Beneficial Results to Laborers and Merchants from the Reduction of the Rate of Interest, ... 178

SECTION XIX.

The Low Prices of Labor in European countries not caused by their Low Rates of Interest,.......... 185

CHAPTER IV.

THE BANKING SYSTEM.

SECTION I.

	PAGE
The Nature of Banks, their Institution, and the Principles by which they are governed,	193

SECTION II.

The Amount of Specie owned by the Banks, and the Interest paid by the people on Bank Loans,	203

SECTION III.

Basis of the Bank of England,	215

SECTION IV.

The Balancing Power of Bank Notes and Deposits,	217

SECTION V.

The Management of the Banks, and the Effects of their operation upon the Prosperity of Trade and Productive Industry,	219

SECTION VI.

Remarks on the Repeal of the Usury Laws,	249

CHAPTER V.

The Amount of a Currency should be Limited *only* by the Wants of Business,	254

CHAPTER VI.

The Necessity of Credit,	261

CHAPTER VII.

A well regulated Currency Impossible under Present Laws, ... 263

Recapitulation, ... 265

PART II.

A TRUE MONETARY SYSTEM.

CHAPTER I.
The Security of a Paper Currency, ... 269

CHAPTER II.
THE SAFETY FUND.

SECTION I.
The Formation of the Money, and the Mode of Issue, 273

SECTION II.
The Security of the Safety Fund money, ... 278

SECTION III.
The Rate of Interest on the Safety Fund money, ... 282

SECTION IV.
Organization and Management of the Safety Fund, .. 286

SECTION V.
The probable Amount of Safety Fund money, ... 288

CHAPTER III.

The Advantages of the Safety Fund money over Specie, ... 290

CHAPTER IV.

OBJECTIONS TO THE SAFETY FUND CONSIDERED.

SECTION I.

Objections to a Paper Currency on account of Foreign Trade considered,........................... 295

SECTION II.

Sundry Objections—the Effects of the Safety Fund on our Banking Institutions, etc., considered,........ 300

CHAPTER V.

Advantages of the Safety Fund, ... 307

CONCLUSION, ... 318

APPENDIX, ... 325

BIOGRAPHICAL SKETCH OF THE AUTHOR.

As an introduction to the fifth edition of my father's work, and in compliance with repeated requests, I shall offer a sketch—though it must be an imperfect one—of his life; chiefly for the sake of telling why and how this book was written.

Edward Kellogg was born at Norwalk, Conn., on the 18th day of October, 1790. He was the son of a substantial farmer, enjoying the comforts of life; each child of the numerous family, however, was expected to do its part toward the common support; and he was early set at work, bringing the cows from the pasture, riding the horse while his older brother ploughed, and doing, when he was ten years old, half a man's work hoeing corn. The hired men who harvested for his father, observing the lad's deep set, deep blue eyes, said to each other in their homely phrase that he would make a smart man. Soon after he was of age, he began to buy goods in New York and sell them to country storekeepers in New Jersey, Pennsylvania, Maryland and Virginia, learning a great deal about men and things in the journeys he made for this purpose. In 1817 he married Esther F. Warner, daughter of Lyman Warner, of Northfield, in his native State. Two or three years later he was established in New York as a wholesale dry goods merchant; soon as senior partner of the firm of Kellogg & Baldwin, and later as chief of the firm of Edward Kellogg & Co. of Pearl street.

When he was about thirty years old his mind was deeply wrought upon by questions of theology and morals, and reading the Bible only, he abandoned the so-called orthodox tenets; when matters of business were not immediately before him, he studied ardently in his own thoughts the relations of man to his Creator and to his fellow-man; on his way from one engagement to another, he usually pondered the meaning of some text of Scripture. He read very few books, but he talked much with other men, and always weighed new thoughts that were thrown out. Singularly fearless and free in mind, he was continually investigating opinions to ascertain whether they were true; and whenever he had learned anything he was quick to communicate it to others. But he chiefly sought to draw out their minds and induce them to think for themselves. To this end he used to talk much with young persons; and, in the intervals of business, with the young men who were employed in his counting-house. His thirst for knowledge was so great that he seriously contemplated giving up business and devoting himself to study. At the same time he was eminently practical. No facilities then existed for ascertaining quickly the commercial standing of men, and the firm often sold on credit to persons living in remote parts of the South and West. When a new customer appeared the clerks would call Mr. Kellogg to talk with him a few minutes, and then he would say whether to sell or not. One of these young men, who learned business under him and is now the president of a national bank in the city of New York, says of him: "He was the best judge of men that I ever knew; his judgment of them was almost infallible." A man of stainless character and reputation, he conducted a large business with honor and success. His advice was frequently sought by younger men; and he was called upon to fill various offices of trust. During those years he did not speak of business matters at home, but he talked much with friends and neighbors about theological doctrines, principles of morality, about political questions and the management of the banks. As a child I used to sit down near him to listen, being greatly attracted by his animated and earnest discourse.

In 1837, the financial panic occurring, he was unable to make collections from his debtors, and, though having assets largely in excess of his liabilities, was obliged to suspend payment, and saw his affairs thrown into what seemed to be almost inextricable confusion. But, gifted with indomitable energy and courage, he met misfortune for himself unflinchingly; maintaining his integrity and reputation, saying afterward, "If I lost everything I had, I was determined not to lose myself." When an old acquaintance, who died a few years ago leaving a princely fortune, came one evening with his wife to drink tea and said, in lugubrious tones, "Mr. Kellogg, what *are* we coming to?" my father instantly replied in his pleasant way, "It is plain what you and I are coming to, Mr. P.: we are coming to our tow trousers again;" whereupon the questioner laughed heartily for the first time since the panic, and they spent a cheerful evening.

Yet, while he thought carefully and anxiously of his obligations and attended faithfully to all that was to be done, his mind turned with earnest and eager inquiry to the cause of the great calamity in which he saw so many involved. He perceived that it was the result of the existing monetary system, and he began to study out the origin of the evils. He soon became convinced that the money of a country, being a public medium of exchange, ought not to be put under the control of private corporations, but ought to be instituted by the government for the benefit of the whole people, and so managed that usury could not be exacted, and that losses in exchange in sending money from one part of the country to another should not be incurred. His soul was moved with indignation at the extortions of usurers, which came continually under his notice; and he caused a friend to write a pamphlet setting forth some facts that he furnished. This was printed in 1841 by Harper & Brothers, and was called "Usury and its Effects: A National Bank a Remedy. By Whitehook." His idea then was that a national bank should be created with a capital of fifty millions, with branches in every State, limited in dividends to five or six per cent., and compelled when its surplus profits exceeded five per cent. on the capital to reduce the rate of interest on its loans. He had not yet ascertained the real nature of money nor devised the true remedy.

He still worked in his mind at the problem, for he knew he had not solved it. He saw that money ought not to be made of gold and silver, which cannot be had in sufficient quantities to meet any great financial crisis, and which nobody wants when confidence exists; that it must be a legal representative of value, and thought it ought to be founded on real estate, or on the public credit resting on the national resources; he saw how to issue it in exchange for mortgages of productive real property—there was no great public debt—but how to redeem it? He tried it in every way he could imagine; he knew there must be some right way of doing it, but what was it? it was of no use to point out the evil unless he could show a remedy for it. He thought upon it by night and by day, and at last, after looking for it three years, one night in the spring of 1843, as he lay in his bed revolving once more his problem, it dawned upon him like an inspiration, "REDEEM IT WITH A BOND BEARING INTEREST." He turned it to and fro for a moment and exclaimed, in the very words of the old philosopher, "*I have found it!*"

Deeply impressed with the value of his discovery, he began at once to write out his ideas. He had had only a common school education, and, as he used to say, "very little of that." He thought himself "the furthest man in the world from writing a book." He disliked to write letters, and made his clerks write for him if possible. But now, morning and evening in the midst of his family, and in moments snatched from business at his counting-house, he set down upon paper the new and stirring thoughts with which his mind overflowed. He had ever been apt to teach, adapting himself carefully to the minds of others, and taking the greatest pains to make facts and ideas intelligible to them; and he wrote simply and vividly. But thinking some revision was desirable, and not having the time nor the practice to do it easily himself, he caused one of the young men in his employment to copy and amend for him. One evening—I was then seventeen years old and was always hovering about him—he showed me some leaves of the manuscript. In my secret heart I thought the amendments were not well made; but I only said to my beloved father, "I think I could do that." A little surprised, he rejoined, "Do you? well, you may try." The next morning he left some pages with me; at night I had a copy ready for him, which he altogether approved; and from that day I became his "scribe," and presently his devout disciple. He was intensely moved by the wrongs that he saw everywhere weighing on the workers of the world through this gigantic, hidden power of money; he knew he had devised the means to overthrow this power, so he worked on at a white heat. Now his relatives and friends began to remonstrate with him. One man of mark, a lifelong friend whom he greatly valued, said to him: "Mr. Kellogg, this is the most difficult part of political economy; no one has ever understood it. It has puzzled the wisest heads from the beginning until now, and you cannot solve it: you will only succeed in bewildering yourself. Besides, your own affairs are in a very perplexing condition and require all your attention; and it is *against your interest* to do anything about it." To which he replied: "I have an interest in the human family, and I have discovered something that is for their benefit. I shall write it; I should if I knew that I could make a million of dollars if I did not; and that if I did, I should live on a crust of bread and die in a garret." So the writing went on.

About the last of July, 1843, enough had been written to cover, as he thought, the important points. He cast about to see whom he could interest in it, and how he should get it printed. Having a high opinion of Mr. Horace Greeley's character and benevolent aims, he invited him to come and hear it read. Mr. Greeley, ever prompt to consider any proposition for bettering the condition of mankind, accordingly came twice to Brooklyn—whither the author had removed in 1838—and my father assigned to me the pleasant task of reading the manuscript to him. The good man heard it through, and said it ought to be published: he seized upon it and carried it away with him, giving it, with my father's consent, to Burgess & Stringer, 222 Broadway, to be published. It was printed at the author's cost, in newspaper form, of which, so far as I know, only the one copy now in my possession is extant. It was entitled, "Usury: the Evil and the Remedy;" and contained the following paragraphs, this being the original of what is now attributed to many different persons and called the interchangeable bonds and money proposition. I quote as follows:

"For the purpose I have before mentioned [to supply the people with a good and sound currency], the United States should establish an institution, which I shall here call a Safety Fund. I give it this name because I think it will be the means of securing to the producers a fair remuneration for their productions. It will save us from the power of any foreign nation over our Internal Improvements, or anything else of great importance. It will enable the nation—as far as man can have such control—to decide its own destiny. Therefore it will be a NATIONAL SAFETY FUND.

"In order to explain the nature of this Safety Fund, I will here write out, in full, two bills, one for a circulating medium, the other for a Treasury Note. By reading these the system may be almost entirely understood. Should such an institution be established, the bills might be more brief, as the laws on the subject would be known, and it would be unnecessary to have as much expressed as in the following:

(*Circulating Medium, or Safety Fund Note.*)

"The United States promise to pay to A. B., or bearer, at their Safety Fund, in the City of ———, One Hundred Dollars, in a Treasury Note, bearing interest at the rate of two per cent. per annum, payable half-yearly in gold or silver coin; and until such payment is made this note shall be a legal tender for debts, the same as gold and silver coins are now a tender."

(*Treasury Note.*)

"One year from the first day of May next, or any time thereafter, the UNITED STATES promise to pay to A. B., or bearer, in the City of ———, One Hundred Dollars, in Safety Fund Notes; and until such payment is made, to pay interest thereon half-yearly on the first days of May and November, at the rate of two per cent. per annum in gold or silver."

"It will be perceived that the note intended as a circulating medium is made a tender for all debts, that it is issued by Government, and payable in Treasury Notes. The Treasury Notes are to bear interest; hence there can be no money in circulation but what the holder can at any time put on interest where the loan would be entirely safe, and the interest payable half-yearly in specie; so that money can, at all times, be loaned for a certain income secured by the nation. One year after the first of May ensuing, the holder can convert the loan again into the legal currency of the country, so there never can be a surplus of money which may not be made productive."

The newspaper contains no date of publication, but the leading article of the New York *Tribune* of August 17, 1843, evidently from the pen of Mr. Greeley, had the heading, "Usury: the Evil and the Remedy," and began, "Such is the title of a powerful essay which has recently been published in this city, in a cheap newspaper form designed for general circulation. The intent of the author is evidently to probe the evil to the bottom, and not to rest in mere grumbling at it, but devise and suggest adequate means for its removal." The main features of the plan are clearly and forcibly stated in this article, with a recommendation to all who think excessive interest an evil to procure and read the paper.

My father then did his utmost to circulate the essay. He sent it to many editors, the paper itself containing a request that they would copy parts of it for the good of the public. On the 28th of October of the same year, a synopsis of it in four columns was printed in the *Tribune;* and, in December of the same year, it was issued, at his cost, as a supplement to the New York *Commercial Advertiser.* Then he had it put in pamphlet form, with some additions, and stereotyped. It was called "Currency: the Evil and the Remedy," by Godek Gardwell, these words containing the letters of his name.

About this time or a little later, he gave up business as a merchant, and, retaining an office in New York, spent his time in the care and improvement of his property. He continued to think and to write on the money question. Sometimes he wrote at length, but oftener a few pages only on any point that was in his mind. When a "good idea" occurred to him he set it down. Sometimes the same in slightly varied form appeared often, especially in regard to the representative value of money. The subject was so important, the need of clear ideas and simple illustrations to combat the old errors so evident, it was all so urgent that he could not say it too emphatically or too much. Then the subject ramified in such a way; it was so vast, touching upon most of the material interests of men; it lay at the foundation of public justice and good morals: the new system was capable of effecting a beneficent revolution, and would, too, by and by. All these things and more were seeking expression. His mind worked so deeply that he often went along the street, noticing nobody, seeing only the idea that he was pursuing and endeavoring to seize.

Some time after the essay was published, when he had a mass of papers thus written, various in subject and length, he told me he wanted me to "arrange them in some order," copy, and get the whole ready for the printer. Though dismayed at being called upon to set in order the subject-matter, it did not occur to me to say I could not do it; I must at least try, if my father expected it. After a time I thought I saw the proper sequence of the argument, and sorted and arranged the papers in chapters and sections accordingly. Perhaps a less formal mode might have been better; but the author himself found no fault with it: he, with his originating mind, "would rather write ten than arrange one;" and he was occupied in searching out ideas and principles. Almost every day there was something new; a page or two came home on the back of a letter or on a sheet of paper doubled up in his pocket, and must be assigned to the proper place; sometimes a section rewritten because the new was better, or to introduce fitly a fresh idea or illustration; then a large part of the chapter on the banking system was written. I used to go over it all again and again by myself during the days while he was away at his office, occasionally suggesting the writing of something on this or that point to fill out the course of thought; and in the evenings and on Sundays he read it over, or we read it over together; sometimes spending hours on a single paragraph, to make it clear and simple. Unwearying thought and care were bestowed on the whole; but the chapter on the nature of money received specially vigilant and repeated revision. For recreation we used to talk together, often into the midnight hours, of the blessings that would flow to mankind from this grand new truth; and we said, that some day the nature of money would be so well understood, and the system so much a matter of course, that people would wonder it had ever been needful to write such a book, or take such pains to argue the question. When it was nearly finished he invited a friend to hear it read, who suggested further omissions and condensations. Then my father went over it several times more, always making some emendations, and five years from the time he began to write it, it was copied out for the printer; containing then in substance all and in length about one-third of the original matter.

The book was published in the winter of 1848–'49, under the title of "Labor and other Capital: the rights of each secured and the wrongs of both eradicated; or, an exposition of the cause why few are wealthy and many poor, and the delineation of a system which, without infringing the rights of property, will give to labor its just reward. By Edward Kellogg." It was stereotyped and printed at his expense, and he had it for sale at his office, then at 47 Stone street.

He hoped he had now written something that would awaken the public attention and direct it to this momentous question; but his book failed to attract much notice, and his plan was called visionary, impracticable, Utopian. Here and there a man read it who perceived its power. One old friend of his, president of a bank in Maryland, said, "Mr. Kellogg, I have read your book, and it is all true, every word of it; but nobody will buy it, nobody will read it, and it will lie on the shelf: but if you will write one on the other side of the question, it will go like hot cakes." A year or two after it was printed, a gentleman, to whom he had lent a copy, said to him, "Mr. Kellogg, your book is true; it is in advance of the time, and the people of this generation do not appreciate it; but future generations will raise monuments to your memory." An editor, too, said to him, "Do you know that this book of yours is the most radical one that ever was written?" Yes, he knew it; nothing was new to him in regard to the deep-reaching nature of his work. He remarked, "This will break down every despotism. As soon as the system is adopted in this country and its results are seen, the people of other countries will compel their governments to establish it; these principles are of universal application, and will be ultimately adopted by all nations; then 'a nation shall be born in a day.'" This last was a favorite expression with him; he often quoted texts of Scripture in connection with his plan. He said, too, "They cannot bring me any question relating to this subject that I cannot answer, when I have had a little time to consider it."

At various times he had written papers expressly for certain public men, setting forth the advantages of his project, hoping to gain the ear of some one who might speak of it effectively to the people. He wrote to Henry Clay, and paid him a visit, making a great effort to interest him; but nobody cared for this newly-discovered truth. He spoke often of the oppression of the laboring classes of England, and wrote an article showing how to remedy it, which he sent to the London *Economist*, but it was not printed. When the book was first published he sent it to Proudhon, and the prominent members of the French Assembly, as well as to other statesmen in foreign countries; ever hoping somebody might perceive its worth, who would endeavor to put it in practice for the good of the people. He placed it in the hands of editors, members of Congress, and Cabinet officers at home. He used to say, "Some men tell me this is a very good theory, but it would not work in practice; but a theory is of no value unless it can be put in practice; the practicability of a theory and the good results flowing from it are what make any theory valuable." It burdened his soul that he could not make men understand, nor even fairly look at a subject laden with the liberty and well-being of mankind. The few instances I have noted are almost the only ones I can recall of a cordial recognition of his work.

He continued to write occasionally when some fresh thought or striking illustration occurred to him; and he spoke of making a new book; thinking again that perhaps he could produce something different in expression and illustration, yet the same in principle, which would reach the public ear. But when he considered that the people were not yet alive to the importance of a better monetary system, and that a great deal of thought and labor had been given to the book, he resolved to take it as a basis, and make it more valuable and interesting by incorporating the new matter with it. Remarking to him once in reference to a passage, "Father, that is so simple it does not seem as if there were any need of saying it," he replied, "It is perfectly simple; but people do not know it." And, "What astonishes me is that no one has ever found this out before. I cannot see how the world has gone on so long without any one understanding the real nature of money." "I do not need to hear the history of the monetary laws of nations. If I take the present condition of the people, I can tell pretty nearly what sort of money they have had." "Political economists fill their books with accounts of things as they are, but they do not show us any means by which the old evils they depict can be done away." Sometimes he used to call money, because of its present elusive, deceitful, and hidden power, a money-devil, and say that it ought to be chained, so that it could not devour the substance of the producers.

He was the most companionable of men: and though his conversation naturally turned to matters of government, law, or religion, he liked lighter topics too; was quick at repartee, could tell a good story, was fond of games, and ever loved a joke. He had a great respect for the common mind; he loved little children and tenderly drew out their thoughts: he had a lively sympathy for the pleasures and occupations of others, and everybody could do his best in that cheerful and inspiring presence. He was withal a man of an unusually beautiful and dignified aspect; of a manly form, above the middle height, having finely cut features, a pure red and white complexion, dark blue eyes, a firm mouth, and soft gray hair lying in abundance on a noble head. His countenance was expressive of power, refinement and benevolence. When he was conversing on some of his favorite topics, and especially when speaking of the excellent results to flow from just laws, his face sometimes assumed the innocent and joyful expression of a child. The moral effect of his system was always uppermost with him. While he foresaw, perhaps as few others can, the physical benefits to follow upon its establishment, the prospect of peace and good-will among men was the one which most delighted him. "The millennium can never come," he would say, "until this system goes into operation; but then it can come!" The foundation of contracts being laid in justice, order and beauty in the state and in society could arise.

As I listened day by day to his conversation, I often thought of making a written memorandum of it, but did not. In arguing a question he frequently began at a distance so remote that one did not see the connection; and as he approached the point, he brought, by means of the train of thought, an unexpectedly great force to bear, carrying conviction to the mind of his hearer. He talked of righteousness, and of justice and mercy, drawing much from the Bible: how often he quoted, "Justice and mercy have met together;" adding, "There is no justice without mercy; it is just to be merciful." He said he had thought a very great deal more about religion than he ever had about the currency, and that he could not have written the book if his mind had not been free on religious subjects. He spoke of writing a book on faith, but he never began it. He said, too, that he could write a code of laws; but he always added, "When my system goes into operation the laws will be very simple; they will be few and easily understood; there will be much less litigation." He remarked that if the laws were just it would not make much difference which political party administered them. He conceived that party strife would be diminished; that legislative bodies would come together less frequently, and he inclined to favor direct taxation for government expenses. He said it was supposed that a country might be so wide, and a nation so numerous as to fall apart because of the bulk, but if the laws were just, and a true system of money were instituted, the country might enlarge and the people multiply without disadvantage.

It was during the later years of his life, while his mind was occupied with these subjects, that a committee of gentlemen invited him to take the presidency of a bank, urging that if he would consent, such confidence was felt in his management that the stock would be taken immediately; and the United States Government appointed him to appraise the value of some lands; but he declined these offices, as he had previously declined a minor political one. I mention these otherwise trivial incidents to show his reputation as a practical man.

In the summer of 1857 it became evident that his hitherto vigorous health was declining, and a few months later the presence of a painful and fatal disease was disclosed. During the financial pressure of the autumn he felt intensely for the general suffering, which, in his then weak condition, seemed almost beyond his endurance; and said, "It is not the trouble in my own affairs, but it is the *cause* of these calamities that wears me out." He wrote an article for the New York *Tribune*, copied in the appendix of this book. The announcement of his approaching departure he received with the equanimity that distinguished him; saying, "It is usually our duty to prepare for life, but circumstances change; there is a debt of nature that we all must pay, and I have considered our duty in relation to it for many years; and it does not alarm me at all—not a bit. I shall still be in the presence of the same Being before whom I have lived; there will be no change in that."

He continued to go to his office as his strength permitted, and to attend to his affairs. At home he caused me to read his book through to him, after the lapse of seven or eight years listening to it with marked satisfaction, and saying that it was much better than he had thought it. When we came to the passage where it is said that those who neither lend nor borrow money, and have not the mental grasp to understand how the rate of interest affects the reward of their labor, shall yet benefit by the institution of the new system, he was visibly affected, and said, "If I did not know who wrote that book I should say, that sounds like Christian legislation!" He changed the title for the present one, made some amendments, dictated a few paragraphs, and from time to time spoke to me of some points which he desired to have enforced; especially that the rate of interest ought not to exceed the expense of instituting and circulating the money; but he added that at one per cent. it could not be made oppressive to the producers. He had previously said that no doubt an attempt would be made to lower the rate of interest gradually; but, in his judgment, it would be much better to bring it at once to the just standard; then every thing would adjust itself to that, and there would not be a series of readjustments consequent upon lower and lower rates. He said, "If there should be a war in this country, my system would be much more likely to go into operation; for the government would be compelled to issue a large amount of paper money to carry it on." * In those days of physical weakness and suffering, when greatly oppressed by the general lack of appreciation for this truth, it soothed him to have me talk to him with faith and hope of the coming day of recognition for it. I promised him that I would print a new edition of his work, and make additions to it from his manuscripts. He gave me all his manuscripts, though long ago I had often said to him that those were my perquisite, valuing them highly, and he had assented, remarking. "There are some good ideas in those old papers that you have not got out yet." But now he gave them to me definitely, and the copyright, and all the

---

* Those who proposed and carried the legal tender act can tell what strength they derived from the facts and arguments of the *New Monetary System*, which was freely circulated among members of Congress and others at Washington.

remaining copies of the essay and the book—and I received them as one who takes a sacred trust for the people. He said, "Mary, I love my friends, I love my family; I take a great interest in their welfare; but I care more for that book than for any thing else, it is of such vast importance to the world."

Soon after this he could no more go out, nor go to his writing-room, and for three weeks his family watched beside his dying-bed. He bore intense suffering with resolution and uncomplaining fortitude. Once as he lay apparently asleep I heard him say, "That is shortly expressed," and asking what he said, he replied, smiling, "I was dreaming—about usury, I guess." Again when I heard some word, he said again, "I was dreaming—pleasant dreams—all my thoughts are pleasant." To an old and valued orthodox friend, who, knowing he did not hold the usually received religious opinions, asked him how he should appear before a just God, he replied, in tones of solemn sweetness and serenity, "In regard to that I feel a perfect peace. You may think strange of it, Judge, but I do." Each day until the very close he gave directions respecting his affairs; in the extremity of death he did not neglect to greet a friend; and in perfect possession of his faculties up to the instant of his departure, on the 29th day of April, 1858, this great soul went hence.

We who sat beside him day and night, and saw his grand composure, could but think of the old philosophers, to whom, in mind, he always seemed to me akin. My spirit went up with him to the company of the saints and reformers of every age. We laid the wasted body in a grave on Chestnut Hill in the Greenwood Cemetery; but not until a cast of his head had been taken, that the sculptor might reproduce in marble his lineaments, for those who shall some day desire to see his face.

I have now told, according to my ability, who and what he was who wrote this book, and how he was moved thereto; trusting that it may comfort and encourage those who are to endure the stress of the coming struggle; that they may know more intimately their pure and benign leader, to whom was denied this conflict which he so ardently sought; that he was not a closet thinker, as some have called him, but up to the close of a long life actively engaged in affairs; mingling freely with men and partaking of the ordinary cares and joys; though having endured toil and hardship, not a disappointed, but, in the main, a successful man; known to most of his business acquaintances in no capacity but as one of themselves, yet, with his deep nature, having, as he himself said, "an inspiration of the truth" on this all-important subject. In closing I must add, that a few days before his death I said something to him, I do not remember what, about writing some recollections of his life, and he answered me, "I don't think much of these biographies. Every child thinks its own father and mother the best in the world. My book will show what my character was."

M. K. P.

ELIZABETH, N. J., *December*, 1874.

PREFACE.

The laboring classes of all civilized nations have been, and are, as a body, poor. Nearly all wealth is the production of labor; therefore, laborers would have possessed it, had not something intervened to prevent this natural result. Even in our own country, where the reward of labor is greater than in most others, some cause is operating with continual and growing effect to separate production from the producer. The wrong is evident, but neither statesmen nor philanthropists have traced it to its true source; and hence they have not been able to project any plan sufficient for its removal.

The design of the present volume is to show the true cause; and to illustrate its operation so plainly and variously, that any ordinary mind may easily perceive how it has produced and continued this unnatural oppression of laborers. It will also be shown, with equal clearness, that a simple and effectual remedy can be applied to the removal of the evil. A good government must have some system by which it can secure the distribution of property according to the earnings of labor, and at the same time strictly preserve the rights of property: and no government, whether republican or not, that fails in these particulars, can insure the freedom and happiness of the people and become permanent. The plan proposed to secure this distribution is obviously safe and certain; and it contemplates no agrarian or other similar distribution of property, nor any interference in contracts between laborers and capitalists, or in the usual course of business. Fulfilling these requirements, it can hardly fail to recommend itself to all thinking men. Therefore, it is confidently believed that when the plan shall become generally known, it will be quickly put into operation, and thus save the producers of this nation from the oppression, degradation and misery which have befallen the laboring classes of all other countries.

A NEW MONETARY SYSTEM.

INTRODUCTION.

All civilized nations enact certain fundamental laws. These are governing powers, and subsequent laws are intended to carry them out into practical use. The most important fundamental law in any nation is that which institutes money; for money governs the distribution of property, and thus affects in a thousand ways the relations of man to man. If wrongly instituted, it cannot be rightly governed by any subsequent laws; and the wrong distribution of property consequent upon it must corrupt society in all its branches. The evils engendered can never be remedied except by altering the fundamental law. Changes in the subsequent laws, so long as they are founded on a wrong base, can only result in the exchange of one evil for another. The proposition that wrong premises will produce wrong conclusions is often stated, yet it is seldom fully understood and properly appreciated. We will therefore, by means of one or two simple illustrations, show the governing power of a fundamental principle.—A good house cannot be built except upon a good foundation. The mason-work above may be laid of the best material and by the best workmen; but if the foundation be not sound, and sink at each corner from five to twenty inches, although the house should not fall, yet this movement of the foundation will distort the floors, ceilings, roof and rooms from their proper shape; and no propping or patching up of floors, ceilings, roof or rooms will ever make the house a good one. It will be directly the opposite, it will be a poor one; and as the foundation continues to move, will constantly need repairs. A valuable machine cannot be invented except upon true mechanical principles. Let a man invent a machine founded upon a false principle. Every part of it may be well made of the best material, and when finished it may present a plausible appearance, yet it either will not work at all or it will work imperfectly, and can never be good until it is founded on true mechanical principles. The stability of a house shows the character of its foundation; the results produced by a machine show the worth or worthlessness of the principle on which it was invented; and with equal certainty the centralization of property in a nation shows the character of its monetary laws. If great wrongs prevail while there is a general conformity to laws apparently designed to secure justice, there must be, in spite of appearances, some defective law or institution, which is a sufficient cause of those wrongs. The general evils naturally and inevitably flowing from it are easily seen, like the parts of the building above ground, and like the wheels of the machine that are open to view, while the great radical defect in the groundwork may be so hidden from public sight as to attract comparatively little attention.

One of the chief objects for which governments are constituted, is to insure the protection of the rights of property. The security of these rights is essential to the welfare of a people. Their infringement is the cause of nearly all legal procedures. Such crimes as theft, gambling, fraud in business, bribery in courts of law, etc., consist in unjustly obtaining property without ren dering an equivalent. To obtain *labor* without rendering a fair equivalent, is also a violation of the rights of property.

Property is almost entirely the product of labor, for even food of spontaneous growth in the seas or on the land cannot be gathered without labor. Labor has effected every improvement in our country; it has built our cities; cleared, fenced, and improved our farms; constructed our ships, railroads and canals. In short, every comfort of life is the fruit of past or present labor. If any one is in doubt whether labor is the actual producer of the wealth, let him consider what would be the situation of this or any other civilized nation, if the laborers should cease their toil for the brief term of five years, letting the earth for that period bring forth only her spontaneous productions. Let man neither sow nor reap, let manufacturing cease, commerce be suspended, and what would be the condition of our country at the end of the five years? Would not a large proportion of the people have sunk into their graves from starvation; and would not many who were living be almost naked like the barbarians? If the earth should open her chasms and spew out pure and malleable gold and silver, as plenty as the rocks in the mountains, it would afford no relief. But if she should cast out wheat, corn and vegetables, beef, pork, mutton, poultry, besides garments, houses, furniture and so forth, the people would be supplied with the means of subsistence. In such a case we might do without the labor of man. But if we had all the gold and silver money and all the paper obligations that have been made from the creation of the world to the present day, they would not be the least substitute for the productions of labor; and yet our laws make these legal instruments in the hands of the few to trample in the dust the rights of the laborer, on whom we depend for every morsel of food that we eat, for the clothing we wear, the houses we live in, and in fact for every comfort and luxury of life.

A moderate amount of labor readily produces an abundant supply of necessaries and comforts for man; but the present distribution of these products is such, that a large number of those who labor much more than their share in the production, receive a very small proportion of the products, while the larger proportion accumulates in the possession of those who are employed neither in producing nor in distributing them. The greater portion of the human family toil day by day for a scanty subsistence, and are destitute of the time and means for social and intellectual culture. The industrious poor, as a class, do not obtain even a competence. Their destitution often induces them to trespass against existing laws, to obtain a small proportion of that, which, under just laws, would be abundantly awarded to them as a fair compensation for their labor. All candid men will acknowledge this truth, that the wealth is not distributed in accordance with either the physical or the mental usefulness of those who obtain it. Opposed to the masses who live in toil and poverty, is a small proportion of the human race, surrounded by all the appliances of luxury, and living in comparative idleness; while their abundant means of social and intellectual culture are too often neglected, or rendered useless by indolence and self-indulgence. These extremes of wealth and poverty, of luxury and want, of idleness and labor, are great, somewhat in proportion to the antiquity of a nation, or the length of time that its monetary law, or system, has been in operation.

The wealth of this nation, like the wealth of other nations, is rapidly accumulating in the hands of a comparatively few persons in our large cities. Still it is indisputable that cities are great consumers of wealth, while they are comparatively small producers. The labor of the country furnishes nearly the whole support of the cities. The rewards of labor paid by the cities and the country respectively to each other, to be justly reciprocal, ought to be in proportion to the services rendered to each other ; but the immensely greater amount of wealth flowing to the cities, and the less to the country, is clearly opposed to this just reciprocity. This will be more apparent by supposing the large Atlantic cities to be cut off from all interchanges with the country. In a short time their citizens would be destitute of food, fuel, and clothing, for exchanges of their productions among themselves would do very little toward supplying their wants ; while the people of the country and the small manufacturing towns, if they had a just medium by which they could exchange their productions with each other, would have an abundant and vastly more bountiful supply than at present of nearly every necessary and luxury of life. They would save for their own use nearly the whole difference between what they now produce for the large cities, and what these cities produce for the country. But even in these cities, where a great part of the national wealth is owned, a majority of the people toil for a scanty subsistence, and thousands of miserable poor are dependent on public charity.

In all probability, four thousand of the most wealthy citizens of the city of New York own a greater amount of real and personal property than the whole remainder of its inhabitants. Their wealth is vested in real estate in the city and country, in bank, railroad, State, and other stocks, loans of money, etc. Allow five persons to form a family, and the four thousand men and their families would form a population of twenty thousand, or two and a half per cent. on eight hundred thousand, the present population of the city. Upon this estimate—and a little observation and reflection will show that it is not an extravagant one—two and a half per cent. of the population are worth as much as the remaining ninety-seven and a half per cent. Take the disproportion of wealth on a greater amount of population. We may reasonably estimate that a hundred and fifty thousand of the wealthiest men in the United States own as much real and personal property as the whole remainder of the nation. Allowing five persons in a family, these hundred and fifty thousand men, with their families, make a population of seven hundred and fifty thousand, or two and a half per cent. on thirty millions, the present population of the country. This calculation will make two and a half per cent. of the population own as great an amount of wealth as the remaining ninety-seven and a half per cent. Our government professes to establish laws for the benefit of the whole people; and such laws, if justly administered, should secure to every individual a fair equivalent for his labor; yet probably half the wealth of the nation is accumulated in the possession of but about two and a half per cent. of the population, who to say the most, have not done more labor toward the production of the wealth than the average of the ninety-seven and a half per cent., among whom is distributed the other half of the wealth.

Let those who doubt whether two and a half per cent. of the population own half the property of the nation select in their own neighborhood, or in a village containing, say, four thousand inhabitants, the twenty most wealthy men, and see if the twenty are not worth as much as all the rest. Or, if the village contain ten thousand inhabitants, take the fifty most wealthy men, and see if they are not worth as much as all the rest. Allowing the families of the fifty men to average five persons each, they would amount to two hundred and fifty individuals—just two and a half per cent. of the population. If it be found that the fifty men and their families own one-half of the property, then see if they have contributed more labor physically, intellectually, or morally, for the general benefit, than the rest of the villagers. We do not now speak of what their wealth may have done in hiring others to make improvements, but of the improvements that the fifty men and their families have effected by their personal labor. If they have not accomplished as much as all the rest of their townsmen, and yet own half the wealth of the town, some wrong to the majority of the people has been done. Not that these men have not acted in as good faith, or with as upright intentions as other citizens; or that others would not be equally glad to accumulate wealth in the same manner; but we ask *how* it occurs that the comparatively few have so large a proportion? They have not earned it, for they could not have performed the labor of building half the town, nor of providing half its inhabitants with food and clothing; nor could they have given half the instruction in the various trades and in the school education of the villagers. And if they have not done one-half the labor, why is it that they possess one-half the property? Why is it, too, that we see one industrious man rise from poverty to wealth, apparently because his business is prosperous, and another man, who is equally diligent in an equally useful employment, remaining with a mere subsistence?

These facts are sometimes attributed to the ignorance and extravagance of the laboring classes. But if all our people were learned in Greek and Latin, as well as in other languages and in the sciences, the ground must continue to be tilled, and railroads, houses, and so forth, built by labor. Not all the education, nor all the money in the world, would make these improvements without the physical labor; and it ought to secure to those who perform it a just and much larger share than it at present does of all the comforts of life. Many good scholars and industrious and intelligent men are poor, while very indifferent scholars and rather ignorant men have often accumulated fortunes. The ignorance of the laboring classes does not account for their poverty. Nor does want of economy better account for it. What opportunity has the laborer to be extravagant, when the price of his day's work would hardly pay that day's board and lodging in a comfortable house in our cities? Do the factory operatives in England, France and Germany live extravagantly, or the seamstresses in London and New York? They earn three, four or five times more products than they actually consume, and these go into the possession of that class of persons who live comfortably or luxuriously without performing much, if any, productive labor, or advancing the moral and intellectual well-being of society. The wealthy men of a nation are not usually those whose genius makes improvements in the mechanical arts, or who, by any species of labor, contribute much to actual production. Their attention is generally directed to the accumulation of wealth by indirect means, which do not require labor.*

The injustice of the present distribution of products is still more conspicuous, when we consider that *present labor* is indispensable to human existence. Although all discoveries, inventions, and improvements, made by all previous labor, are transmitted, free of expense, to successors, yet the property, thus improved and inherited, cannot give support without *present* labor. The spontaneous productions of the earth cannot supply one-twentieth part of the population with food. Clothing can last but a few years, and buildings, unless repaired, must decay. Therefore, each generation must in the main provide its own means of subsistence. If a generation enact laws through which one-third of the succeeding

---

* *Labor* signifies toil, which produces or distributes something actually useful; and this is the sense in which the term is used in this volume. When toil is directed to wrong ends, it does not deserve the name of labor.

generation can live in luxury without labor, then the labor of the other two-thirds, besides supplying their own necessities, must also supply the wants of the first third. Although the idle rich man inherits wealth, yet he owes his present support to the labor of others. Others must raise the grain that he consumes, manufacture cloth for his use, build his house, etc. If one-third of a generation own all the property, they have the means of supplying their wants by labor upon their own possessions; but the two-thirds who have no property, have not even the means of preserving their lives, unless the one-third allow them the use of property on which to expend their labor.

In addition to this evil of greatly centralized wealth, all civilized nations are every few years visited with great revulsions in trade. Outstanding debts become unsafe, and many debtors bankrupt. There is usually an apparent overstock of goods and products, for which there is no ready market; houses will not sell or rent; manufactured goods lie in the stores and cannot be sold for the cost of making; and therefore laborers are out of employment, for why should more be produced to decrease still further the ruinous prices at which those already in market must be sold? At such periods, in our cities, one house is filled with families, one in each room from cellar to garret, and the adjoining house stands empty for want of tenants able to pay the rent. Goods are piled up in stores without sales, while great numbers of the laboring community are ragged and are begging from door to door for old clothes to shield themselves and their families from the piercing cold, and for the crumbs that fall from the tables of the rich to keep them from starving. When people look about to ascertain the cause of these things, seeing houses and stores untenanted, and great quantities of agricultural products and manufactured goods on hand for which there appears to be no market, they generally come to the conclusion that over-production and over-trading have caused these calamities. If this be really the case, public measures should be taken to avert such disasters, by preventing an excess of labor. Is it not strange that at the times when the amount of surplus production is a subject of national lamentation, the people who produce by their labor the very things which they need for their own use and comfort, are the ones who are often destitute of them; while a few capitalists who do little or nothing toward the production and distribution, are supplied with all the comforts and luxuries of life at half, or less than half their usual price? But a surplus of cotton has never remained because no one needed it. In 1844, nearly sixty thousand citizens of New York received the aid of public charity. All these needed additional cotton clothing. At least one-half the population of the whole country would have made a yearly purchase of five dollars' worth of additional cotton clothing, if they could have spared the means from their earnings. In one year ten millions of persons would have consumed $50,000,000 worth of cotton clothing, in addition to the previous quantity. Cotton would then have maintained a good price, and the crops would have been consumed. If, during the years included between 1837 and 1844, the laborers in the city of New York and its vicinity, whose occupation was the building of houses, had been furnished with the work which they would have been willing to perform, they would have built a house for nearly every poor family in the city. If the unemployed laborers in the districts where the materials for building, bricks, mortar, timber, boards, nails, etc., are usually prepared, had been set at work, the materials might have been furnished, and the buildings erected and paid for by labor. The laborers, too, would have been much happier, for they begged for work without obtaining it, and many were dependent on public charity.

It is plain that there can be no real over-production unless a large surplus remains after all the people have been fully supplied with the necessaries and comforts of life. The public cannot over-trade by distributing each year's productions among those who really need them to use. Too high prices cannot be paid for labor, unless the laborers in general actually gain more than their equitable share of the year's productions. Neither can there be an over-stock of laborers so long as thousands are suffering for want of the very articles these laborers would gladly produce, if they could be employed. There cannot be too many houses, when they would be filled with tenants able to pay the rent if work could be obtained. We must look for the real cause of these calamities, not in over-production, but in the power that governs the distribution of the products.

But, taking another view of the subject, it may be said that we are a free people, and many suppose we enjoy all the rights that a government can confer. Every one employs himself in labor, trade, speculation, or otherwise, according to his own choice; sells his labor or products at such prices as he can obtain, and buys the labor and products of others at prices that he agrees to pay. Our government is also deemed beneficent because poor-houses and schools * are provided for the

---

* In the various States, a tax is levied to provide schools for the children of the laboring classes. Under existing laws, this species of charity is, doubtless, very important. But wealth being the product of labor, the laborers should have abundant means to educate their children; and if a fund be established for the purposes of education, it should be necessary for those only who are unable or unwilling to labor. It is unreasonable for the laws to be such as to compel the producers of wealth to ask alms of non-producers.

needy. If a farmer or a mechanic should be told that our laws oppressed him, probably he would say, that he worked at what he pleased, and sold either his labor or its products to whom he pleased, and had no law suits, and, therefore, the laws did not in the least infringe his rights, and would not those of any other man who was upright in his dealings. The laboring classes make their own bargains with capitalists, and one another; and all are equally protected in the property which they lawfully acquire. Why then do not laborers get all they are justly entitled to receive? Looking at the matter in this light, it wears an appearance of freedom and equal justice; yet results prove the existence of some radical wrong lying below this surface view. For we all know that wealth is produced by labor, and that the people of the country send the best products of their incessant toil to supply the luxuries of the wealthy in cities; and that the laborers in these cities build splendid mansions for the opulent, and poor tenements for themselves, most of which are also owned by capitalists, and rented to their occupants. True, all this labor is paid for by capitalists according to their agreements with laborers; yet, notwithstanding these voluntary agreements according to the law of supply and demand, the wealth of the nation continues to accumulate in large fortunes in the hands of a comparatively few non-producers, leaving a very large number of its actual producers in poverty. These are facts that stand out to public view, and cannot be denied. Freedom of contract, choice of location and occupation, and protection of property, are manifestly proper and right, and ought to be enjoyed by every people; yet we see they fail, and entirely fail, to secure any equitable distribution of property, and any adequate compensation for labor. They fail for the same reason that good materials and workmanship on a bad foundation fail to make a good house. Their foundation is unsound and variable, perverting their natural good tendencies, and engendering defects corresponding with their wrong basis. A bad foundation for a house affects the edifice above, and the few individuals who are interested in its building and use. A machine not founded on true mechanical principles, affects the few who own it, and those interested in its working. But a national standard of value like money, which forms the foundation of contracts, and regulates the award of property, thus greatly modifying and limiting all minor rights of freedom of contract, location and occupation, and which a whole nation is compelled to use, must, if it be variable and uncertain, affect injuriously the interests of every individual, family and association, as far as the money circulates.

The present rates of interest on money enable the owners of property to demand an undue proportion of the products of labor for the use of property, and laborers are compelled to make their agreements with them under these circumstances. Undoubtedly both parties are governed by their own interests in making their agreements; but the circumstances under which contracts are made, render them very unjust toward laborers. Suppose one of the contracting parties to be in water, where he must drown unless he receive assistance from the other party who is on the land. Although the drowning man might be well aware that his friend on shore was practising a very grievous extortion, yet, under the circumstances, he would be glad to make any possible agreement, to be rescued. The monetary laws of nations have depressed the producing classes to a similar state of dependence upon capitalists, and they are similarly obliged to make their contracts with them under great disadvantages. A very large proportion of the people are actually wronged out of their property, and the earnings of their labor, by the operation of the laws, although their contracts are voluntarily made, and honestly fulfilled. Neither of the contracting parties may know that either is injured by the laws, although both may be sensible that justice is really not done them.

In all ages and nations, philanthropic men have endeavored to devise some means of securing to labor a better compensation. Labor-saving machines have been invented; associations have been formed for the purpose of producing with less labor, the earnings being equitably distributed, according to the work performed. But these benevolent efforts have failed of any general success. The reason is this: no individuals, nor associations of individuals, can withdraw their labor or their products from the influence of the national laws which regulate distribution. The great disparity in the conditions of the rich and poor is the natural result of unjust laws, and, therefore, this disparity must continue so long as these laws are in force. If, however, a father should so dispose of his property, that all his children, except one, should be compelled to work twelve or fourteen hours a day for a mere subsistence, while one son should receive an immense fortune, which would supply him with every luxury without toil, the injustice and injury to both parties would call forth the censure of every right thinking person. A government is no more justifiable in legislating so as to produce these results, than a father is justifiable in a similar treatment of his children. Governments are established to protect the just rights of the governed, as much as a father holds his position to protect the just rights of each child.

Present laborers, who produce present products, should receive a very large proportion of them, and capitalists who do not labor, should receive a correspondingly small proportion. How shall this change in the reward of labor and capital be effected? Shall laws be made to determine the prices of various kinds of labor, and thus prevent the laborer and employer from making contracts upon their own terms? This would be impracticable, and, if practicable, not desirable. Each man should be at liberty to make his own contracts. There is no need of interference with this liberty, in order to prevent capital from taking too large a proportion of the products of labor.

The unfair distribution of wealth is caused by an unjust legal *standard of distribution*. Distribution is regulated and effected by the standard of value, which is money. Money, as will be hereafter shown, exercises astonishing power throughout every department of business and industrial occupation. When monetary laws shall be made equitable, present labor will naturally receive a just proportion of present products, and capital will likewise receive a just reward for its use.

The necessity for the *exchange of commodities* is generally acknowledged. Few, however, even among thinking men, are aware how indispensable these exchanges are to the subsistence and comfort of the human family. Men are social beings, and mutually dependent. To appreciate this important truth, we must consider the inability of each man to provide for the numerous wants of his nature; and the ignorance and discomfort to which each would be exposed, were he not benefited by the labor of others. If every man could build his own house, furnish his own food and clothing, and make all the instruments and utensils that he needs to use: if the materials for all these things were placed upon every acre of land, and every man, woman and child, were endowed with sufficient skill and strength to produce them, there might be no need of an exchange of commodities.

But all men are, in many, in most things, dependent on the labor of their fellow men. For example, take the farmer, who is acknowledged to be the least dependent of men, and see for how many things even he is indebted to the labor of others. He must have implements for the cultivation of his farm, a plough, harrow, shovel, hoe, sickle, cradle, scythes, a fan, or fanning-mill, and a cart or wagon. The farmer is dependent on the miner for the iron ore; on the collier to dig the coal; on the furnace-worker to smelt the iron; and on the forger and the smith to make his iron and steel instruments. He is dependent on the wagon-maker for his wagon; on the machinist for his fanning-mill; on the carpenter for his house; on the nail-maker for nails; on the glass-manufacturer for glass; on the stone-cutter and the mason for mason-work; on the brick-maker for bricks; on the cooper for barrels, tubs, and pails; on the saw-maker for a saw, and on the rolling-mill to roll out the iron or steel for it; on the tin-plate-worker for kitchen utensils; on the moulder and caster of iron for iron pots; on the miner of copper, and on the copper and brass founder for brass and copper kettles; on the pump-maker for a pump, etc., etc. He is dependent on the needle-maker, the pin-maker, the button-maker, the silk grower, the tanner, the shoe-maker, the hatter, the saddle and harness-maker, the cabinet-maker, and the type-maker, type-setter, and printer. Not one of these artisans, in attending to his particular employment, produces his food and clothing; and all would be destitute of them, unless supplied with them by the labor of others The farmer raises all his food, except salt, tea, coffee, sugar, molasses, spices and the like; these, and the ships to transport them, must be furnished by others. These wants call into employment ship-carpenters, sailors, compass-makers, surveyors, chart-makers, etc. The farmer must raise wool, cotton, hemp, or flax, or else be dependent on others for clothing. If the farmer, who is the least dependent of men, receives from others so many supplies, how is it with the hatter and the shoe-maker? The former makes an article to cover the head, the latter one to cover the feet; and all the additional supplies of both must be furnished by the labor of others. Artisans, too, depend upon each other for the different parts of their work; the cotton manufacturer must be assisted by others to carry forward his manufacture. Many articles, such as watch-springs, are useless unless they are combined with other parts. It is, then, of paramount importance that no obstacles be thrown in the way of a ready exchange of commodities.

A certain quantity of one kind of produce is worth as much as a certain quantity of another kind; and all civilized nations have adopted some *medium* by means of which all kinds of produce may be more easily exchanged than by direct barter. We hear it sometimes asserted that there is no need of a medium of exchange. But the articles of trade could not be divided and distributed to supply the numerous wants of a people without a representative of value through which the distribution could be made. For example, a man brings to market five hundred bushels of wheat. The purchaser tenders corn in payment; and they agree that seven hundred and fifty bushels of corn are worth as much as five hundred bushels of wheat. The seller can use but a small portion of the corn, and finds a purchaser, with whom he exchanges the surplus for hams. He disposes of the hams for hats and shoes. If he endeavor to divide the hats and shoes, and exchange them for the articles that he needs, he may spend two years before he can return to his farm to raise a second crop of wheat. Yet he is fairly dealt with. All those with whom he exchanges, give him, as nearly as possible, an equivalent of actual value for the actual value that they receive; and all the articles are such as all need. In fact, all trade is simply a barter of one useful thing for another. A person who produces more of an article than he needs for his own use, exchanges his surplus for the surplus articles of others. If the farmer had sold the wheat for *money*, the money would have been a tender for any other article that he wished to purchase.

The value and prices of all products are estimated by money, the legal standard of value. In making out a bill, the articles sold are set down at the prices agreed upon, extended and footed up, and they amount to so much *money*. How could contracts for various articles be made, and bills of them be made out and summed up, without money? Should it be said that a pint of Indian corn was equal to four rows of pins, and a pound of cotton to twenty needles; and, if so, must there not be a description of the quality of the pins and needles, as well as of the cotton and corn? If it should be said that ten pounds of sugar were of equal value with a boy's cap, would it not be necessary to describe the quality of the sugar, as well as the material, workmanship, and size of the cap, in order to make the contract just? A *standard of value* is manifestly indispensable to a just and convenient exchange of commodities.

Monetary laws are the most important that are enacted; for, by these laws, money is made the tender for debts and the medium of exchange for products. All individuals are compelled to found their contracts for the necessaries of life upon the standard fixed by law. However good the intentions of the parties, their contracts will partake of the evil of the monetary laws upon which they are founded, and every law that goes to support the fulfilment of the contracts will partake of the same evil. We have laws to prohibit the fulfilment of contracts made upon certain acknowledged unjust principles. Contracts made in gambling are void in law. In gambling, each player stakes a certain sum, and all agree that the winner shall take the whole. This contract would be perfectly fair or just, if the first or fundamental principle were just. But the principle upon which gambling is founded is, that what one gains, others lose; for no production is made by gambling, and no equivalent is given to losers for their money. The laws make money the foundation for all business contracts. The value of this foundation is unjust and continually varying; so that parties in fulfilling their contracts are compelled to give either more or less than a just equivalent for their purchases. The results of all contracts are as varying and unjust as their foundation. The continual fluctuations in the value of money make a sort of gambling system of all trade.

For an example of the effects of variations in the value of money, suppose the bonds of the government be issued, payable in twenty years, and bearing six per cent. interest. If we had no foreign market for these bonds, and the interest on money in our own country were unalterably fixed at six per cent., the bonds would be worth exactly par, and would continue of the same value throughout the twenty years. But if the interest on money should rise to nine per cent., and to obtain a loan at that rate the best security were required, the government bonds would fall, and would not be good security for more than three-fourths of their par value. If the government issue a bond at par, and, by pressure in the money market, the holder be compelled to sell it at three-fourths of its par value to meet his engagements, the government takes, or allows others to take, one-fourth of his money, for which he no more receives an equivalent than the gambler receives an equivalent when he gambles away one-fourth of his money. The government reserves the right to coin money and regulate its value, and yet allows its value to change incessantly, and thus, by its own acts, deprives a man of a fourth of his money without rendering to him any equivalent.

Under our present monetary laws, when interest is low

and money plenty, if a contract be made for the purchase of a farm, of which one-half the purchase money is to be left on mortgage for a term of years, the purchaser runs nearly as great a hazard of losing a large proportion of the money that he pays for the farm, as if he had staked the amount on the turning of dice. For if, at the time the money becomes due, interest should be as high as it was from 1837 to 1840, it is doubtful whether the farm would sell for enough to pay one-half the purchase money remaining on mortgage. The farmer's loss, in this case, would be owing entirely to the change in the value of the dollar, and not to any change in the actual value of the farm; for the farm would produce as good a crop as if money had continued to bear a uniform interest of six per cent. The laws of the United States are supposed to be highly favorable to productive industry; but the standard which regulates and effects distribution is so made as, in a great degree, to defeat its own object, and to exert a disadvantageous influence upon production. The effects of high and varying rates of interest upon all classes of producers will be hereafter more fully exhibited.

Among political economists, the nature and regulation of money appear to have been subjects of the utmost difficulty. We have no full account of its functions, and no satisfactory answer to the numerous and perplexing questions which arise concerning its value and regulation. The alternate abundance and scarcity of money, and the variations of interest, are supposed to be irremediable evils. It would seem that gold and silver coins inherently possess a mysterious power, which defies all regulation, and renders impossible a comprehensible monetary system. It is doubtless true, that while the nature of a thing is not understood, all attempts to regulate it must prove ineffectual, and legislative bodies have hitherto instituted money in a very imperfect way. The money of a nation, instead of being a power by which a few capitalists may monopolize the greater part of the earnings of labor, ought to be a power which *should distribute products to producers*, according to their labor expended in the production.

The labor-saving machines that have been invented within the last half century, have greatly facilitated production. Improvements in implements of husbandry have materially lessened agricultural labor; and most articles manufactured by machinery are made with less than one-fourth of the labor that was formerly required. We should naturally suppose that these improvements would be a great relief and advantage to the laboring classes; and that they would feel grateful to those who have studied out the laws of nature and invented the machines. Yet both the inventors of machinery, and the operatives, in general, continue to toil on in want, and many of them have neither means nor leisure to educate their children. Increased facility in production seems to increase the number and multiply the wants of those who live in idle luxury, instead of affording the desired relief to actual producers. Fifty years ago, the farmers raised, carded and spun their wool; they raised flax and spun most of their linen; and cotton was also mostly carded and spun by each family to supply its own wants. Now, farmers who raise wool, cotton and flax, sell the raw materials, which often pass through a number of hands before they reach the manufacturer. The manufactured goods again pass through several hands before they reach the consumer. Machinery has collected the people into towns and villages to work in large factories, where they sell their labor, and buy their board and clothing This greatly augments the necessity for the exchange of goods—the more machinery the greater the necessity for exchanges of products—yet there has been no new invention in financial affairs, by which the exchange may be more equitably and easily made. True, we have increased the amount of gold and silver coins, and the number of banks, bank-notes, and money-brokers, but this is no more an improvement in the medium of distribution, than an increase in the number of pack-horses on the old muddy roads would be an improvement in conveying products, while it would still take the same muscular power to convey a given weight. A railroad made and a steam-engine substituted for horses and oxen, are great improvements in the mode and means of transportation. Though the quantity to be conveyed may be increased tenfold, railroads and steam-engines will fulfil all requirements; whereas if we depended on an increased number of horses and oxen, want of teams and bad roads would often cause great inconvenience. But no inconvenience of this kind could equal that experienced by the producers in consequence of the defects of our monetary system. Just monetary laws are of more importance to the laboring classes than all the machinery that has been invented during the last fifty years. And when the needed reformation is made, the producing classes, who will gain the benefit of all improvements, will rejoice at every advance in machinery, and the inventors will be hailed as the benefactors of man.

Many people seem to be opposed to *innovation*. They do not consider that all improvements in the mechanical arts, or in laws, are innovations upon former things and former laws. The establishment of our republican government was an innovation upon monarchies. People do believe that changes may be made for the better, for each year they assemble legislative bodies to remodel old laws, and to make new ones. Every modification of a law is an innovation, and every new law is an innovation upon former laws. Every moral improvement is an innovation upon the previous evil. Those who talk against innovation are often great innovators. They are doing, or advocating something to improve the condition of man.

INTRODUCTION. 39

The antiquity of laws and customs is not a proof of their excellence. In all ages, and in all nations the producing classes have been ill paid for their labor. Let us no longer recur to ancient laws and usages to uphold our unjust standard of distribution. Our producing classes are vastly more interested in knowing how the products of their own daily labor are disposed of, than in knowing how the ancients disposed of theirs. We cannot alter the evils of the past; we must act for the present and the future. Suppose a legislature enact a law which gives a certain part of their constituents great advantages over the remainder. They discover the error, and amend the law so as to operate equally upon all. The alteration is not an infringement of the rights of those who received undue advantages from the former law. It only renders justice to those previously injured. Money is as much the representative of the property of the people, as the legislature are the representatives of their constituents. Its erroneous construction and undue power have made a few rich, and have plunged thousands into poverty. They have sent hundreds to premature graves, starved the widow and the orphan, and given untold wealth to the miser. They have been the cause of incalculable moral and social evils. It is not to be understood that those who now possess the wealth are worse than others who do not possess it, or that others, if they could have obtained it, would not have appropriated it in the same manner. But one thing is certain, that an enormous and universal wrong exists, which nothing but an entire change of our laws, respecting money, can remedy. Money is the *national* standard of distribution, therefore the evils inevitable upon its present institution, are *national* evils, which can only be removed by the action of the general government.

A defective standard will, doubtless, appear to many an inadequate cause for the wide spread wrongs of unjust distribution; but the fact can be established by the clearest proof, and such will be adduced in the progress of the work. It will also be shown, that a safe and just monetary system can be easily established by the government, which will so regulate the standard, that the general distribution of products will be in accordance with actual earnings. When the farmers and mechanics, and other producers, and laborers, understand the system which is to be developed, and perceive its adequacy to secure to them a just compensation for their labor, they will as surely cause it to be put in operation, as they would send their products to Philadelphia or Boston, rather than to New York, if in the former markets they could sell them for a third more than in the latter.

The correction and due regulation of money will make no change in the present ownership of property. The changes effected by the establishment of a sound monetary system will be gentle, immediate, gradual, sure. Only such will ensue as will naturally result from securing to the laborer a fair compensation. Its object will be to protect producers in their rights, and not to retaliate for past injuries. No agrarian distribution will be necessary, but a just standard, that will at once begin to regulate the distribution of products, so as to reward the labor performed, and which will in process of time distribute property in accordance with individual and general rights and interests. Although the bearings of money upon labor may be deemed a somewhat dry subject, yet, under its present new aspect, it is believed that it will prove deeply interesting to all classes. The patient and continuous attention of the reader is solicited to the important facts and principles now to be presented relative to the uses and abuses of money, and to the new plan to be suggested for its institution and regulation.

PART I.

THE PRINCIPLES OF DISTRIBUTION.

———•••———

CHAPTER I.

OF VALUE.

VALUE consists in *use* ; it is that property, or those properties, which render anything useful. A house that could not be occupied would be worthless, unless its materials could be employed for some other purpose. A horse is valued for his useful qualities; if he becomes disabled, he is worthless, for his use is destroyed. So of everything necessary to the support and comfort of man, it is valuable because it is useful.

The same is true of ornaments. They are valuable because they are useful for ornamental purposes. If diamonds were deprived of their beauty, their use, and therefore their value, as ornaments, would cease to exist. A valuable portrait might be rendered worthless by erasing the features. The canvas and the paint, the material of the picture, would remain, but its use would be destroyed.

The value of all property is estimated by its *usefulness*. For instance, the income that a city lot can be made to produce, determines its value. The interest on the money that its improvement will cost, must be first deducted, together with the taxes, insurance, and repairs necessary to keep the improvement permanently good The surplus it will yield after making these deductions, determines the true value of the lot.

There are two kinds of value: *actual value*, and *legal value*. *Actual value* belongs to anything that inherently possesses the means of affording food, or which can be employed for clothing, shelter, or some other useful purpose, ornamental or otherwise, *without being exchanged for any other thing*.

Legal value belongs to anything which *represents actual value*, or *capital*. Its existence depends upon actual value. The worth of things of legal value depends upon their capability to be exchanged for things of actual value.

The following illustration shows the distinction between actual and legal value, and the dependence of the latter upon the former. The national debt of England exceeds £800,000,000 sterling, say $4,000,000,000. It bears interest at about an average of three per cent. per annum, amounting to an annual sum of $120,000,000. A hundred and twenty millions of dollars' worth of the products of labor, of actual value, must be sold annually to pay the interest; to pay the principal would require a large proportion of the wealth of the country. If the paper, the legal value which represents and secures the debt and interest, were collected and burned, it would not diminish the real wealth of the nation. It would merely cause a change in the individual ownership of property. But alter the circumstances, and suppose a similar amount of actual value to be consumed, houses, manufactories, machinery, fences, grain, etc., to the amount of $4,000,000,000, and nearly every improvement would be swept from the British Islands. Destroy merely the three per cent. interest of actual value or the debt for one year—*i. e.*, products to the amount of $120,000,000, and a famine would ensue; for actual value, the products of labor, would be destroyed, instead of a legal representative, as in the case of the conflagration of the paper securing the interest.

The power of money, like the power of a bond and mortgage, is legal. A mortgage upon a specific piece of land gives the owner of this paper instrument a right to a certain portion of the value of the land. A mortgage is a specific lien, by which one individual binds a certain portion of his property to another. A lien on property, in the technical acceptation, is a judgment recorded on the docket of a court, or a mortgage recorded in the county clerk's office. These instruments hold a right over the property of the debtor, in defiance of him, or of any other person who may have the property in possession. Money is a public lien upon all property that is for sale in the nation; and the holder of money can, at all times, procure with it the amount of property which it represents, as much as the holder of a mortgage can procure the specified amount of property upon which the mortgage is a lien. Money is, however, a lien superior to all mortgages and judgments; because, if the specified amount of money be tendered, the owner of the mortgage, or judgment, is compelled to cancel it.

Notes of hand are deemed by all business men to be liens upon the property of their drawers; otherwise, although a man owned ten thousand dollars' worth of property, his note for five thousand dollars would be deemed no better secured than if he owned no property. If money were not a lien on property, it would be valueless, and people would cease to part with their property for it.

The value of notes of hand, bonds and mortgages, book accounts, and money, depends upon their capability of being exchanged for property. Their power to accumulate is given by law, and they accumulate a mere legal representative; that is, interest in money, which is valuable only because, like the principal, it can be exchanged for a certain amount of actual value. Hence, the value is in the property, and not in the money or in the obligations. Money, and all obligations, are mere representatives, and depend upon property for their value.

CHAPTER II.

MONEY—THE MEDIUM OF DISTRIBUTION.

SECTION I.

THE NATURE AND PROPERTIES OF MONEY.

Money is the national medium of exchange for property and products. It must be instituted, and its value must be fixed by the laws of the nation, in order to make it a public tender in payment of debts. No debt can be paid with property or with individual notes, except by consent of the creditor; but when *money* is tendered, all creditors are compelled to receive it in full satisfaction of debts. The aim of legislation in regulating the value of money is to insure to all individuals, in making exchanges of their property for money, the full value of their products or property. Debts are postponements of the time of payment for the property or products received; and loans of money, and all rents of property are mere rents of the use of certain amounts of legal or actual value, which use is to be paid for at the expiration of a specified period. Money is the legal tender, and must be offered and received in payment for all these debts.

Certain properties are by law given to some substance, which bears the name and performs the functions of money. The term *money*, then, signifies a legal, public medium of exchange, which possesses all the qualifications necessary to effect a just exchange of property. In the discussion of the nature of money, it will appear that its properties are, in truth, the creation of law, and entirely different from the properties of the things which it exchanges.

Money has four properties or powers, viz.: *power to represent value, power to measure value, power to accumulate value by interest,* and *power to exchange value.* These properties are co-essential to a medium of exchange: it is impossible that any one of them should exist in such a medium independently of the others. The *material of money* is a *legalized agent,* employed to express these powers, and render them available in trade. The powers of money, which alone render it useful, are created by legislation; therefore, money can possess none but legal value. As all legal value depends upon the actual value which it holds or represents, money must represent actual value—that is, the value of property or labor.

SECTION II.

THE POWER OF MONEY TO REPRESENT VALUE.

Money must be a *legal representative* of property, for it is impossible to find any light and portable material possessing the requisite inherent value to equal and balance the value of the property and products to be exchanged. The real value is in the property and products, and the money is only the legal medium by which this value is represented and by which exchanges of the property and products are made.

Every representative is distinct from the thing which it represents; and its presence implies the absence of the thing represented. A representative has power to act for, or in lieu of something else. The power to represent is always independent of the natural or inherent powers of the representative; it is superadded and delegated, and cannot alter the original capabilities and qualities of the agent. Delegated authority gives the agent, the person or thing, power over other persons or things, which, with merely his natural capabilities, he cannot possess. Acting for himself alone, his acts are all individual, and incapable of binding any but himself. For instance, he cannot give a note, bond or deed, which will bind others, or the property of others, unless the power be expressly delegated to him. He *may receive authority* to give a note or bond binding the property of the people for its payment. This authority does not diminish or alter his capabilities as an individual; it is superadded to his natural endowments. An ambassador represents our nation at a foreign court. If he be lost at sea, the nation loses but one individual, although he represents and acts for thirty millions. But if the nation should be annihilated, and the ambassador should reach his destination in safety, he would cease to be a representative: he would have nothing to represent. He would, however, possess all his powers as an individual—he would lose only his delegated authority as a representative.

A representative in Congress is chosen by the people, and is empowered to act for or in lieu of them. Still it is not supposable that he possesses as much knowledge and skill as all his constituents. They are farmers, mechanics, manufacturers, and merchants. Of many of the arts with which they are familiar, the member of Congress is ignorant. He is their representative for one specific purpose—*i. e.*, to make laws to govern the people. He has a moral perception of justice corresponding to their perceptions of justice, and this fits him to be their representative in making laws. Money is made solely to facilitate the exchange of products. To be capable of effecting this exchange, it must be endowed with a *legal power to represent actual value;* for it possesses no inherent quality which makes it equivalent to products or labor more than the representative in Congress possesses all the knowledge and abilities of his constituents. It is held for the time being in lieu of property; we cannot use it as property, and if we wish to use actual property we must obtain it by giving the legal representative, money, in exchange for it. A representative in Congress has the sole authority to act there; and the people whom he represents can neither control him, nor be heard in lieu of him. They have no authority nor voice in making the laws except through their representative; but the laws which he helps to enact have a binding force on his constituents and others. So of money; when it is made a representative of value it controls and determines the value of labor and property, while these have no power to control and regulate the value of the money. The money is the only legal tender for debts; and all property and labor are as powerless to discharge an obligation as the constituents of a representative are to act in Congress after they have delegated their power to their member. The representative of value should no more have power to accumulate property in the hands of a few than the representative of the people should be allowed to legislate for the benefit of a few of his constituents. Both are mere representatives, endowed with powers for specific purposes; the former to exchange products, the latter to enact laws. The producing classes elect and support the members of Congress, who are bound to make laws for the equal benefit of the people. The people also furnish the material of money and the property which it represents; and the representative of value should be such as to conduce in the highest degree to their welfare.

The following is another example of delegated or representative power: A man gives a note for a thousand dollars. He thus delegates to the paper on which the note is drawn a power that increases its legal value millions of times. Before the drawing of the note, the paper possessed a small amount of actual value, but was not a legal representative of other property; for, as paper only, its worth depended upon its inherent qualities. But when the note is drawn, the paper becomes a representative, and has, according to law, a delegated control of a thousand dollars' worth of the property of the drawer. The drawing of the note does not add a fraction to the actual worth of the paper; its value in holding the property is legal, and superadded to its inherent qualities; the same value might be superadded by law to a plate of steel, or of any metal. The note and the property are distinct existences; but the legal value of the note depends on the actual value of the property. The paper material of a note good for a thousand dollars, is not as valuable as an ounce of flour; but it has a legal power which makes it capable of being exchanged for two hundred barrels of flour, worth five dollars each. A trifling labor will provide the representative note, but a great amount of labor is required to produce such a quantity of flour, or actual wealth. All individual notes are, however, payable not in flour, nor in actual products or property, but in money, the legal representative of all commodities and property.

According to law, the owner of an estate represents the value of the estate in his own person; but by a simple power of attorney, he can give to another the entire control of his property during his life-time. The receiver of the power may not be worth a dollar, but the power of attorney may make him the representative and controller of millions of dollars' worth of property. The paper that secures to him the control of the property has no greater inherent value after the writing of the instrument, than it had before; it is merely made to represent the property and control its use. The actual value which the paper represents, exists in the property, and, without the property, the paper would be worthless. The power of attorney is confined to an individual; but if a man, instead of making the power to a single person, should make it to bearer, whoever held the paper would have power over the property controlled by it. The negotiable power of money is inseparable from it, otherwise it would not be money. The holder of money has power over a certain amount of property for sale, and can appropriate it to himself. Money has a legal power or value as much superior to the natural value of its material, as a paper which secures authority over property has a value superior to blank paper.

Money is, then, a legal existence, being constituted a national representative of property; consequently it is a public lien on all property for sale in the nation, a public medium for the exchange of products, and a tender in payment of debts. If money be made a representative of the earth and its productions, it cannot fail to be permanently valuable, for the earth and its products are necessary to the existence of man; and anything which legally represents them, and can be exchanged for them, must be valuable to its holders.

It is a popular error that the value of money depends upon the *material* of which it is made. As this misconception of the nature of money is of long standing, we shall endeavor to point out its inconsistency, in connection with each property of money. The value of money perpetually depends upon its power to represent value, and not upon its material, because money never reaches a point at which it can be used as an article of actual value. Suppose twenty-six individuals owe $100 each, payable on the same day: A. owes B., B. owes C., and so on through the alphabet to Z. In the morning, A.

borrows from a bank a bank-note for $100 and pays it to B., B. pays it to C., C. to D., and so on, until it passes down to Z., who owes and pays it to the bank from which A. borrowed it. The same bank-bill pays twenty-six debts, and in the evening is in the ownership, and possession of the same bank as in the morning. Suppose that, instead of money, each of the twenty-six persons owes in the same order a loaf of bread, and each must have the loaf to use on the specified day or suffer from hunger. In the morning A. goes to a baker, borrows a loaf and pays it to B., B. pays it to C., C. to D., and so on through the alphabet to Z., who pays it over to the baker. The money in passing through this routine answers every man's purpose, and in meeting the contract fulfils the function for which money is designed, but the bread does not fulfil the purpose for which bread is designed, nor can a single loaf short of twenty-six answer the purpose. But one bank-note pays the twenty-six debts, and is ready to fulfil as many contracts more the next day, whereas twenty-six new loaves would be required to meet an equal number of contracts. It may be objected that the comparison is not a fair one, because bread is consumed by use and money is not: take then any other article valuable for its material and not consumed in the use. Twenty-six individuals have land to plough on the same day; can they borrow one plough and make it answer the purpose of twenty-six?

The value of lands and of goods, wares and merchandise, does not depend upon any act of legislation, upon any power to represent and exchange, but upon their utility for food, clothing, etc. If the gold or silver material of money be used for any other purposes than to represent and exchange property, if it be used for spoons, or ornaments, it at once ceases to be money: it is no longer a legal representative of value, but finds its level as a commodity. But the inherent properties of all articles of actual value, are their only valuable properties. However various the employment of articles of actual value, their properties do not change, or become useless: For example, cloth is useful to make a garment, and when made, is a *cloth* garment. The nature of the cloth does not change; it is only applied to a specific purpose, and the cloth retains its properties of durability, etc. Metal buttons are used upon the garment, and continue to be metal buttons. But silver money converted into a spoon, makes a *silver* spoon, and *not a money* spoon. The silver is no longer a legal representative of actual value; it is no longer money, for it has ceased to have the properties of money, which are creations of law. Neither a spoon nor bullion can legally represent, measure, accumulate nor exchange property; and the mere metal is, consequently, not a medium of exchange, nor a tender in payment of debts. The sole value of gold and silver coins, when not used for a currency, consists in the worth of their materials for spoons, ornaments, etc., which are a very small part of our actual wealth, and not indispensable to human existence. The metals cease to be money, as the power of a representative ceases when the term for which he was elected expires. He may be reëlected and receive his former power; and the gold may be recoined by the government, and thus be endowed with its former power as money. So, if the paper of a bond or note be ground to dust its value ceases; but it may be remade into paper, and by the requisite writings receive its former value.

The laws of nations have established money as the standard of value. These laws are immaterial; they are principles, and not material substances. The power of money is also immaterial: it is its legal authority, and not its material substance that establishes its value and power. The laws have professedly established the value of money in its material substance, but the groundwork being false, they have failed practically to establish money upon this basis; yet they have so far succeeded as grossly to deceive the public. That the worth of money to exchange property does not reside in its material, but in its legal power to represent value, will appear in the following illustrations: A. hires B. and C. to work for him at ten dollars per week each. At the end of the week he pays B. a ten-dollar gold piece, and C. a ten-dollar bank-note; taking in both cases a receipt in full for the week's work. B. is now the actual owner of the gold, and C. the actual owner of the paper in the bank-note. C. can buy in the market just as many of the necessaries of life with his paper money as B. can buy with his piece of gold. B. gave no more labor for the gold money than C. gave for the paper money, and can buy no more products with the gold than C. can buy with the paper. If there be any intrinsic value in gold money which does not exist in paper money, B., when he parts with his piece of gold, loses all the difference between the intrinsic value of the gold money and the intrinsic value of the paper money. But all the difference in the intrinsic value of the gold and paper disappears when both are used as money; hence it is evident that it is the immaterial power, that it is its legal authority over other things, and not the intrinsic value of its substance, that establishes the market value of the money. B. did not work the week because he needed the gold, neither did C. work the week because he needed the paper. They both labored for the same object, which was to procure the necessaries of life; and they both knew that either kind of money was legally competent to pay for these things. A yard of cloth measured with a gold yard-stick is neither longer nor shorter than if measured with a wooden one; and property purchased with gold or silver money is neither more nor less valuable than if bought with paper money. A person intends to purchase a farm and settle in Ohio. He has a thousand dollars in silver, but, as it is inconvenient to transport the specie, he exchanges it at a bank in New York for a thousand one-dollar bank bills. The bills readily purchase the farm. The individual who receives them in payment lends them on interest, and the borrower purchases wheat with them. Thus the bills circulate as money, and can be loaned for as good an income, or will purchase as much grain, as a thousand dollars in silver. They fulfil every purpose for which money is designed as well as the silver would. If the notes should remain permanently in Ohio, and the people should believe the bank secure, the notes would be a much better currency than coins, for they would make purchases as well, they could as well be loaned for an income, and could be much more easily transported. Why could not a thousand axes be deposited in Wall street, and a thousand pieces of paper be taken for them, on each corner of which was engraved "*one axe*," and in the body a written promise to pay one axe on demand, and these paper axes be taken to Ohio, and made to answer every purpose for which axes are designed, in clearing forests, etc., in lieu of the steel axes? There is as much resemblance between a paper axe and a steel axe as there is between a paper dollar and a silver dollar. If a paper dollar, that represents a silver dollar, is as good for all the purposes for which money is designed as a silver dollar, why is not a paper axe, that represents a steel axe, as good for all the purposes for which axes are designed as the steel axe? The reason that the paper dollar will answer as well as the silver dollar is, that the silver and the paper dollar are both representatives, the silver dollar equally with the paper dollar. (See *Chap. III., The Banking System.*) If the value of money be in the worth and weight of its material, it cannot be representative; and if its value be not representative, it would be as impossible to make paper money fulfil, as it now does, the functions of coins as to make a paper promise to pay a loaf of bread on demand as nutritious as the bread; or to make paper representatives of ploughs promising to pay real ploughs on demand capable of tilling the ground. If a city bank have $100 in coins and issue $600 in banknotes, the amount of money is as much increased as if $600 in specie had been issued. Each dollar of the banknotes will pay for as much labor, and for as many of the necessaries of life as any one dollar in specie; and so long as these bank-notes continue to circulate and to be on a par with specie, they continue to hold the same power and value in the market that are held by gold and silver money. Hence, if the value of money is inherent, this must prove that it inheres in bank-notes as well as in coins. The fact that it takes many thousand times more labor to mine the gold and silver and coin them into money, than it does to make the paper and engrave the bank-notes, makes no difference in the market value of the money, because the value of the money depends on its immaterial power—that is, upon its legal authority, and not at all upon its material substance. The law can and does designate the substance out of which money shall be made, but human laws do not in the least alter the intrinsic value of any substance. We might as well undertake by legislation to make saw-dust as nutritious as bread, as to undertake to make paper money on a par with specie if the value of the specie were dependent on its material substance. It takes as much labor and material to make a one-dollar bank-bill as it does to make a one thousand dollar bill; yet the latter is worth in the market precisely one thousand times more than the former.

The reason that the value of bullion is equal to that of coins is, that coins are made at the expense of the nation. The government coins all the gold and silver offered at the mint free of charge. It will give, in exchange for them, an equal weight in coins. If the government would take wool, and make cloth at the public expense, and return to those who furnish wool an equal weight in cloth, the cloth and wool would command the same price, because the expense of manufacturing the cloth would be borne by the government. If a charge were made for manufacturing, the wool would be worth less than the cloth; and if a premium were charged for coinage, the value of bullion would depreciate below that of coins. It is clear that gold and silver have no special inherent value which makes them naturally money; for they are not money until made so by conversion into coin.

SECTION III.

THE POWER OF MONEY TO MEASURE VALUE.

The *power to measure value* is another property of money. Measures are definite quantities of length, weight, bulk, and value, by which the amount of length, weight, bulk, and value in any substance is defined and ascertained.

Length, weight, bulk, and value, must necessarily be indefinite, unless some limit be fixed upon for a standard to which all other lengths, weights, quantities, and values may be referred, and by which they may be computed. *Length* may be the circumference of the earth, or the unknown distance to a star, or it may be the one-thousandth part of an inch; therefore, to convey any definite idea of length, reference must be made to a fixed standard. Weight, quantity, and value, are equally indefinite; hence the necessity for some *limit* or *standard*, to which they may be referred, and by which their amount may be ascertained.

The length, weight, quantity, and value of all articles, in business transactions, are settled by certain measures fixed upon by the government. The length of the yard-stick measures and determines a before undefined length of cloth; the size of the bushel measures and defines the before undefined quantity of grain; and so of the pound weight, it defines the quantity of cotton or other substances. The cloth does not define the length of the yard-stick, neither does the grain determine the size of the bushel, nor the cotton the pound weight. The value of the *dollar* measures and determines a before undefined value of land, labor, or products; the value of land, labor, and products, does not measure and determine the already defined value of the dollar. When the yard-stick measures cloth, it does not determine its own length; and when money exchanges property, it does not determine its own value. Both the length of the yard-stick, and the value of the money, were previously determined by the laws which instituted them, and gave them power to measure length and value, which are their sole objects and uses as measures.

The pound weight, or the standard of weights, determines the amount of the weight of all commodities; and the dollar, or money, the standard of value, by its own fixed legal value, determines the amount of the value of all other things. The weight of the pound, the length of the yard, and the value of the dollar, are presumed to be invariably fixed by national laws, and, therefore, every variation from their legal standard is a fraud upon the public. If the yard be variable, the measure of length will commit frauds when it is used; and if its value be fluctuating, the measure of value will commit frauds whenever it is used to measure the value of labor or property. If measures be strictly just and uniform, they will equitably determine quantities and values, whether of land, labor, or commodities.

It appears that the government considers the dollar of more importance than any other measure, for it reserves the right to coin it, and makes it a criminal offence for individuals to coin or issue money, even if it be equal to the government standard in purity and weight. Individuals are also prohibited from making and issuing paper money as a substitute for gold and silver money, unless especially authorized by law; and when this privilege is granted, the amount that may circulate and the security that shall be given to secure the public against loss, are also prescribed by law. But any individual may make and use any other measures, or may make and sell them in market, the government having merely a supervision over them as to weight, size and length.*

Money measures its own amount or value of actual property as often as it passes from one individual to another, as the yard-stick measures its own length as often as it passes over the cloth; consequently a given sum of money measures in a given time more or less property, according to the frequency of its transfer. In one morning, a dollar, passing through several hands, may be laid out for food, buy various articles of clothing, be loaned out with other dollars on bond and mortgage, and then purchase a dozen articles more. Every time it passes, it determines the market value of the thing that it buys.

If there were no distinction between measures of value and articles of value, the same principle would apply to both; one yard of cloth, rapidly measured, would answer the purpose of two, slowly measured; a pound of food, rapidly weighed, would answer the purpose of two, slowly

* Notwithstanding the care the government has taken to guard the use of money, there is in this nation more litigation, fraud and oppression, growing out of the corrupt use of money, in one week, and often, doubtless, in a single day, than all the evils that occur in a century from the fraudulent use of all other measures.

weighed. The value of money cannot consist in the amount or kind of the metal in which its properties are embodied; for, in its rapid circulation, it can be used neither as a utensil nor as an ornament, and is only useful to *exchange* property. Eagles and dollars are seldom used for ornamental purposes: and when they are so employed they cease to exchange products.

The value of money balances the value of the commodity sold, as the weight of the pound balances the weight of the thing weighed; or the yard, the length of the cloth measured. Measures of quantity remain stationary, their only function being to determine the exact quantities of the commodities transferred from the seller to the purchaser. But the measure of value passes into the possession of the seller, who holds it as a representative of value in lieu of his commodity. And it is on this account that the measure of value is frequently confounded with articles of value.

Money, like all other measures, is *divisible*. The yard is divided into feet and inches, that it may determine any required length. The pound weight is divided into half-pounds and ounces; the bushel into the peck, quart, etc., that they may accurately determine the various weights and quantities of various substances. Money is divided into pounds, shillings, and pence, dollars, half-dollars, dimes, etc., that it may determine the precise amount of the value of all commodities.

The government reserves the right to fix the length of the yard, the weight of the pound, the size of the bushel, and the value of the dollar, that they may be fitted for public use. Money is the public measure of value; and the government is bound to make it just and uniform, that it may correctly determine the value of all commodities.

SECTION IV.

THE POWER OF MONEY TO ACCUMULATE VALUE BY INTEREST.

Money, the representative and measure of value, has also *the power to accumulate value by interest.* This accumulative power is essential to the existence of money, for no one will exchange productive property for money that does not represent production. The law making gold and silver coins a public tender, imparts to dead masses of metal, as it were, life and energy. It gives them certain powers which, without legal enactment, they could not possess, and which enable their owner to obtain for their use what other men must earn by their labor. One piece of gold receives a legal capability to earn for its owner, in a given time, another piece of gold as large as itself. Or, in other words, the legal power of money to accumulate by interest compels the borrower, in a given period, determined by the rate of interest, to mine and coin, or procure, by the sale of his labor or products, another lump of gold as large as the first, and give it, together with the first, to the lender. If the borrower of the gold pay interest half yearly at the rate of seven per cent. per annum, he must double the lump in about ten years. If he pay interest half yearly at the rate of six per cent. per annum, he must double the lump in less than twelve years; at three per cent., in less than twenty-four years; and at one per per cent., in about seventy years.

In popular phrase, money is said to be a *producer of value;* but this expression conveys a false idea, for money possesses no power to produce. The earth produces by actual increase—by the growth of additional quantities of the seed sown. But money possesses no natural capability to produce its like. It can only accumulate things already produced. When a loan of a hundred dollars is repaid with interest, the six or seven dollars given as interest have not grown upon the original one hundred. Nothing grows upon the mortgage that bears interest. The interest on the money, or on the mortgage, must be paid in money received in exchange for property, products, or labor.

The worth and amount of the interest on the dollar constitute and determine the value of the dollar, and make it equal to a certain amount of actual value or property, as much as the amount and kind of labor that a man can perform, determine his value as a workman; or as the quality and quantity of the fruit of a tree determine the value of the tree. In the same manner, and for the same reason, if the interest on the dollar be good, the dollar will also be good. The value of the workman and of the tree is natural to them, and consists in their power to produce; the value of money is artificial, and consists in its arbitrary power to represent actual value and to accumulate by interest.

Demand and supply are sometimes said to give value to money; but it would be as reasonable to assert that demand and supply fix the length of the yard, the weight of the pound, or the size of the bushel, as that demand and supply regulate the value of money. One is a legal instrument to determine value, its own value being fixed by law; the others are legal instruments to determine length, weight, and quantity, their own length, weight, and size being fixed by law.

Money is valuable *in proportion* to its power to accumulate value by interest. A dollar which can be loaned for twelve per cent. interest, is worth twice as much as one that can be loaned for but six per cent., just as a railroad stock which will annually bring in twelve per cent., is worth twice as much as one that annually brings in six per cent. The value of state, bank, railroad, or any other stock, is estimated by the dividends it will pay during the time it has to run. Any increase or diminution of the power of money to accumulate by interest, increases or diminishes proportionably its value, and consequently its power over property.

Money becomes worthless whenever it ceases to be capable of accumulating an income which can be exchanged for articles of actual value. Take the following example. Suppose, during the Revolutionary war, A. had lent to B. a thousand dollars in gold or silver coin, at six per cent. interest, for a term of fifty years, and had taken as security a mortgage on B.'s farm, which was worth $10,000. A. had agreed to receive the six per cent. interest from B. in Continental money. This currency soon after proved to be worthless; and the interest proving worthless, the principal would have been worthless to A. during the fifty years for which he lent it, although the loan was made in gold and silver coin, and, at the expiration of that period, the principal would have been paid him in coin.

Now reverse the circumstances, and suppose A. had lent to B. a thousand dollars in Continental money on the same farm for fifty years, and had made the interest payable in gold and silver coin. Although the principal was lent in Continental money, which soon after became worthless, it would have continued as valuable to A. for fifty years, as the interest in coin which he received upon it. The interest continuing valuable, the mortgage would have been a binding lien upon B.'s farm for the fifty years, and would have taken a part of the yearly produce of the farm for that period. At the expiration of the fifty years, the principal would have become worthless, for it could not have brought in a further income. But in the former case, in which specie was lent and the interest made payable in Continental money, the interest being worthless, the contract would not have been an encumbrance upon B.'s farm; for no part of its yearly products would have been required to pay the interest. At the expiration of fifty years, the principal could have been demanded in specie.

The value of money as much depends upon its legal power to be loaned for an income, as the value of a farm depends upon its natural power to produce. If the Continental money, or the assignats of France, had been made representatives of property, and capable of being always loaned for a good and uniform income, they would have been as permanently valuable as a mortgage in perpetuity on a farm, which could yearly collect from the farmer a certain quantity of products, as interest, or income. The value of a horse depends upon his ability to perform useful labor for his possessor; and the value of money depends upon its capability to earn for its owner by being loaned on interest. Take twenty mortgages for ten years on twenty different farms. Suppose each of these farms to rent for sixty dollars a year, just the interest on each of the mortgages. It would take the whole produce of each farm to pay the interest on each mortgage. The twenty mortgages would take the rent or produce of the twenty farms for ten years. In one month, one thousand dollars could be easily loaned so as to take the entire income of twenty farms for ten years. Consequently, each time the money was lent it would accumulate an income which would be as valuable to its owner as a farm of equal value leased for the same period; for the income on the money would yearly purchase the whole yearly produce of the farm.

The difference between money and the farms is, that the former is a legal representative and measure of value, and the latter are of actual value. The money is as capable of representing and measuring its own amount of value a hundred times in a year, and creating a hundred incomes, as the pound weight is of determining its own amount of weight a hundred times. The quantity of cloth measured, and the weight of things weighed, cannot be increased by the number of times that the measure is applied to them. But money being a representative of value, and being endowed by law with the power to accumulate by interest, makes an income whenever it is transferred from one to another as a loan.

Anything that exists in perpetuity, is valuable in exact proportion to the income it will yearly bring to its owner. The market value of a house, store, or farm, rises or falls with the rise or fall of its yearly rent; and the value of the dollar rises or falls with the rise or fall of its rent or interest. If we admit both the property and the money to be merchandise, this principle cannot be true in one case without being equally true in the other; therefore, whether we assume money to be of actual, or of legal value, to keep its value uniform, the rate of interest must be kept uniform. Doubling the capability of the dollar to accumulate, doubles the value of the dollar. Its nominal value may, and does remain the same—that is, it retains the name of *dollar*, although it possesses twice its ordinary value, or power over property and labor.

The same principle applies to all measures. The length of the yard-stick being doubled, although it might still retain its name, it would measure twice as much cloth as with its present limits. And money, while its denominations remain the same, measures more or less property, according to the rate of interest. We may imagine a measure fluctuating, expanding and contracting between certain points; as a yard-stick, made of some elastic material, susceptible of being stretched to twice or thrice its ordinary limits, and still called a yard-stick, and used as such. But no one would deem himself acquainted with the actual length of anything measured by this yard-stick, although, if it were the legalized one, it could, and must be used in business.*

Measures of quantity are instituted, and their length, bulk, and weight are fixed by law, and not by individuals. The measure of value is instituted and made by law; and, consequently, it is fraudulently used when the rate of interest upon it, which determines its value, is altered by individuals. The fundamental proposition of Jeremy Bentham, in his "Defence of Usury," is as follows:

"No man of ripe years, and of sound judgment, acting freely and with his eyes open, ought to be hindered, with a view to his advantage, from making such bargain, in the way of obtaining money, as he thinks fit; nor (what is a necessary consequence) anybody hindered from supplying him, upon any terms he thinks proper to accede to."

According to Mr. Bentham's theory, when money is loaned, the rate of interest to be paid must be a matter of agreement between borrower and lender. This makes the rate of interest belong to the system of free-trade, whereas it no more belongs to this system than the length of the yard-stick or the weight of the pound. By increasing the rate of interest, both the principal of the money and the interest upon it have an increased power over property, just as the pound increased in weight would call for an additional quantity of products to balance it. The right to fix the value of money is as much reserved by the government as the right to fix the length of the yard or the weight of the pound; and the regulation of its value is a thousand times more important to the people.† The value of money is no more fixed

---

* See Appendix, A.

† Although the value of money is now professedly fixed by the government, we can form no correct idea of what its value will be at the end of three or six months. But we should think it ridiculous to ask what would be the length of the yard, or the weight of the pound, or

or regulated by the laws ordering each piece of money to be coined of a certain weight and kind of metal than the length of the yard would be fixed by ordering it to be made of a certain weight and kind of wood, without regard to its length.

The value of money depends upon its power to accumulate value for its owner, by interest, and not upon the worth of its material; as the value of a paper instrument, which secures a ground-rent, depends upon the productiveness of the land on which it is secured, and not upon the inherent qualities of the paper. If the land were permanently unproductive, the lien could command no products, and would be worthless, except so far as the paper on which it was drawn possessed inherent value. Suppose the lien to be engraven on a silver plate, instead of on paper, and to be made in perpetuity for $10,000, at six per cent. interest per annum. Let the annual products of the land be sufficient to pay for the labor expended upon it, and to pay the ground-rent, and the silver on which the ground-rent was engraven would be

the size of the bushel three or six months hence; or to express great anxiety when the crops were coming in and the fall trade commencing whether enough measures could be procured to measure the grain, or scales and weights to weigh it, or yard-sticks to measure the cloth manufactured. We should think farmers, manufacturers and merchants crazed, if they should come to New York to ascertain whether enough measures could probably be had to determine the weight and quantity of their products; and under a just and sound monetary system, it would be equally absurd to ask whether enough money could be obtained to buy or exchange the goods, or to make any internal improvement; and it would appear as ridiculous to ask what the rate of interest would be at the end of three or six months as to ask how many feet it would then take to make a yard. Money properly instituted would be as definite and uniform as the latter measure, and would no more govern the amount of production than the yard-stick does the quantity of cloth manufactured. It could be about as easily procured to facilitate all desirable production, trade and improvements as yard-sticks to measure any quantity of cloth.

worth ten thousand dollars, whether the plate of silver on which it was drawn were three feet square, and weighed three hundred pounds, or whether it were three inches square, and weighed but three ounces. If the ground-rent on each plate were in perpetuity, and it were necessary to preserve each in its proper form, to keep the title good, although so great a difference existed in the weight, there would be no difference in the value of the two plates, for both would secure the same annual amount of interest. If, however, the ground-rent should fail because of some defect in the title, of course the larger plate of metal would be worth more than the smaller, for it would make more useful and ornamental articles. A ground-rent made in perpetuity for $10,000, secured on good property by paper instruments, would be as valuable to any owner as the larger silver plate. For this and for similar purposes, the paper is as much superior to the silver as, in manufacturing, the power-loom is superior to hand-weaving. The value of these liens on specific pieces of land, does not more depend on the productiveness of the land than the value of money depends upon its power to accumulate an income from the labor or property of borrowers. The value of the papers which secure the National Debt of England would cease if the government should pass a law to pay no more interest upon the debt. A mere legislative enactment could annul the value of the papers. Laws, then, give them their worth, and their worth consists in their power to collect a yearly income, which may be exchanged for the products of labor.

Money could not answer the purposes of a medium of exchange unless it were necessary to part with it to make it valuable. For this reason it is made to accumulate no interest in the possession of its owner; for if it would accumulate interest in his hands, it would be legally equivalent to a bond and mortgage bearing interest, or to productive property, and the owner would not need to part with it to make it productive.

SECTION V.

THE POWER OF MONEY TO EXCHANGE VALUE.

Another power of money is *to exchange property*. When it is made the public representative of value, and the interest is fixed at a just rate, it is fitted to perform the duty of money, which is the equitable exchange of property. All goods, wares, and merchandise, although they may be exchanged for money a number of times, soon find a place where they are consumed; but money never reaches a point where it can be used except as a tender in exchange for property. Making a silver dollar an equivalent or tender in payment for a debt contracted by the purchase of a bushel of wheat, does not make the dollar possess the nutritious qualities of the wheat, more than giving a note upon the purchase of a hundred bushels of corn makes the note of as great actual value as the corn. The value of the note depends upon its power to exchange itself for the property of the drawer, and not on the worth of the paper upon which the note is drawn. But the value of the corn depends upon its nutritious qualities, and not upon any power to exchange itself for the property of the person who raised or sold it. The note must be exchanged for property before it can be useful to its owner; money must also be exchanged for property to become useful.

This, then, is the distinction between articles of actual value and the medium of exchange. The former are designed to be actually used or consumed; the latter is designed to be continually exchanged for articles for actual use and consumption. Hence money is not merchandise, for if its material be used as a commodity—if coins be converted into watch-cases and ornaments, the owner must keep them to make them useful.

The object of the institution of money is to facilitate the exchange of commodities; and this it could never do unless it were possessed of as much legal value as the thing for which it is to be exchanged possesses actual value. If a farmer has five hundred bushels of wheat, with which he wishes to buy sugar, coffee, tea, molasses, clothing and so forth for his family, he will not sell the wheat for five hundred dollars, unless the money will be a legal equivalent for all the articles for which he wishes to exchange his wheat. He does not want the money to keep; he wants it to exchange for other articles that he needs to use or consume, and he sells his wheat for money because the money is a legal equivalent for every species of property. It would be very difficult for him to divide up the wheat and barter it for various articles in different places; and the wheat is not a tender. But he can divide up his money in amounts to suit all his purchases, and the money is a legal tender in payment. A man may carry a piece of paper money in his pocket that is a legal equivalent for a valuable farm in any part of the country, when if he had the same amount of actual value, it might be impossible for him to move it; but he can sell it for money, and the money he can carry in his pocket and buy with it where he pleases.

Some writers, instead of considering money as a medium of exchange, call it *capital seeking investment.* If money be capital, it is already invested; because the capital would consist in the inherent value of the material of the money, and not in the thing the money seeks to obtain. But, when money has found one investment, it is as much a seeker for a second and a third investment, as if it had not been invested at all. It is always seeking investment, without being invested.* It is no more real capital than a very poor horse, of which the appearance is such that he will do very well to exchange off. But if he should finally fall into the hands of a person who had not the good fortune to exchange him again for something else, the owner would have to depend upon his few useful qualities. And if a currency were formed in the various nations independently of gold and silver, and coins should cease to be a tender in payment of debts, the value of coins would depend upon their inherent qualities, as metals, as much as the value of the horse when he could be no longer exchanged for more than his actual worth, would depend upon the little labor that he could perform, or upon his hide and bones. The price of the gold and of the horse would then depend upon their actual usefulness, and not upon any capabilities for exchange.

Money is, then, a combination of legal powers, expressed upon metal, paper, or some other substance; its value is the standard or determiner of the value of all other things, and it serves as a public medium of exchange for land, labor, and all commodities.

---

* We are accustomed to say that money is invested in property, but this is not true. Money is no more invested in property than the yard-stick is invested in the cloth that it measures. When money has passed from one person to another either as a loan or in payment for property, it is ready to be lent again or to be paid for another piece of property. The money is no more used up by passing from one person to another than the yard-stick is used up by measuring a single piece of cloth. We are often told in the money articles of the daily newspapers, that the money of the country has been used up in railroads; but upon travelling over these roads we see evidences that a great deal of *labor* has been expended in grading them, furnishing the iron and timber and so forth, but we do not see any money. If the money has been invested in these roads, it has now gone somewhere else; and it is still going to and fro in the earth, and up and down in it.

SECTION VI.

THE MATERIAL OF MONEY, AND THE DISTINCTIONS BETWEEN MONEY AND THE MATERIAL OF WHICH IT IS MADE.

The *material* of *money*—gold, silver, paper, or any other substance—is a *legalized agent*, made to express the four properties, or powers of money, and render them available in business transactions.

Common usage has applied the term *measure* to the material, by means of which, length, weight, etc., are ascertained; as, for instance, the yard, pound, and bushel, instantly suggest the stick, iron, and wood, the means employed, rather than the abstract length, weight, and size, which are, in reality, the things signified by the terms. It matters not whether the yard-stick and pound weight be of wood, iron, or gold—length and weight are the only properties necessary to be expressed by them, and possessing the standard limits, their *material* is a matter of indifference. Of course, *some* material is indispensable; but the only thing that makes one substance preferable to another, is its superior convenience. So of money; it is a matter of indifference by what material the powers or properties of money are expressed, for the material is merely a substance fixed upon by law.

The natural powers of any material do not make it money. Its powers and agency as money are delegated to it by law, in addition to its natural capabilities When gold is used, the powers conferred upon it make it an equivalent for every species of property. If gold had not been selected for the material of money, and a legal power given to it to exchange property, and to accumulate interest for its use, a man would have as little occasion for more gold than he needs for utensils and ornaments, as for more clothes than he can wear, or more tools than he can use. It would have been subjected to the same laws of trade as other merchandise, and must have waited a demand for consumption before it could have been sold. It is clear that gold possesses no peculiar or inherent excellence to endow it with power to determine the value and control the use of all other things. But when it is made the agent of these legal powers, it becomes necessary to acquire the gold in order to discharge debts; and the quantity of the metal being limited, its owners are enabled to extort from the necessitous a very high price for its use. If gold were not used as the material of the currency, its abundance would cause no inflation of business, nor would its scarcity produce distress, because, compared with other metals, its use is very limited.

The following statement will show the different effects upon our own people of the use of the precious metals as utensils, and their use as the material of money. All will probably admit that there were, in 1846, twelve thousand families in the city of New York, owning, on an average, $800 worth of gold and silver ware, such as tea, coffee, and dinner services, vases, ornaments, etc. Including jewelry, the amount of the metals probably far exceeded the sum named. But calculating the twelve thousand families to have owned $800 worth each, they owned, in the aggregate, $9,600,000; while, according to the Bank Reports, the specie in all the banks in the State of New York on the 1st day of November, 1846, amounted to but $8,048,348. Suppose the twelve thousand families owning these silver and gold utensils and ornaments, had in one week collected them together, and shipped them to England. The shipping of these wares would have had no more effect upon the monetary affairs of the State or nation, nor upon business, than the shipping of the same amount in cotton and tobacco. But had the people drained the $8,048,348 of coins from the banks, and shipped them abroad, the banks throughout the State, and throughout the United States, would have been compelled to suspend specie payments, and hundreds of thousands of our people would have been bankrupted or thrown out of employment. Yet, by shipping the gold and silver wares, more than one million and a half more of the precious metals would have left the country, than by shipping the coins. The shipment of the smaller amount would have shaken the country to its centre, while the shipment of the larger amount, could not have unfavorably affected business. And yet our gold and silver utensils and ornaments are more in use than our coins; for the coins are mostly in kegs and boxes in the vaults of banks, and if they are moved at all, it is usually from one bank vault to another, without even emptying them from the kegs. If money is merchandise, why would not the shipment of our gold and silver utensils affect the business of the nation, as much as the shipment of our coins? The same twelve thousand families were doubtless the owners of a much larger amount of the capital stocks of the banks than the $9,600,000; and could at any time have sold stock enough to draw all the specie from the banks, and thus have caused a suspension of payments; and distressed producers, even without shipping the specie.

If the value of money inhere in the precious metals, so that a certain weight naturally possesses a certain amount of power to exchange property, and still is itself a commodity, the value of which is fixed by law, other commodities made of the same naturally precious metals, watchcases, spoons, etc., should likewise be subject to the scrutiny and restriction of government, that the public may not be imposed upon in the receipt of them by any mixture of alloy. If money be a commodity, why do governments pretend to fix a value upon coins, and not upon any other commodity, although it be made of gold or silver? If a definite value be assigned to one commodity by legal enactment, a definite value should also be legally assigned to every other commodity, that each may sustain a just relation according to the amount of labor necessary to manufacture or produce it. If money be a commodity, goods sold might as well be made payable in other commodities, sugar, beef, etc., as in money. Why not as well sell money on time payable in goods, as goods on time payable in money? If money be a commodity, why should the government force the public to convert every other commodity into this one to pay debts? If the sale and purchase of all other commodities will cause debts to exist, why should one commodity only be competent to pay them? And why should the value of every other commodity be determined by this one commodity? If money be a commodity, why does the government reserve the right to coin it, making its private coinage a criminal offence? Why not let any one make it, and dispose of it in market as of any other commodity? If money be merchandise, why is it, that it can be at all times exchanged for property and products, in any part of the country, and that all other more necessary commodities are at certain times esteemed almost worthless, compared with it? It is answered, that it is because it is made by law a legal tender in payment for debts—that it has this superiority over every other commodity. But the very answer proves that it is not a commodity; for a legal tender is a creation by law of certain properties which do not naturally belong to any substance, but which are made to represent all substances, and to control their exchange. Governments have enacted their monetary laws upon the false principle that the gold and silver metals had an intrinsic value, and consequently a power in their material, before they were instituted as money, equal to their legal power and value after being so instituted.

It is sometimes said, that commodities are a sort of currency, because they can be and are exchanged for money. But though a bushel of wheat may be exchanged for money, it does not possess any of the legal and distinctive properties of money. The wheat does not become money more than a watch would become land by being given in exchange for land.

Some argue that the dollar derives its value from the labor required to mine and coin the silver for it. They say that if a day's labor be required to mine the silver for a dollar, and a day's labor be required to raise a bushel of wheat, the silver and the wheat are of equal worth, and that the legal acts of the government cannot alter the value of either. But if the equal amount of labor expended make the dollar and the wheat of equal value, why will the dollar at certain periods buy two or three times more wheat, or more labor, than it will at other periods? Why does not the value of labor and of wheat increase equally with the value of the dollar?

When the products of labor command a high price, labor also commands a high price. A given quantity of wheat or of other products will pay for nearly the same amount of labor every year. But if the price of products be low, the employer cannot pay to labor a high price in money. In seasons of depressed prices, a dollar will purchase double, treble, or quadruple the amount of labor that it ordinarily will, and this difference occurs when no more labor is required to mine and coin the silver. Let those who maintain the theory, that the labor required to procure money constitutes its value, account, if they can, for these facts, so as to satisfy laborers and producers, the reward of whose labor, and the price and sale of whose products it so nearly affects.

Because money is held in lieu of labor performed, and in lieu of everything valuable, the public have been accustomed to consider money an actual equivalent in value to the commodity or labor it will pay for; whereas in fact, it is only a legal equivalent or balancing power. Air, water, food, clothing and a vast variety of other things are essential to the existence and comfort of man, and no one thing can be an *actual* equivalent for them. It is as impossible that ten pounds' weight of gold should possess equal actual value with the four thousand bushels of corn, or four thousand days' labor which the gold will purchase, as that a small quantity of poison, frequently necessary as a medicine to restore man to soundness and health, should be of equal value with the corn or labor. As many elements for the support of man exist in the poison, as in the money. Both are useful in their spheres, the former to remove obstructions to health, the latter to facilitate the exchange of products. Poison is of little value compared with food; and money is as little valuable compared with property. It would be as reasonable to esteem the comet which appears once in a century, more valuable to us than the sun that daily sheds its fertilizing beams upon the earth, as to esteem the actual value of gold and silver equivalent to that of all the necessaries of life. If the quantity of gold were unlimited, not a thousandth part as much of it would be used as of iron. The notion that gold and silver are endowed by the Creator with some mysterious value and capabilities, which render them of greater importance than the ordinary products of labor, is an erroneous and pernicious one. Legal enactments cannot alter the inherent properties of metals.

The common opinion that the material of a currency must be something scarce and difficult to procure, that the limited amount may render it permanently valuable, arises from a misconception of the nature of money, the properties of which are entirely independent of the material. Money consists in the legal powers to represent, measure, accumulate, and exchange property and products. It receives its powers from law. If gold and silver should become as abundant as iron and lead, the only difficulty in maintaining them the materials of a currency, would be the difficulty of protecting them from counterfeit. Could they be protected, it would be as unnecessary to abandon them for a currency on account of their abundance, as to abandon the use of paper in making obligations, because more exists than can be used for that purpose. If the quantity of gold and silver were unlimited, and that part of it which was needed for a currency were made a lien upon and representative of property, there would be nearly as great a difference between the value of the metals so used and bullion, as there now is between a paper obligation that is a lien upon valuable property and a piece of blank paper.

For ages gold and silver have been esteemed precious metals, containing a large amount of intrinsic value, although their inadequacy to supply natural wants is manifest, when we imagine a man, with a bag of coins, on a desert island, and without the power to exchange them for other articles. These metals have intrinsic, or actual value, and this value consists in their utility for utensils and ornaments; their malleability, ductility and beauty rendering them, for some purposes, superior to all other metals. But it will be confessed, that we could far better dispense with them than with any of the abundant metals, which are in more general and constant use, and the loss of which would seriously impair our comfort.

In early ages, gold and silver were, doubtless, selected for the material of money on account of their scarcity, and the amount of labor necessary to procure them; the same reason that led the American Indians to select the beaver-skin for a standard of value, by which the value of all other skins and commodities was estimated. It has been already explained, that gold and silver, when used as money, cease to have any other use. These metals have, however, received the sanction of governments as the material of money. The laws require that coins used as a public tender shall contain a certain weight of the authorized metal—without which they are illegal, and cannot be enforced as a tender. But the only reason that they are not received is, that they are unsanctioned by law. If coins of base metal were endowed by law with the properties of money—that is, were made representatives of actual value, capable of accumulating by interest, and a public tender for debts, they would answer every purpose of money, equally well with coins of pure metal. They could represent, measure, accumulate and exchange property, and these are the sole properties and uses of money. Therefore they would be money, for anything that possesses the properties of money, without division, subtraction, or increase, *is* money. But if the metal were used for purposes of dentistry, the difference between the pure and the base would at once appear; for the metal would then be used otherwise than as the material of money, and its utility would not depend upon its legal powers, but upon its natural capabilities as a metal.

The value of money, then, depends upon its powers to represent, measure, accumulate, and exchange value. These powers, given to any convenient material by Congressional enactment, will qualify it for a medium of exchange, and in every particular constitute it money.

CHAPTER III.

THE RATES OF INTEREST THE GOVERNING POWER OF DISTRIBUTION TO LABOR AND CAPITAL.

SECTION I.

THE POWER OF CAPITAL TO ACCUMULATE PROPERTY AND LABOR ACCORDING TO THE RATE OF INTEREST.

In the introduction, labor was said to be the chief producer of wealth, and the preceding chapter has been devoted to the consideration of the nature and powers of money. The present chapter will exhibit the laws which govern the distribution of the wealth, and will show the practical effects of certain rates of interest upon producers.

The Constitution of the United States, Art. I., Sec. VIII. 5, declares, "The Congress shall have power to coin money, regulate the value thereof, and of foreign coin, and fix the standard of weights and measures." Money is the legal standard of value, by which the value of all articles for sale must be determined. The rate of interest fixes the value of money. Its value is no more fixed by the quantity or the quality of its material, than the size of the bushel is fixed by the quantity and quality of its wood. The rate of interest maintained upon loans of money, determines what proportion of the earnings of labor shall be paid for the use of capital, and what proportion shall be paid to the laborers for their productions. If interest on money be maintained at a high rate, rents on property will also be high.

There are but two purposes to which the yearly products of labor can be applied. One is the payment of the yearly rent or interest on the capital employed, and the other is the payment of labor. If laborers pay to capital, as use or interest for the year, their whole surplus products, the laborers, as a body, work for a mere subsistence, and the capital takes their whole surplus earnings. The laborer receives for his year's toil, food, clothing and shelter only, and these perhaps of the poorest kind ; while the capitalist lives in luxury, increases the number of his bonds and mortgages, or with his income buys land or builds houses to let, which will, in succeeding years, take a still greater sum from the laborer. The law of interest, or per centage on money, as much governs the rent or use of all property, and consequently the reward of labor, as the law of gravitation governs the descent of water. If the interest on money be too high, a few owners of capital will inevitably accumulate the wealth or products of the many. With the present accumulative power of interest, there is no more chance of the laboring classes gaining their rights by combining their labor to increase production, than there would be hope of success that by combining their labor they could reverse the course of the rivers, and make them run to the tops of the mountains, and pile up the waters on their summits. The law of gravitation, in the latter case, would not be more sure to overpower all their labor, and frustrate all their plans, than the present governing power of the interest on money is sure to gather up the increased production and add it to the wealth of capitalists. The fault is in the law which governs the distribution of property ; and combinations to increase production would no more effect any general change in the distribution, than combinations against the law of gravitation would effect a change in its general governing powers. The evil is legislative, and the remedy must be legislative.

Money loaned on interest or invested in property, is doubled in a certain length of time, determined by the rate of interest. When this rate is too high, it requires the principal to be doubled in so short a time, that the borrower is compelled to give all his surplus products as interest or rent; whereas, justice requires that he should pay only a moderate per centage for the use of capital, and himself retain the chief surplus of his labor.

The following illustrations, calculating property to accumulate or double at certain rates of yearly per centage, in the same manner as money, will clearly exhibit the various results to laborers from various rates of interest. A., B., and C. are young men, who have just come of age. C. is heir to $10,000, while A. and B. are mechanics, without capital. C. contracts with A. and B. to build a house which shall cost $5,000, on a lot for which he paid $5,000. The house and lot together are worth $10,000. C. leases this property to A. and B., and charges them seven per cent. upon its cost, clear of insurance, taxes and repairs. The interest is payable once a quarter. A rate of interest of seven per cent. per annum, paid quarterly, will accumulate a sum equal to the principal loaned or invested in property in ten years. At this rate, in ten years A. and B. are compelled to buy another lot, build upon it another as good a house, and pay the lot and house to C. for the use of the house they occupy. In twenty years, if A. and B. retain the use of the house and its accruing rents, they must pay C. three houses; in thirty years they must pay him seven houses; in forty years, fifteen houses; in fifty years, thirty-one houses; in sixty years, sixty-three houses; and in seventy years, one hundred and twenty-seven houses. In seventy years all these must be built by A. and B., and paid to

C. as the accumulation on the one that he leased to them. The one hundred and twenty-seven lots which A. and B. earn the money to buy, cost $635,000, and the buildings cost an equal amount, making together, $1,270,000; which sum is paid to C. for seventy years' rent of one house and lot worth $10,000. At the expiration of the lease, the original house must be returned to its owner, as well as the rent. If, instead of being invested in the house and lot, the $10,000 were loaned on interest at seven per cent., and the interest were collected and reloaned quarterly, the money would accumulate in a given period precisely the same amount as the property.

Now, suppose interest to be at three per cent. per annum, and A. and B. to build the house, and pay C. three per cent. annually on its cost of $10,000. This is $300, instead of $700 a year; and, at this rate, the interest on money, collected and reloaned quarterly, requires nearly twenty-four years to accumulate a sum equal to the principal. Therefore, in twenty-four years A. and B. would give C. another house; and, in seventy-two years, seven houses, instead of one hundred and twenty-seven, which they are compelled to do at seven per cent. interest. The labor of building the houses is neither increased by a high rate, nor diminished by a low rate of interest.

If C. let his house to A. and B. at six per cent., in about twelve years the income or rent will equal the principal; therefore, at the expiration of that period, A. and B. must pay C. another house, and in twenty-four years, they must pay him three houses. But if C. lease the house to them for twenty-four years at three per cent., A. and B. return him his house, adding one to it as its rent, and retain two houses as their own surplus. With interest at three per cent., in twenty-four years A. and B. would each own a house and lot worth $10,000;

while, with the interest on money loaned or invested in property at six per cent. both would still be tenants, although they would have performed, in both cases, the same amount of labor. With interest at three per cent., in forty-eight years they would give C. three houses, instead of fifteen, as at six per cent., and they would own twelve as the surplus product of their labor. But at six per cent., C.'s capital would compel A. and B. to continue his tenants, and to build for him sixteen houses more during the next twelve years.

Take another example of the accumulation of property at seven per cent. interest. At the age of twenty-one, D. owns a well improved farm of one hundred acres. He leases it to E. at an interest of seven per cent., payable in land, as the interest on money is payable in money. At the close of the year, E. pays D. seven acres of as good quality as the one hundred rented, and with a *pro ratâ* proportion of buildings upon them. D. continues to let the farm to E. requiring him to pay the rent in land half-yearly, as interest on money is paid half-yearly in money; and to pay rent on the land so paid, as the borrower of money pays interest on the interest which he adds half yearly to the principal. In ten years, E. must pay one farm; in twenty years, three farms; in thirty years, seven farms; in forty years, fifteen farms; in fifty years, thirty-one farms; in sixty years, sixty-three farms; and in seventy years, one hundred and twenty-seven farms; all in as good a state of cultivation as the one originally leased. At the age of ninety-one, D. can bequeath to his posterity one hundred and twenty-seven farms, from the mere rent on one. These farms E. must earn by the labor of seventy years, and pay to D. for the use of one farm. If it were possible for him to earn the one hundred and twenty-seven farms to pay to D., and the rate of interest were reduced to one per cent., he need pay to D. only about one farm as rent for the seventy years, and could retain one hundred and twenty-six as the surplus of his labor.

Again, suppose John and Richard to be poor boys, each ten years old, who expect to be bound out at the proper age to learn the carpenter's trade. But a rich uncle bequeaths to John a house worth ten thousand dollars. It is worth so much, because it will rent for seven hundred dollars a year over and above taxes, insurance and repairs. John's guardian is a lawyer, and will collect the rent, and loan it out for him at seven per cent. per annum, getting his fees from those who borrow the money. John likes Richard, and learns his trade with him, and earns his living by his labor as Richard does. John instructs his lawyer to purchase another house, whenever the rent of the one accumulates to enough to buy a second equal to the first. If the interest be regularly collected and loaned at seven per. cent., and the interest be collected half yearly, it will equal the principal in ten years and one month; when his lawyer can buy for John a second house, so that when he is twenty years and one month old, he will be the owner of two houses. These two houses, rented for ten years and one month more, will buy for John two houses more; so that at the age of thirty years and two months, he will own four houses: at forty years and three months, he will own eight houses: at fifty years and four months, sixteen houses; at sixty years and five months, thirty-two houses; at seventy years and six months, sixty-four houses; and at eighty years and seven months of age, he will own one hundred and twenty-eight houses, each of which is rented at seven hundred dollars a year; and all of them together are bringing in a clear yearly income of eighty-nine thousand six hundred dollars. Now what has John, or his uncle, or his guardian, done, that the public should be obliged to give John one hundred and twenty-seven houses for seventy years' use of one house? These one hundred and twenty-seven houses are all legally his; and our laws maintain that John has as equitable a right to them as if he had bought the lots and built the houses by his own labor. Yet, if we allow labor to be worth a dollar a day, it would take the entire earnings of sixty men for over seventy years to pay for the one hundred and twenty-seven houses, which the use of the one house has in seventy years legally acquired for John, without the performance of any labor on his part.

Let us see how different would be the results in this case if the interest on money, and consequently the rents on property, were at one per cent. per annum, instead of at seven per cent. John's uncle bequeaths to him the house worth ten thousand dollars; but, instead of renting it at seven per cent. on its value, John can rent it at but one per cent. over and above taxes, insurance and repairs, and regularly collects and loans out the rent as in the former case. It would be about seventy years before the rent and the accruing interest on the rent would equal the principal, and buy for John a second house as valuable as the first. With interest legally fixed at one per cent. the use of one house for seventy years would accumulate for John, out of the earnings of others, one additional house of equal value, whereas, at seven per cent. it would accumulate for him one hundred and twenty-seven houses. Whether the government fix the rate of interest at seven or at one per cent. the public must provide the same quantity of material and perform precisely the same amount of labor to build the one hundred and twenty-seven houses; but with the interest at seven per cent. John would lawfully own them all, whereas with interest fixed at one per cent. he would lawfully own but one house out of the one hundred and twenty-seven houses, and others would lawfully own the remaining one hundred and twenty-six houses. To furnish the materials and build these houses, requires not only skill in the mechanical arts, but also the performance of an immense amount of manual labor. But to give the one hundred and twenty-seven houses to John, who is fairly entitled to but one of them for the use of the one he rented, is the legitimate operation of the law fixing the interest at seven per cent. What chance have the producing classes by any combination of labor to contend successfully against such an accumulating and centralizing power? They might as well venture into the sea, with the wind blowing a hurricane, and expect by their bodily strength to turn back the waves. The sea would not be more certain to sweep over them, and pursue its onward course, than the accumulative power of money at seven per cent. interest yearly to gather up the surplus earnings of labor despite all combinations of labor against it. If the producers ever gain their rights, it will be by legally controlling the power of money, and not by any combinations of labor.

If a hundred dollars can be lent at seven per cent. interest, the borrower pays seven parts of the whole for the use for one year. The borrower must invest the money (for it is of no use to keep) in land or other property, and therefore must pay seven parts of the value of the property for the use of one hundred parts for a year. But if money be borrowed at one per cent., of course the borrower pays but one part for the use of one hundred parts either of money or property for a year, hence at this rate laborers would receive six parts of their net yearly earnings now paid to capital. A man who labors on his own property gains for himself its whole product. The rate per cent. interest determines what proportion others shall pay him for the use of capital, which he does not need for his own use. Suppose seven per cent. to be the fixed rate of interest, and V. to be a farmer, who, at the age of twenty-one, inherits five farms, worth ten thousand dollars each. He wishes to cultivate one himself, and to sell or rent the remaining four. A., B., C. and D. are farmers without property, and are obliged to hire their farms. They cannot expect V. to rent them his for less than the interest on the money for which they would sell. Suppose these men to rent V.'s four farms at seven hundred dollars a year each; and V. to collect his rent yearly, and lend the money to others at seven per cent., and yearly to collect and reloan this interest. The rent and accruing interest upon the rent, in ten years and three months, would enable V. to buy four additional farms, worth ten thousand dollars apiece, which he could rent to four more tenants. In ten years and three months, the rent and interest upon the rent of these eight farms would furnish V. with money to purchase eight farms more of equal value, which he could rent to eight other tenants; in a third period of the same length, the rent and interest upon the rent of the sixteen farms would buy sixteen additional farms; in a fourth period, the rent and interest upon the rent of the thirty-two farms, would purchase thirty-two more farms; in a fifth period, the rent and interest upon the rent of the sixty-four farms, would buy sixty-four more; in a sixth period, the rent and interest upon the rent of the one hundred and twenty-eight farms would buy one hundred and twenty-eight more; and in a seventh ten years and three months, the rent and interest upon the rent of the two hundred and fifty-six farms then owned by V., would buy for him two hundred and fifty-six farms more, of equal value with the first farms which he rented to A., B., C. and D. Thus V., in seventy-one years and nine months, would become the owner of five hundred and twelve farms, worth ten thousand dollars each, and bringing in a yearly income of seven hundred dollars apiece. Five hundred and eight of these farms would be added to V.'s wealth by the labor of his tenants, not to mention the improvement made on their original value by the labor; and V. would have had besides, the entire produce of the one farm reserved for his own cultivation.

We will now see what would be the result to V. and his tenants from the simple change of the rate of interest from seven to one per cent. Suppose V., as before, to inherit five farms, each worth ten thousand dollars, one of which he cultivates himself. If he should sell the remaining four for ten thousand dollars each, he could lend the money at one per cent., that is for four hundred dollars; but he rents the farms to A., B., C. and D., at one per cent. on their value, and thus receives the same income. If V. should loan this yearly rent of one hundred dollars on each farm, yearly collecting and reloaning the interest, nearly seventy years would elapse before the rent paid him by A., B., C. and D., and its accruing interest, would buy four more farms of equal value with those rented; whereas, in about the same period, at seven per cent. the rent and its accruing interest would buy five hundred and eight farms. Whether the interest were at one or at seven per cent., V. would equally receive the products of his labor on the farm that he kept for his own use; but at seven per cent., he would gain by the labor of his tenants five millions and eighty thousand dollars' worth of land; while at one per cent. he would gain by their labor but forty thousand dollars' worth. The agreements between V. and his tenants appear on the surface as fair where they pay the larger as where they pay the lower rent; because, in each case, they conform to the groundwork or foundation established by law; but, in the latter instance, V.'s tenants would as much pay to him the full yearly market rent of his farms by paying one hundred dollars apiece, as in the former by paying seven hundred dollars apiece. If one acre of land would produce twenty-five bushels of wheat worth one dollar per bushel, each of V.'s tenants must yearly sow, gather and sell twenty-eight acres of wheat to pay seven hundred dollars rent. Suppose wheat to continue worth one dollar per bushel, and the rent to be diminished to one per cent.; with the same industry and economy, each tenant could pay the one hundred dollars rent, and retain for himself six hundred bushels of wheat as the surplus of his labor. If V.'s tenants, in about seventy years, could earn and pay to him five hundred and eight farms, in the same period, with the interest at one per cent., they could earn for themselves five hundred and four, for the other four farms would pay all their rent to V. Having the entire produce of one farm for his own support, the low rent of the other four could do him neither injustice nor injury; while compelling A., B., C. and D. to pay the larger rent would deprive them and others of the just reward of their labor; and V. would not be really benefited by the hardships imposed upon them.

The interest on money at seven per cent. is as oppressive as the same rate per cent. rent on land. Suppose V., instead of renting his four farms, should sell them for $10,000 each, and loan the money at the legal rate of seven per cent., collecting and reloaning the interest yearly. In ten years and three months, the principal and interest together would amount to $80,000; in twenty years and six months, to $160,000: in thirty years and nine months, to $320,000; in forty-one years, to $640,000; in fifty-one years and three months, to $1,280,000; in sixty-one years and six months, to $2,560,000; and in seventy-one years and nine months, to $5,120,000. Multiply $10,000 by five hundred and twelve, the number of farms, and it will give the same sum. If V. should sell the four farms for $40,000, and lend the money on bond and mortgage at seven per cent., requiring, as is usual, double the value in land as security, he would have mortgages covering $10,240,000 worth of landed estate; and the people occupying this land would be hard at work to pay him the interest; thus rapidly concentrating wealth in his hands, instead of diffusing it to supply their own wants.

But with interest at one per cent., $40,000 loaned for seventy years, would accumulate but $40,000 more; whereas, at seven per cent. it would accumulate $5,080,000. This difference in interest of $5,040,000 would be added to V.'s wealth from the earnings of others, while V.'s accumulation of money or increase of lands would not add either a dollar to the quantity of money, or an acre to the quantity of land. It would only have monopolized it for V.'s benefit. It would have caused the people to owe V. $5,080,000, and make them $5,040,000 poorer than if interest had been at one per cent. The contracts between V. and his tenants being made in conformity with the standard at seven per cent., they must pay him the $5,040,000, or defraud him of what is legally his due; and if he voluntarily take less than this from them, it is an act of charity. Seven per cent. is not the standard for V. only; it is a public standard that favors other capitalists equally in the various branches of business, and imposes upon the producing classes generally obligations similar to those it imposes upon V.'s tenants.*

---

* We do not question the right of V. to inherit the five farms, and to enjoy all the produce of the one he cultivates: nor do we object to his receiving a just rent for the use of any other farms which he may own; but the rent of the latter should be only equivalent to a proper support of the money by which their value is represented; and we claim that one, or one and one-tenth per cent. is ample to pay for the necessary material and labor to furnish a representative that shall be and remain perfectly secure and good. . . . As labor in all useful departments should be fairly compensated, so also the necessary labor to furnish and issue the money of a nation should be justly remunerated; and the per centage interest on the money should be equivalent to pay for the needful material and labor to furnish and lend it. The interest ought not to exceed the expense of the institution and circulation of the money. (See Sec. XVII. and Part II., Chap. II.)

To give some idea to what extent the power of interest operates, it can only be necessary to say, that all the money lent on bonds and mortgages by individuals, by insurance and trust companies; all the money lent for United States, State, County, City, Railroad, Canal and other bonds, made to raise money for public improvements, whether these improvements be made by corporations, by the States or by individuals; also all the money lent by banks, brokers and individuals on promissory notes—all these loans are operating with a like centralizing power against the producers and in favor of money-lenders. This power also establishes a like rate per cent. rent to be paid for the use of all property, real and personal. The rent of houses and lots in cities, and of farms and houses in the country, must conform to this standard. All the goods, wares and merchandise on hand in the nation, and that are in process of being produced and manufactured, are governed in their value by money, and are under tribute to its centralizing power. It is an unavoidable power, because it is instituted, upheld and enforced by the national laws, and is the basis upon which all market values are founded.

The following statement shows the effect upon producers of a rate of interest on capital of six per cent. per annum. The yearly income of our most wealthy citizen from dividends on State, bank, and other stocks, money lent on bonds and mortgages, and rents of property, is said to amount to $2,000,000. Take the farmers of the six New England States, include those of New York and New Jersey, and it is very doubtful whether, after paying necessary expenses, each makes a yearly gain of more than one hundred dollars. According to this calculation it would require the use of twenty thousand farms, and the surplus earnings of twenty thousand farmers and their families, to clear $2,000,000 a year. However difficult it might be to trace the ways and means by which this income is gathered, it takes $2,000,000 worth of the surplus products of labor to pay the legal accumulation on the capital. Suppose able-bodied men to earn one dollar per day, for an average of two hundred and seventy-five days in each year—*i. e.*, $275. Two millions of dollars would annually hire and pay for the labor of seven thousand two hundred and seventy-six men. Allow the receiver of the income to expend yearly for his own support as much as seventy-three laborers earn, and he will still receive a clear gain of $1,980,000 yearly, the entire earnings of seven thousand two hundred and three men. Calculate the interest on $1,980,000 at six per cent., and the next year it will make an addition to his income of $118,800; which sum would pay for the labor of four hundred and thirty-two men, in addition to the number employed in the preceding year. What is the probable surplus that each of these laboring men would yearly retain, after deducting from the $275 their own expenses, and those of their families? Can any laboring community be prosperous, and pay so great an amount of interest on capital? The legal power of money to accumulate an undue rate of interest, compels these laborers to give all their surplus products to one man for the use of capital, while they and their families are deprived of a good subsistence, and are obliged continually to increase that capital, which yearly exercises a greater power over their labor.

In order that the power of the ordinary rates of interest to concentrate property in the hands of capitalists may be more clearly seen, in the following illustration the contracts shall be based upon wheat instead of upon money. Take the yearly income of Mr. A., say $2,000,000. If his money be loaned, or his property be leased at six per cent. on its valuation, he must be worth thirty-three and a third millions of dollars. Suppose Mr. A., instead, to own thirty-three and a third millions of bushels of wheat,

Let him lend the wheat instead of the money at six per cent., and the interest will be precisely two millions of bushels. The farmers who borrow the wheat, and give their bonds and mortgages upon their farms to secure the payment of the principal and interest, must sow, reap, and thrash out two millions of bushels, transport them to New York, and put them into Mr. A.'s storehouses, to pay the interest for one year. What a pile of wheat is this for one man's use, gained too, without his sowing or harvesting a bushel of it. But suppose the interest to be at one per cent. instead of at six per cent. and Mr. A. to lend these same farmers the thirty-three and a third millions of bushels of wheat at this per centage; at the end of the year they will have to pay him only three hundred and thirty-three thousand three hundred and thirty-three and a third bushels of wheat, to satisfy the interest. The farmers will then retain one million six hundred and sixty-six thousand six hundred and sixty-six and two-third bushels for their own use, or to sell to others, or to pay toward the principal of the debt. With interest at one per cent. they will as much satisfy Mr. A.'s yearly claims, by paying him the smaller quantity of wheat, as they would at an interest of six per cent. by paying two millions of bushels. If each acre of land produce fifteen bushels, and the farmers cultivate on an average ten acres each, it will take the labor of thirteen thousand three hundred and thirty-three farmers, and the use of one hundred and thirty-three thousand three hundred and thirty-three and a third acres of land to pay the yearly interest of six per cent. on the thirty-three and a third millions of bushels of wheat borrowed of Mr. A. But if interest be at one per cent. and the farmers continue to pay Mr. A. the two millions of bushels yearly, in eighteen years and four months they will pay off both the principal and the interest of the debt.

Suppose the farmers to pay six per cent. interest, *i. e.*,

two millions of bushels of wheat on the loan for twenty years, they will pay forty millions of bushels to satisfy the interest, and will still owe the thirty-three and a third millions principal. If Mr. A., as he yearly receives the interest from the farmers, say two millions of bushels of wheat or $2,000,000, should lend it out to mechanics at six per cent. interest, and continue to do this for twenty years, adding yearly to the loan the interest so accrued, it would accumulate, in the twenty years, to $73,571,180. The interest on this interest for a year amounts to $4,414,270, which would yearly be due from the mechanics. If the mechanics, instead of paying the interest in wheat, should pay it in manufactured articles, they would pile up an enormous quantity of goods in Mr. A.'s storehouses for his yearly use. With interest at six per cent., at the end of twenty years, the farmers would owe Mr. A. $33,333,333, or the same number of bushels of wheat, and the mechanics would owe him $73,571,180; together, $106,904,513; which would annually require from the farmers and mechanics $6,414,270 worth of their products merely to pay the interest.

Now let interest be at one per cent. per annum, and let Mr. A. lend $33,333,333 at this rate, and in twenty years the interest compounded yearly would amount to but $7,339,666, instead of $73,571,180; making by this simple alteration of the rate of interest for twenty years, a saving to the farmers and mechanics of $66,231,514.

These calculations of the centralizing power of money are not based upon any usurious rates of interest, but upon six and seven per cent., and the latter rate is established by the State of New York as just and equitable; and judgments in the courts of law are rendered and entered upon the records accordingly. These rates of interest are certain to take the wealth from the producers and give it to the financiers. It will be hereafter shown that the rate of interest may be easily reduced to one per cent., or to any other per cent. that shall be deemed most conducive to the general welfare; and if the people think it more just that the interest should cease to accumulate wealth so rapidly in a few hands, they will enact laws to prevent it. If they will stop such accumulation by interest, they will live upon the products of their own labor, instead of living upon the charity of capitalists. If in twenty years Mr. A. should bestow on the needy $66,231,514, or the same number of bushels of wheat, it would be an unheard-of liberality. But if the law of interest were such that he could not legally take this amount from the people, they would retain it in their own possession, as the natural product of their labor, instead of being compelled to receive it as a charity.

Mr. A. now uses the most of his capital by investing it in State and other stocks, buying business notes at large discounts, lending money on bond and mortgage, buying up mortgages bearing seven per cent. interest below their par value, purchasing property under foreclosure, etc. Doubtless his object is to obtain the best possible per centage income for the use of his money or property. All that he gains by these means above six per cent. interest, takes a still greater sum from the earnings of producers.

Now suppose from this time forward Mr. A. should determine to pursue a different course, and to lay out his capital in such a manner as to conduce in the highest degree to the welfare of the people around him. To support them in idleness would be a disadvantage; but to employ them, and pay for their work such a price as would give them a good subsistence, and furnish them with the means of educating their children, and to provide for the aged and needy, would be a very benevolent disposition of his wealth. To do this he invests all his property in the manufacture of cotton goods. With thirty-three and a third millions of dollars he could carry on an extensive business. He builds his manufactories, and purchases machinery. He contracts with a number of planters to supply him for a certain number of years with a given quantity of cotton. He also contracts with workmen to perform the labor in his mills, and agrees to give to all such prices as will afford them and their families a comfortable subsistence, make suitable provision for the education of their children, and support those who are unable to work and dependent upon them. The cotton will, of course, be always furnished at a uniform price, and the price of labor will be about the same each year. Mr. A. now fixes the prices of his goods so as to sustain the various people in his employment. Let Mr. A. invest all his means in mills, in stock, and labor, on these terms, while the planters hire their plantations, and the mechanics, manufacturers and laborers employed by Mr. A. hire houses to live in, etc., from others at a rent of seven or eight per cent. per annum, and it will be impossible for him, with all his capital, to sustain himself. In a very few years he will become bankrupt, for he must enable his workmen to pay their rents, and give them, besides, a comfortable support. This obliges him to use his own property at a low rate of interest, while, through his workmen, he is compelled to pay a high rate of rent or interest for the use of the property of others. The operation is, virtually, that the owner of thirty-three and a third millions of dollars borrows an equal or large amount at six, seven, or eight per cent. interest, and reloans the borrowed money, together with his own, at an interest of one, or one and a quarter per cent. By so doing, his fortune will soon pass into the hands of other capitalists.

The present monetary laws of all nations are opposed to the reward of labor; and no individual or national attempts justly to reward it, except by changing these laws, can secure any permanent success.

SECTION II.

THE WEALTH OF CITIES, AND THE MEANS OF ITS ACCUMULATION.

The following illustration shows the capability of money, at an interest of six per cent. per annum, to centralize the wealth of nations in large cities.

Suppose an uncultivated island, ten miles square, and a few miles distant from the coast of the United States. Ten thousand wealthy citizens of the States intend to build a city upon it. These citizens are worth $150,000 each; in the aggregate, $1,500,000,000. The legal interest on money is fixed at six per cent. per annum. For two years previous to their removal to the island, the people prepare upon it houses for themselves, and suitable accommodations for merchants and mechanics. Each of these families expends $3,000 yearly for its support. Each family being worth $150,000, the interest on which, at six per cent. would be $9,000, each has an income of $6,000 a year, over and above expenses. They expend their surplus income for two years, *i. e.*, $12,000 for each family, in the aggregate $120,000,000, in making improvements on the island. They dispose of their property on the main land on credit, securing it by bonds and mortgages, State stocks, or otherwise, so that they insure an interest payable half yearly of six per cent. per annum, on the whole amount of their property. These obligations merely represent the value of the property they leave upon the main land, and must yield an income from the products of the land and labor of the purchasers. The annual interest on $1,500,000,000, amounts to $90,000,000. The paper obligations held by the creditors legally empower them to demand an interest of $90,000,000, in specie. The mere giving of obligations is all that is required in the transfer of property. The conversion of their property into bonds and mortgages and other securities, may not have required the use of a million of dollars of money. But the payment of both principal and interest must be made in money.

The ten thousand families contain, on an average, five persons each, making, in the aggregate, a population of fifty thousand. They employ, on an average, three domestics in each family, increasing the population to eighty thousand. The yearly expenses of each family amount to $3,000; or, for the whole, to $30,000,000. Hatters, tailors, shoemakers, cabinet-makers, mechanics of every sort collect about them to supply their wants, and receive the sums which they expend in living. More than fifty thousand laborers and artisans are needed to supply their wants. In a few years the centralization of capital collects a city of three or four hundred thousand inhabitants. The ten thousand families expend $30,000,000 yearly, and draw besides, from the people of the main land, a clear income of $60,000,000 a year, which they can reloan. The debtors cannot send the $60,000,000 in money, and are therefore obliged to send the products of the soil, manufactured articles, etc., to this city for sale, to procure money to meet their payments of interest. The city soon becomes the market-place of the nation, and engrosses the principal business. The people are astonished at its wealth and prosperity, and congratulate themselves on having so fine a market for their products.

In the course of a century or two, the ten thousand families and their descendants can, if they choose, without labor on their part, build a wall around their city as high and as broad as the walls of ancient Babylon. Meanwhile, the people upon the main land are obliged to supply all the wants, the food, clothing, etc., not only of the ten thousand families and their descendants who do no work, but also of the laborers employed in the erection of the wall, in the building of houses, and in all other improvements. Producers and manufacturers from different parts of the country carry their goods to the city, and the citizens, after selecting the choicest for their own use, resell the remainder to laborers, who are only able to purchase the poorer kinds. If an account were kept of those sold to the country, it would be found that they were minus nearly the whole support of the people of the city. Now what compensation is received by the people of the main land for the supplies which they furnish? The citizens, indeed, pay money for the supplies, but this money is the interest on capital loaned to the people, without whose labor it would have been useless. In a similar manner, under the present monetary laws of the United States, a few rich men in cities engross the wealth of the country. It is as natural under these laws for the wealth to fall into a few hands as for water to find its level by its own gravitation; and while our present rates of interest prevail, no combination or success in production, either by machinery or the muscular power of labor, will ever effect any important change for the better. But when the laboring classes combine to have good national monetary laws in lieu of the present evil ones, their united efforts will effect a change in these laws, and thus accomplish the object they have so long and so anxiously sought after. If the interest in the case supposed were limited to one per cent., the income for each family would be only $1,500, or one-half of what they each year expend; consequently, they must either labor for the other half, or take a portion of their principal each year for their support. It would, therefore, be impossible for them to build or sustain such a city.

The ten thousand most wealthy men in the United States are probably worth, on an average, at least $300,000—in the aggregate $3,000,000,000. The annual interest on this sum at six per cent. would be $180,000,000. If these men should sell their property, and invest the proceeds in bonds and mortgages bearing six per cent. interest per annum, and remove from the country, they would impose a tribute on the productive industry of the nation which would impoverish it for ages. It is doubtful whether the people would ever be able to pay and satisfy the interest and principal of the debt. They would pay $180,000,000 of their products yearly, without receiving any equivalent. And yet, without the labor of the buyers or borrowers, the property would be useless; and if the owners received any benefit from it, they would be obliged to remain and cultivate it themselves. Ought the laws to be such, that ten thousand wealthy men, on leaving their country, could impose such a burden upon the millions left behind? If interest were reduced to one per cent., and the ten thousand men should sell their property, leaving the proceeds on interest at one per cent., this nation would pay them $30,000,000 interest annually. And this would be quite enough for producers to pay for the mere use of capital.

To show conclusively that the present rates of interest are the cause of the accumulation of the wealth in our cities, we will enter at length into a calculation which each can test and examine for himself. No one will dispute that in the city of New York there are several hundred families whose collective wealth is equal to $250,000 for each family. For our illustration, however, we will take but one hundred families, and supppose each of them to be worth equal to $250,000—in total, $25,000,000 As five or six of our citizens might be pointed out who are, in the aggregate, worth at least double the sum total, this calculation is a moderate one. Suppose these one hundred families to emigrate to some desirable section of the country, and settle upon two hundred acres of land, so that each family owns two acres. They convert all their property into money, or into bonds and mortgages bearing six per cent. interest, the lowest legal rate of interest in any State of the Union. Each family expends yearly for its support $3,000, or the interest at six per cent. on $50,000. This sum would supply each family with the necessaries and luxuries of life without the performance of labor by any of its members. Besides the $50,000 of which they expend the income, each family has $200,000—in the aggregate, $20,000,000—loaned at six per cent. interest, the annual income of which would be $1,200,000. The yearly expenditure of $300,000 (the interest on $50,000 for each family) soon collects near them merchants, mechanics, laborers, and others, to supply their wants; and farmers find here a market for their produce.

These families and their posterity live without labor, being determined to incur no hazard of business. They intermarry for five generations, thirty years being the average duration of each. Upon marriage, each couple receives $50,000, the income on which, at six per cent., amounting to $3,000 a year, is appropriated to their support. They also receive their average proportion of the principal. They are forbidden to exact a higher rate of interest than six per cent. per annum, payable half-yearly, and are not at liberty to call in the principal so long as the interest upon it is regularly paid. The families consist of five persons each, exclusive of servants, amounting, in the aggregate, to five hundred individuals. Suppose them to increase twenty-five per cent. every twelve and a half years. Each family at the emigration had $200,000 loaned at six per cent. interest, amounting to $12,000 per annum; and, in the aggregate, on the $20,000,000 owned by all, to $1,200,000 per annum. This interest, collected and reloaned half-yearly, will double the principal, $20,000,000, in about eleven and three-quarter years; but, to leave time for the collection and reinvestment of the interest, allow it twelve and a half years to double. The following calculations exhibit the sum which would be owned by the families at the end of five generations of thirty years each, or at the end of one hundred and fifty years. This calculation of the centralization of wealth by interest is no idle theory, but a mathematical demonstration of facts, based upon the lowest rate of interest established by law in any State— a much lower rate, too, than the average one at which money is actually loaned.

The following table exhibits the accumulation at the rate, and under the circumstances, as above:

TABLE

OF THE INCREASE AT SIX PER CENT. OF THE WEALTH OF A HUNDRED FAMILIES WORTH $250,000 EACH, DURING A PERIOD OF ONE HUNDRED AND FIFTY YEARS, WITH A DEDUCTION OF THEIR ANNUAL EXPENSES.

100 families worth $250,000 each	$25,000,000
Yearly expenses of each family, $3,000, or the income on $50,000 at six per cent.—total for 100 families..	5,000,000
Deduct $5,000,000 for expenses, and there are left to accumulate......................................	20,000,000
The interest at six per cent. paid half yearly, and re-loaned, will equal the principal in 11¾ years; but allow 12½ years, and then add........	20,000,000
	40,000,000
Add 25 per cent. increase to 100 families in 12½ years —*i. e.*, 25 families, and deduct $50,000 for the support of each of the 25	1,250,000
Left to accumulate.............................	38,750,000
Add 12½ years interest, at 6 per cent.	38,750,000
	77,500,000
Add 25 per cent. increase to 125 families—*i. e.*, 31 families, and deduct $50,000 for each of the 31	1,550,000
Left to accumulate.............................	75,950,000

Left to accumulate (brought forward).......	$75,950,000
Add 12½ years' interest at six per cent............	75,950,000
	151,900,000
Add 25 per cent. to 156 families—*i. e.*, 39 families, and deduct $50,000 for each of the 39.............	$1,950,000
Left to accumulate.................................	149,950,000
Add 12½ years' interest at 6 per cent..............	149,950,000
	299,900,000
Add 25 per cent. to 195 families—*i. e.*, 49 families, and deduct $50,000 for each of the 49...............	2,450,000
Left to accumulate.................................	297,450,000
Add 12½ years' interest at 6 per cent..............	297,450,000
	594,900,000
Add 25 per cent. to 244 families—*i. e.*, 61 families, and deduct $50,000 for each of the 61...............	3,050,000
Left to accumulate.................................	591,850,000
Add 12½ years' interest at six per cent............	591,850,000
	1,183,700,000
Add 25 per cent. to 305 families—*i. e.*, 76 families, and deduct $50,000 for each of the 76...............	3,800,000
Left to accumulate.................................	1,179,900,000
Add 12½ years' interest at six per cent............	1,179,900,000
	2,359,800,000
Add 25 per cent. to 381 families—*i. e.*, 95 families, and deduct $50,000 for each of the 95...............	4,750,000
Left to accumulate	2,355,050,000
Add 12½ years' interest at 6 per cent..............	2,355,050,000
	4,710,100,000
Add 25 per cent. to 476 families—*i. e.*, 119 families, and deduct $50,000 for each of the 119..............	5,950,000
Left to accumulate	4,704,150,000
Add 12½ years' interest at 6 per cent..............	4,704,150,000
	9,408,300,000
Add 25 per cent. to 595 families—*i. e.*, 149 families, and deduct $50,000 for each of the 149	7,450,000
Left to accumulate.................................	9,400,850,000

Left to accumulate (brought forward)............ $9,400,850,000
Add 12½ years' interest at 6 per cent...............$9,400,850,000
                                                    ─────────────
                                                    18,801,700,000
Add 25 per cent. to 744 families—*i. e.*, 186 families,
  and deduct $50,000 for each of the 186............   9,300,000
                                                    ─────────────
Left to accumulate.... 18,792,400,000
Add 12½ years' interest at 6 per cent...............18,792,400,000
                                                    ─────────────
                                                    37,584,800,000
Add 25 per cent. to 930 families—*i. e.*, 233 families,
  and deduct $50,000 for each of the 233............   11,650,000
                                                    ─────────────
Left to accumulate......................... 37,573,150,000
Add 12½ years' interest at 6 per cent...............37,573,150,000
                                                    ─────────────
                                                    75,146,300,000
Add 25 per cent. to 1,163 families—*i. e.*, 291 families,
  and deduct $50,000 for each for the 291 14,550,000
                                                    ─────────────
Left to accumulate $75,131,750,000

Add the two hundred and ninety-one families to the eleven hundred and sixty-three, and their sum is a thousand four hundred and fifty-four, which is the increase of the one hundred families, by the addition of twenty-five per cent. every twelve and a half years. The calculation is continued for a hundred and fifty years, or for five generations of thirty years each. The sum of $50,000 is assigned to each family, which, loaned at six per cent., secures to each a yearly income of $3,000. Each family has an income of ten dollars per day for three hundred days in the year. If each family average five individuals, each man, woman and child receives an income of two dollars per day. This is twice as much as a laborer can earn in a day, and the single dollar must support both himself and his family. Besides this yearly income, the people of this nation would owe the fourteen hundred and fifty-four families $75,131,750,000. Suppose this sum to be equally divided among the families, each would have $51,672,455. The interest upon the sum total, at the rate of six per cent., would amount to more than $4,500,000,000 annually. An immense amount of the products of labor must be yearly sold for money to pay this interest. Is the law which thus accumulates interest or products, a power for actual production? No—the law which exacts this interest does not increase the quantity of money, nor of products; it simply requires that the proceeds of $4,500,000,000 worth of products shall be given over to the fourteen hundred and fifty-four families to satisfy the interest. More than half the present valuation of the whole property of the United States, both real and personal, would be required to pay the interest for one year. And yet these families exact less than our laws permit, for they take but six per cent. interest, and in a number of our States, the legal rate is seven or eight per cent.

Now let one per cent. be the legal rate of interest; and suppose the families to loan the twenty millions for the same period of a hundred and fifty years at one per cent., instead of at six per cent., and to collect and reloan the interest half yearly. The people have the same amount of money to use; and at the expiration of the hundred and fifty years, the sum of the principal and interest does not exceed $90,000,000, while at six per cent. it amounts to $75,131,750,000. At one per cent., the principal and the interest do not amount to one eight-hundredth part as much as at six per cent., nor does the sum require one eight-hundredth part as much labor to pay it. If the people borrow the money at six per cent., at the end of six months they give back a portion of the borrowed money to pay the interest. The interest is reloaned to them, and thus continually increases their indebtedness. With interest at one per cent., the people would have the same quantity of money, and at the end of six months would give back a half per cent.

to pay the interest, and the families would reloan the half per cent. to the people, instead of reloaning the three per cent. A high rate of interest cannot increase the quantity of money, but it increases the indebtedness of the people.

If interest were at one per cent., each of the one hundred families would have but $2,500 income on its whole capital; and if they should continue to expend $3,000 apiece yearly, each family, in order not to encroach on its original capital, would have to produce, by its labor, $500 worth of products yearly, for its own use or for sale, instead of being able to lay up $12,000 yearly, without labor. The producing classes could never be oppressed by the capital of these families. But with interest at six per cent., in less than a century and a half, the whole nation would be subject to their control, besides being obliged to support them and their posterity in idleness during the hundred and fifty years.*

---

* It is not reasonable to suppose that man's morals will be pure so long as we make laws which deprive him of his physical rights. A standard that will deprive producers of what they justly earn, and bestow on non-producers what does not belong to them, cannot fail to corrupt the morals of both parties. No ingenuity in the invention of machinery, and no physical force or combination of labor, has power to change this wrong; because the evil is not in the production, but in the wrong distribution, which proceeds from the invisible power or law that governs it. For all laws are spiritual or mental powers, which operate upon and affect visible things; and their effects can only be altered by altering the spiritual or mental law. This power of money is not the product of labor, nor even a visible thing, more than the attractive power of the magnet is visible. Money, whether of gold, silver or paper, is visible, but the power of interest is invisible, and yet gathers to itself things visible as metals are attracted to a magnet.

SECTION III.

INTEREST RECEIVED BY THE CITIZENS OF THE CITY OF NEW YORK ON LOANS TO THE COUNTRY.

Doubtless the city of New York has at this time more than $50,000,000, and probably more than $100,000,000 lent in various ways to the country at six or seven per cent. interest. Some part of it is invested in State bonds, bank and railroad stocks, stocks of manufacturing companies, etc.; and some lent on bond and mortgage, the dividends or interest on all of which must be paid in New York. Estimate this sum at only $25,000,000, and allow it to draw seven per cent. interest. Suppose the citizens to support themselves independently of the income from this loan, and allow it, by collecting and lending the interest half yearly, to accumulate for a century. It matters not in what way the capital may be lent, producers are compelled to add all the interest from the proceeds of their products. In ten years and one month the $25,000,000, will increase to $50,000,000; in twenty years and two months, to $100,000,000; in thirty years and three months, to $200,000,000; in forty years and four months, to $400,000,000; in fifty years and five months, to $800,000,000; in sixty years and six months, to $1,600,000,000; in seventy years and seven months, to $3,200,000,000; in eighty years and eight months, to $6,400,000,000; in ninety years and nine months, to $12,800,000,000; and, in one hundred years and ten months, to $25,600,000,000. This is as certain as any other mathematical calculation, and nothing can prevent the accumulation of enormous sums in the hands of a few capitalists in this city, unless it be the inability of the inhabitants of the country to pay the interest on their loans. This rate of interest compels farmers to give the value of one farm every ten years for the use of another; the tenant of each manufactory to give the value of another manufactory, once in the same period, for the use of the one occupied; and the passengers and transporters upon each railroad and canal, to pay a sufficient fare or freight to construct, at the expiration of that period, another railroad or canal. It is manifest that the producing classes are unable to fulfil such requirements. Each additional railroad and canal must be added to the original one by the producing classes, and is given to the capitalist without labor or production on his part. He gains them by the legal power of money to accumulate, which is equally great, whether the money be lent on interest or invested in property. If farmers, manufacturers, mechanics and merchants, were compelled to pay only a just rate of interest, they could devote the labor now expended in the payment of high rates to non-producers, to the supply of their own wants and of general comforts and conveniences.

Large cities accumulate the wealth of nations without earning it. According to the State Register, in 1845, the city of New York contained a population of 371,233, and the State of New York contained a population of 2,604,495. The population of the city was less than one-seventh part that of the State. And yet the assessed valuation of the real and personal property of the city at that period was $239,995,517, while all the other property in the State was valued at only $365,650,574. This estimate does not include Brooklyn and Williamsburgh, which are in fact parts of the city of New York, as they have grown up and are sustained by its business. Taking the city of New York alone, it appears that it owns more than two-fifths of the assessed property in the State, while it contains less than one-seventh of the State population. But it is doubtless true that its citizens are worth *more* than all the other inhabitants of the State. They own large tracts of land in different parts of the State, and these lands are taxed in the counties in which they are located. If these taxes were estimated as being paid in the city, where the property is owned, and were taken from the taxes of the country, the transfer of taxes on the amount of $62,827,530, would make the valuation of the property of the city equal one-half the property of the whole State. The citizens of the city of New York own large tracts of land in other States, which are taxed in those States. They have also a large amount of money lent to the country on bond and mortgage, and large amounts invested in United States, State, and bank stocks, and in stocks of manufacturing and railroad companies, etc., in various States, all of which property, if taxed, is estimated and taxed as belonging to the country. There are doubtless many loans of money and much personal property, which, although lent and used in the city, escape any taxation. The people of other parts of the State own a considerable amount of property, stocks, etc., in the city; but the amount owned by them in the city is very small compared with the amount owned by the citizens of the city in the country—probably not one-twentieth. It is reasonable to conclude that the inhabitants of the city and county of New York own as much, or even more property, than all the people in all the other fifty-eight counties in the State.* Does any one suppose

* If, to show the relative gain in wealth of the city and the State, from 1845 to 1859, we include with the county of New York the neighboring counties of Kings and Westchester—which are, in fact, suburbs of the city of New York—we have the following result:

Assessed value of real and personal property.

COUNTY.	1845.	1859.
New York,	$289,995,517	$552,008,742
Kings,	80,750,472	106,914,629
Westchester,	10,086,817	40,487,671
	280,782,806	699,411,042
Other Counties,	324,863,789	716,879,795
Total State Valuation,	$605,646,095	$1,416,290,837

that the citizens of this city earn more by their labor than all the other inhabitants of the State? Do they do more toward supplying the people of the State with food, clothing, building materials, etc., than the people of the State do toward supplying them with these things? If they do not, why should they possess and continue to accumulate so great a proportion of the wealth?

The means of arriving at the truth in relation to this, would be to take for a series of years an exact account of all the products which are sent out of the city, and see if the products that leave the city are increased above, or diminished below the products that are sent from the country into the city. If the money be taken into account, the interest and dividends on both sides should be excluded. Allowance should be made for the labor performed in exchanging goods, in shipments, etc., in the city, equal to the allowance for the same amount of labor on a farm, so that the population of the city should be fairly compensated for their labor. If it be found that tne 371,233 citizens of the city have not performed one-half the labor for the 2,604,495 inhabitants of the State, and yet have obtained more than one-half the whole property, it is evident the distribution has been unjust. Our producers are continually endeavoring to overcome their poverty by their industry, but while our present rates of interest prevail, capital will continue to take their surplus earnings, and leave them poor.

It appears that, in 1845, these three counties owned 46½ per cent. of the wealth in the State, and, in 1859, they owned 49½ per cent. But, unquestionably, their actual proportion of the wealth was far greater than is shown in the statistics; for their citizens own very large amounts of real estate and other property beyond the limits of these counties. The property, too, of many persons whose wealth was acquired in the city, and who have removed their residences beyond the counties named, might properly be included in this calculation as belonging to the city.—[M. K. P.]

SECTION IV.

THE PER CENTAGE ACTUAL INCREASE OF THE VALUE OF THE PROPERTY OF THE STATES OF NEW YORK AND MASSACHUSETTS, COMPARED WITH THE PER CENTAGE LEGAL INCREASE ON THE PROPERTY OF THESE STATES FOR THE SAME PERIODSS.

The State of New York is deemed very prosperous, and thought to be rapidly increasing in wealth by its industry and enterprise. The following table, taken from the New York State Register for 1846, will exhibit the actual gain of the people of the State for ten years, viz, from 1835 to 1845, according to the assessed value of the property:

TABLE

OF REAL AND PERSONAL ESTATE IN THE STATE OF NEW YORK, AS TAKEN FROM THE STATE REGISTER FOR 1846.

	Real estate.	Personal estate.	Corrected aggregate valuation.
1835	$403,166,094	$128,526,103	$530,653,524
1836	539,756,874	132,615,613	....
1837	498,430,054	122,021,033	....
1838	502,864,006	124,680,778	....
1839	519,058,782	131,602,988	....
1840	517,723,170	121,447,830	....
1841	531,987,886	123,311,644	....
1842	504,254,029	116,595,233	....
1843	476,999,430	118,602,064	....
1844	480,027,609	119,612,343	....
1845	486,490,121	115,988,895	605,646,095

$74,992,571

The table shows that in 1835, the whole valuation of the taxed real and personal estate in the State of New York, was $530,653,524; and that in 1845, it had increased to $605,646,095. In the ten years, the people of the State added to their wealth $74,992,571—equal to $7,499,257 a year, or a fraction over one and four-tenths per cent. a year on the capital employed. This calculation is made without any payment of interest until the expiration of the ten years.

Taking the above as a fair valuation of the property, the people of the State added only about one and four-tenths per cent. per annum to their capital, and the legal interest of the State is seven per cent., and is usually paid oftener than yearly. If we had rented the State of a foreign nation, and at the end of every six months had taken up our obligations and added in the six months' interest, at the end of the ten years we should have added to the principal over $524,000,000. We should have owed the foreign nation, in interest or rent, a sum seven times greater than all that we earned above our own support. If we earned only $74,992,571 more than our own maintenance, how could we return the property to its owners, and pay them $524,000,000 of rent, or seven times more than our labor would have produced? Yet the laws of the State, fixing the interest at seven per cent., make a requisition equal to this upon laborers in favor of capital.

The average of the yearly loans of the banks in the State of New York, according to their own reports, amounts to $70,000,000
According to the annual report, the debt of the State on the 30th September, 1846, was 24,734,080
Debts of the principal cities in the State in 1845, as taken from the State Register :
City of New York...................... $14,476,986
" Brooklyn......................... 545,000
" Albany........................... 500,000
" Troy............................. 772,000
" Rochester 108,000
" Buffalo.......................... 57,131
——————
16,459,117
——————
$111,193,197
The interest on this sum at 7 per cent. per annum...... 7,783,523
Yearly average of the surplus earnings of the people of the State, according to the assessed valuation of the property, from 1835 to 1845..................... 7,499,257
——————
$284,266

It appears that the interest on these debts alone, at seven per cent. would amount to $284,266 more than the surplus earnings of all the people in the State, and this too without compounding the interest. It must be borne in mind, that this debt of $111,193,197 is contracted for money borrowed by the people, or by the State, and the interest paid upon it goes into the hands of a few capitalists, who furnish the capital for banking, and lend the money to the State and its incorporated cities. All the debts contracted by the sale of lands, agricultural products, and merchandise—all the money lent by individuals on bond and mortgage, and all business debts, bearing interest, are additional to the reported debts. The debts yearly contracted in the State by sales of land merchandise etc., amount to several hundred millions of dollars, and two, three, or four hundred millions bear interest. Must not the payment of so great an amount of interest, by the producers, concentrate the wealth of the State in the hands of a few capitalists, and continue more and more to oppress the producers? We might as well expect by labor to dam up the mouths of our rivers, so that they could not empty into the ocean, as to expect by labor, to contend successfully against the power of capital, even at two and a half per cent. interest, and much less against six or seven per cent. An interest on capital of even two and a half per cent. per annum would as certainly break down productive industry, and accumulate the wealth in favor of capital, as the rivers would certainly break down the dams, and force their waters and the obstructing dams into the ocean.

According to the assessed valuation of the property of the State of New York, the increase of its wealth from 1835 to 1845 was about one and four-tenths per cent. per annum, without compounding the interest. This was a period of only ten years. It is probable that, in 1835, property was estimated higher in proportion to its actual worth than in 1845. This statement, then, would not be an exactly fair criterion of the actual increase of wealth in the State. During that period, according to it, we gained, beside our own support, only a fraction over one per cent. a year by all our labor. If this was a correct estimate, the per centage we gained in wealth was only three-fourths as great as our per centage increase in population, for, during the ten years, our population increased from 2,174,517 to 2,604,495, or a fraction less than two per cent. a year. This calculation would make the aggregate wealth of the State in proportion to its population less in 1845 than it was in 1835; and this, we presume, was not the fact. Still there is little doubt that at least one-half the people of the State were poorer in 1845, and are now poorer, than they were in 1835. The increased wealth is accumulated in fewer hands. More and more of the earnings of the producing classes are required to pay the yearly rent, or interest, on the yearly increasing capital. If the men who are now rich had in 1835 an in come that abundantly supplied their wants, an increase of wealth has not added to their happiness; and the increase has been taken from those who toil, and yet are suffering for the necessaries of life. Without improving the condition of the rich, we are continually doing a wrong to a large class of industrious and worthy citizens.*

* In 1859, the valuation of the real and personal property in the State of New York had increased to $1,416,290,837, showing an increase in fourteen years of $810,644,742, or less than seven per cent. added annually. But property was probably estimated lower in proportion to its value in 1845 than it was in 1835 or 1859, and a calculation embracing the twenty-four years, would give a truer criterion of the actual increase of wealth. The property of the State in 1835 was valued at $530,653,524, and the increase in twenty-four years was $885,637,313, or for the whole period an average of not quite seven per cent. per annum; and, added yearly, of about four per cent. per annum. At seven per cent., with the interest compounded yearly, the State would have added to its wealth during the twenty-four years, over $2,100,000,000, that is, over $1,200,000,000 more than was actually added to the wealth of the State by the labor of all its inhabitants. The legal rate of interest demanded from laborers over $1,200,000,000 more than they actually earned. Of course, as a body, they could have had only a bare subsistence, and large numbers of them must have been reduced to the condition of paupers. The following extracts are taken from the Report of the New York Association for improving the Condition of the Poor, for the year 1859. James Brown, President; James Boorman, James Lenox, Horatio Allen, A. R. Wetmore, John C. Green, Vice Presidents.

"It was shown in the Thirteenth Annual Report of this Association, that, according to the ratios of population in the two countries there were about two paupers in the wealthy and prosperous State of New York, to one in Ireland, whose very name has long been a synonym for poverty and wretchedness. The statement appeared so improbable, that it was received with a general expression of incredulity. Since that period, pauperism appears to have augmented more rapidly in our own State than it has decreased in Ireland. If any reliance, therefore, is to be placed in Governmental Reports, that unwelcome fact, so humiliating to our pride, having been confirmed by the statistics of each succeeding year, can, with no show of rea-

An estimate of the increase of wealth in the State of Massachusetts, for fifty years, is contained in an article in the May number, for 1847, of that deservedly celebrated

son, be longer denied or evaded. The Annual Report of the Secretary of the State of New York, to the Legislature, of the paupers relieved in the several counties, at the public expense, during the past year, affords a basis for a comparison of our own pauperism with that in Great Britain and Ireland, for the same period, of which the following is the result:

	Population.	Paupers.
England and Wales	19,045,000	885,000
Scotland	2,035,000	115,216
Ireland	6,500,000	56,910
New York State	3,500,000	261,155

"In other words, the pauperism of England and Wales was in the ratio of *four and six-tenths per cent.* of the whole population; in Scotland, *three and nine-tenths per cent.*; in Ireland, about *nine-tenths of one per cent.*; while in the great State of New York, which is foremost in population, enterprise and resources, the ratio is *seven and four-tenths per cent.* Making, therefore, every reasonable allowance for hypothetical inaccuracies in our State Statistics—for the figures assumed are less than the returns would justify—and we are confronted with the appalling fact, that the pauperism in this State is some five per cent. in advance of that in Ireland; that is to say, there are, according to the ratios of population, five paupers in this State to one in that country. It is unnecessary to extend the contrast, or it might be farther shown, that the legal provision for the relief of the New York paupers is greater *per capita*, than the governmental allowance in Ireland, but proportionately less than the poor rates both of England and Scotland.

"Let it not be supposed that this dread phenomenon of pauperism has come suddenly upon us. Statistics, on the contrary, show that it has reached its alarming prevalence by a steady, gradual growth. The census of the State from 1831 to 1851, and the pauper statistics for the same period, exhibit the following results:

Increase of population in 20 years.................. 61 per cent.
Increase of pauperism from annual tables during the
    same period................................... 706 per cent.

"'In 1831, there was one pauper to every 123 persons: in 1841,

periodical, Hunt's Merchants' Magazine. A few extracts are made to show the difference between the amount of property produced by the labor of Massachusetts during

there was one to every 39 persons; in 1851, there was one to every 24 persons; and this year (1856), there is one to every 17 persons. Let the same ratio continue 15 years longer, and there will be one pauper to every five persons; that is, every five persons in the State must support one pauper. Twenty years, reaching from January, 1831, to 1851, furnish as just a scale as can be obtained, by which to gauge the succeeding 20 years. Indeed, the five years since 1851 show a still larger increase in the ratio of pauperism, so that at the end of 15 years more, the 20 years from 1851 to 1871 would exhibit even a sadder result than the number of years between 1831 and 1851. It is submitted, whether we should act from a blind confidence in the perpetuity of our institutions, or from statistics gathered from the steady action of a quarter of a century, on our history.'

"Since 1856, when the above statement in substance was first published, pauperism has increased in the State above the ratio then anticipated, so that the present proportion to the population is one pauper to about 13½ persons. Is it not astonishing that such facts are unheeded? It is idle to reason against facts, for if there is any reliability in statistics, the facts themselves stand boldly in evidence.

"Ireland and other foreign countries have doubtless been benefited at our expense, by the deportation of their poor, and to them we owe the bulk of our pauperism." . . . .

"But, in conceding this, let not the momentous fact be overlooked, that pauperism, so long regarded as an exotic, is actually germinating in our own soil, with baneful luxuriance. The humiliating proof of this is placed beyond dispute by official statistics. Of the 130,150 paupers relieved in this city, in 1858, 50,251, or 38 per cent., were natives; and that this result was not attributable to the demoralizing influences of city life, is shown by the fact that, of the 261,155 State paupers, 104,744, or 41 per cent., of the whole number, were natives of the United States. It is evident, therefore, that exclusive of emigration, the ratio of our native-born paupers to the population of our city and State is far beyond that of England and more than double that of Ireland. . . . .

"It is the certain tendency of every financial revulsion, to throw multitudes of the self-supporting, industrious classes down to a lower level than they before occupied. Nay, in the ordinary annual opera-

fifty years, and the amount which would have accumulated upon the capital employed during that period at six per cent. interest.

"It is the object of this article to exhibit the progress of wealth in Massachusetts during the fifty years, from 1790 to 1840, as deduced from the six State valuations, taken at intervals of ten years each. These valuations have the legislative sanction of the General Court, and are the bases of apportionment of all State taxation for the ten years following. They are prepared from the returns furnished by the assessors of the several towns and districts, and are intended to embrace all the taxable property of the Commonwealth. They may be relied upon as sufficiently correct for the purposes of comparison, or of showing the progress of wealth during these fifty years; at least they furnish the nearest approximation we have to the true amount of wealth in the State."

The assessors' valuation of the property in the State of

tions of labor, as affected by the seasons, and by the fluctuations of supply and demand common in the most prosperous times, every winter is full of perils to thousands of the respectable poor. Such being the laws of labor, what schemes of economical science will prevent their operation?

"But the subject presents itself in another aspect. The times are always hard with large families, whose miserably insufficient wages just keep them above starvation. By wonderful energy and management, they contrive to live on, unaided, the greater part of the year. But let them be overtaken with sickness, or by the usual contractions of labor during the winter, which takes away their slender pittance, and what is there between them and starvation? They have no work, no savings to fall back upon, and their children and themselves are perishing with cold, and hunger, and nakedness. It is not in human nature to endure such an ordeal, unharmed, especially when driven by stern necessity to consort with the outcast, and to be degraded by public relief. Yet such, alas! is often the condition of many of the deserving poor."—[M. K. P.]

Massachusetts in 1790, was $44,024,349, and in 1840, it had increased to $299,880,338. The increase of wealth in the State during fifty years was $255,855,989. In Massachusetts the legal rate of interest is six per cent per annum, and the value of property is commonly estimated by the per centage income for which it can be rented. If a house and lot, or a store and lot, will rent for $600 per annum, besides the taxes and insurance, the property is valued at $10,000, for the income from it is equal to interest at six per cent. per annum on $10,000.

In Massachusetts, the banks are allowed to discount paper at six per cent. In making loans, they take the interest or discount from the notes for the time they have to run. Take the value of the property in 1790, say $44,024,349, and suppose it to have been loaned at six per cent. per annum, on notes having six months to run. In fifty years the interest on this sum would have amounted to $885,524,246. Add the principal—*i. e.*, $44,024,349, and we have a sum of $929,548,595. The actual increase of wealth in the State during the fifty years, was but $255,855,989. Add to this the principal or property of the State in 1790—*i. e.*, $44,024,349, and the entire wealth of the State amounts to $299,880,338; or not one-third as much as the accumulation on the same capital would have been in fifty years at six per cent. interest per annum. If, in 1790, the people of Massachusetts had rented their property of a foreign nation, and agreed to pay interest on it half yearly at the rate of six per cent. per annum, they would have been bound to pay in the fifty years, about three and a half times more than they earned during that period over and above their living. The results of the establishment of this rate of interest in the State, are manifest in the accumulation of wealth in the hands of the few, and in the proportionate destitution of the many.

According to a pamphlet containing a list of the

wealthy men of Boston, and an estimate of the value of their property, there are 224 individuals who are worth, in the aggregate, $71,855,000, and upon an average, $321,781 each. In this pamphlet no estimate is made of any individual's property that is supposed to amount to less than $100,000. If we take the wealthy men in all the other towns and counties in the State, and suppose that there are 3,000 other individuals who are worth only $30,000 each, their aggregate wealth would amount to $90,000,000. Add this sum to the $71,855,000 owned by the 224 men, and we have $161,855,000, or considerably more than half the value of all the property of the State. Such estimates are liable to be more or less incorrect; but any one who will make an estimate of the wealth of the town or village in which he resides, will find that a very small proportion of the inhabitants are worth more than all the rest. This is still more true of large cities than it is of towns and villages.

If the estimate of the wealth of the 3,224 wealthy men in the State of Massachusetts be correct, these men are worth more than all the other inhabitants of the State. Allowing the families of the 3,224 men to average five persons each, they would constitute a population of 16,120 individuals. In 1840, the State contained a population of 737,700. The 16,120 individuals would not be two and one-fifth per cent. of the population, and yet they would own more than half the wealth of the State. If this estimate even approach the truth, it shows an immense disproportion of wealth for the labor performed by its owners; for it is impossible that they, or their ancestors, whatever may have been their skill or industry, can have performed the labor and made the improvements which constitute this wealth. The interest on money loaned, and the rent on property leased, are the only means by which they could have accumulated it. $44,024,349 loaned on six months' paper at six per cent.

interest per annum, as interest is taken by banks, would increase in fifty years to twenty-one times its original amount. This increase would accrue to the lenders of the money, by merely exchanging their money, or banknotes for the notes of individuals, and collecting the interest.

If the rate of interest on money in Massachusetts were at one per cent. per annum, instead of at six per cent., and the $44,024,349 were loaned on six months' paper at one per cent. interest in advance, in fifty years the money would accumulate $28,879,973. Add the principal—*i. e.*, $44,024,349—and the sum would be $72,904,322, instead of $929,548,595, the accumulation at six per cent.

SECTION V.

INTEREST ON NATIONAL AND STATE DEBTS.

Interest on money at six per cent. per annum, payable half-yearly, will double the principal in eleven years, eight months, and twenty days; but, for convenience, we will call it twelve years. One thousand dollars lent at six per cent., in twelve years, will accumulate to $2,000; in twenty-four years, to $4,000; in thirty-six years, to $8,000; in forty-eight years, to $16,000; in sixty years, to $32,000; in seventy-two years, to $64,000; in eighty-four years, to $128,000; in ninety-six years, to $256,000; in a hundred and eight years, to $512,000; in one hundred and twenty years, to $1,024,000. Multiply this sum by 1,024, and it will give the accumulation for one hundred and twenty years more; $1,024,000 × 1,024 =$1,048,576,000. Multiply this product by 1,024, and we shall have the accumulation during the next one hundred and twenty years, or for a period of three hundred and sixty years — $1,048,576,000 × 1,024 = $1,073,741,824,000.

A rate of interest on money at one per cent., payable half-yearly, will double the principal in about sixty-nine and a half years; but, for convenience, we will call it seventy years. One thousand dollars lent at one per cent., in seventy years will accumulate to $2,000; in a hundred and forty years, to $4,000; in two hundred and ten years, to $8,000; in two hundred and eighty years, to $16,000; in three hundred and fifty years, to $32,000; or in three hundred and sixty years to, say, $37,574.

Deduct $37,574 from the accumulation on $1,000 at six per cent., during the three hundred and sixty years —i. e., $37,574 from $1,073,741,824,000, and the remainder is $1,073,741,786,426; which sum, a rate of interest at six per cent. on $1,000 will accumulate over and above the sum accumulated by a rate of interest of one per cent. on $1000 during a period of three hundred and sixty years. One dollar loaned at six per cent. per annum, the interest collected and reloaned half-yearly for a period of three hundred and sixty years, will accumulate the sum of $1,073,741,824; while the same dollar loaned at one per cent., and the interest collected and reloaned in the same manner for the same period, will accumulate little more than $37. One dollar loaned at six per cent. interest per annum for a period of three hundred and sixty years, would accumulate more than the assessed value of the whole State of New York. The legal interest in the State of New York is seven per cent., and one dollar loaned at this rate for three hundred and sixty years, would accumulate a greater sum than the valuation of the whole United States.

Suppose a foreign nation should lend to the government of the United States $100,000 at seven per cent., on condition that our government should give her bonds half yearly for the payment of the interest, and the sum should accumulate for a term of three hundred and sixty years. However prosperous our people might be, at the expiration of the period the whole property of the nation would not pay the debt. At seven per cent. interest, the debt would double in about ten years. In three hundred and sixty years, $100,000 loaned at seven per cent. interest per annum would amount to $6,971,947,673,600,000; a much larger sum than the valuation of the property of the whole world. These calculations make it evident that six and seven per cent. interest cannot and ought not to be paid by any nation.

We will make a calculation of interest at three per cent. per annum, paid and reloaned half-yearly, as in the former calculations. If the United States should borrow from England $100,000 at three per cent. interest, take up her bonds every six months, and give new bonds, adding in the interest, the debt would be doubled in about twenty-three and a half years. But allow it to double in twenty-four years, and the $100,000 would accumulate in three hundred and sixty years, to $3,276,800,000. The annual interest on this sum at three per cent. would be $98,304,000. The yearly payment of this sum of interest would be caused by merely borrowing $100,000 for a period of three hundred and sixty years at three per cent. per annum, adding the interest every six months. This enormous debt would be occasioned by the accumulative power of interest, which it requires the products of labor to satisfy and pay.

Suppose, when Virginia was settled in 1607, England had sold to the first settlers the whole of the United States for $1,000, and had taken a mortgage for this sum covering the whole property, but instead of paying the interest yearly at seven per cent. the settlers had agreed to take up their bonds at the end of every six months, and add in the interest. Allow the $1,000 and the accruing interest to remain outstanding until 1860, and then become due. Although our prosperity has far surpassed that of any other nation, yet our property of every description would not pay the debt. Interest at seven per cent. doubles the principal in ten years and one month. In one hundred years and ten months the debt would have amounted to $1,024,000; and in two hundred and one years and eight months, to $1,048,576,000. Add fifty years and five months to 1859, and the sum would amount to $33,554,432,000. All the interest which would have accumulated upon the $1,000 would not have increased the quantity of money or the property of the nation. All the increase of the value of the property would have been added by the labor of the people: but all their surplus earnings have not equalled the legal accumulation at seven per cent. interest on $1,000 during this period.

The southern and western States depend upon the yearly products of their labor for their wealth; they are greatly impoverished by the amount of interest that they are compelled to pay to our eastern and northern cities for the use of money. A very large amount of the capital stocks of western and southern banks, and a large amount of western and southern State bonds, are owned by capitalists in the northern cities and by foreigners. The interest on these is constantly transferring the earnings of the people of these States to a few capitalists in the large cities and in foreign nations. All this would be avoided by the establishment of proper monetary laws by our own government. The government ought to furnish money, by making a representative of the property of applicants in their own States, and no State should be compelled to pay to other States or nations millions of dollars' worth of products yearly for the use of money to represent the value of its own property. For if there be property in any State or country, there is a foundation on which to establish a plenty of good money to represent its value; but if there be no property there will be no inhabitants; and, of course, no use for money.

Money has been instituted with such overwhelming power, that it is almost universally understood to be the actual capital, and the property and labor of a nation only representatives of the value of money. The newspapers and periodicals of the day consider capital abundant when money is plenty, and lament the want of capital when money is scarce. New States legalize high rates of interest to induce capital, that is, money, to come into them for investment. But the money is not capital, for if the real capital did not first exist in these States in sufficient amount to secure the money it would never go into them. There could be no use for money in any part of the world unless the capital first existed; for there would be nothing to buy, and the money itself could afford no means of support, and would therefore be entirely useless. But although a new State may have a large amount of capital and improvements, the inhabitants cannot exchange their property without money: it is impossible for the people to make their exchanges by barter, and no States take the products of labor for taxes: all debts are payable in money. The people of every State must have money for the transaction of business, yet money is not their capital, it only represents the value of their capital. Landed property in any new State that is competent to secure permanently a loan of $1,000, made by a citizen of another State, and to secure the payment of the interest yearly, is just as competent to secure permanently a like sum of paper money, if it were created by the Government on purpose to make this loan. Where actual capital exists, it would be as easy, under true monetary laws, to make all the money necessary justly to represent and exchange its value, as it is to furnish measures to determine the quantity of products; and there would be no more necessity for this nation to depend upon England, or upon any other foreign country, to furnish us with money to represent the value of our own capital, than there is for sending to the Czar of Russia for some of his nobles to govern us.

SECTION VI.

NO ACCUMULATION OF PROPERTY BY LABOR EQUAL TO THE ACCUMULATION BY THE LOAN OF MONEY AT SEVEN PER CENT. INTEREST.

Although the business of a nation be conducted in good faith, and all contracts be fulfilled according to law, and no scarcity of money be induced, yet a legal rate of interest of seven per cent. per annum, will inevitably concentrate the wealth in a few hands.

To show that interest at seven per cent. will accumulate property far more rapidly than it can be earned by labor, suppose a nation of one thousand individuals. We will use this miniature nation in illustration, because the operation of the laws will be more readily seen upon so small a community; but the effects would be similar upon a great nation. The thousand persons settle in a new country, and engage in various occupations, agricultural, manufacturing, mercantile, etc. At the settlement of the colony, we will suppose the colonists to be worth an equal amount of property, so that one shall possess no superiority over another. Each pursues some lawful and useful business, without entering into any speculation whereby a fortune may be gained without labor. No one has any means of support besides actual production, except the legal interest of seven per cent. on money loaned, or rent at the same rate on money invested in property. All are diligent in their several occupations, and thus each contributes to the general well-being.

Two mechanics, just come of age, are desirous of accumulating large fortunes. They are good workmen, and each is able to earn a dollar a day over and above his ex-

COMPARED WITH LEGAL INTEREST. 127

penses. Every six months they loan the money thus earned at seven per cent. interest, the interest payable half yearly. They set their affections upon being rich, and therefore do not burden themselves with a house and family. These men earn an average of a dollar a day, beside their expenses, three hundred days in each year, during forty years and four months. Their age is then, sixty-one years and four months. Each earns by labor $300 per year for forty years, or, for the whole period, $12,100 —together, $24,200. The interest on their earnings, loaned half yearly, for a period of forty years and four months, accumulates an amount which will be seen by reference to the following table. Interest at seven per cent. per annum, paid and reloaned half yearly, accumulates a sum equal to the principal in ten years and one month.

TABLE.

INTEREST AT SEVEN PER CENT. on $300.

1st half year they earn by their labor......	$300 00	Amount brought up	$1,308 74
		5th half year's labor..	300 00
6 months' interest at 7 per cent...........	10 50		
			1,608 74
	310 50	6 months' interest....	56 30
2d half year's labor....	300 00		
			1,665 04
	610 50	6th half year's labor...	300 00
6 months' interest.....	21 37		
			1,965 04
	631 87	6 months' interest.....	68 78
3d half year's labor..	300 00		
			2,033 82
	931 87	7th half year's labor..	300 00
6 months' interest.....	32 61		
			2,333 82
	964 48	6 months' interest.....	81 68
4th half year's labor...	300 00		
			2,415 50
	1,264 48	8th half year's labor...	300 00
6 months' interest....	44 26		
			2,715 50
	1,308 74		

INCREASE OF PROPERTY BY LABOR

Amount brought up	$2,715 50	Amount brought up	$5,488 69
6 months' interest	95 04	15th half year's labor	300 00
	2,810 54		5,788 69
9th half year's labor	300 00	6 months' interest	202 60
	3,110 54		5,991 29
months' interest	108 87	16th half year's labor	300 00
	3,219 41		6,291 29
10th half year's labor	300 00	6 months' interest	220 20
	3,519 41		6,511 49
6 months' interest	123 18	17th half year's labor	300 00
	3,642 59		6,811 49
11th half year's labor	300 00	6 months' interest	238 40
	3,942 59		7,049 89
6 months' interest	137 99	18th half year's labor	300 00
	4,080 58		7,349 89
12th half year's labor	300 00	6 months' interest	257 25
	4,380 58		7,607 14
6 months' interest	153 32	19th half year's labor	300 00
	4,533 90		7,907 14
13th half year's labor	300 00	6 months' interest	276 75
	4,833 90		8,183 89
6 months' interest	169 18	20th half year's labor	300 00
	5,003 08		8,483 89
14th half year's labor	300 00	6 months' interest	49 49
	5,303 08		8,533 38
6 months' interest	185 61	Add one month's labor	50 00
	5,488 69		$8,583 38

In the first ten years and one month, the two men earn by their labor	$6,050 00
Interest thereon during this period	2,533 38
	8,583 38
In the 2d ten years and one month, the interest on this sum equals the principal	8,583 38
	17,166 76

Amount brought over		$17,166	76
2d 10 years and 1 month's labor, and interest thereon		8,583	38
		25,750	14
3d " interest		25,750	14
		51,500	28
3d " labor and interest thereon		8,583	38
		60,083	66
4th " interest		60,083	66
		120,167	32
4th " labor, and interest thereon		8,583	38
		128,750	70
In 40 years and 4 months the men earn by their labor		24,200	00
Remainder accumulated by interest		$104,550	70

The interest on the sum, $24,200, earned by their labor is $104,550 70—over four and a quarter times more than they have earned by their labor. Suppose the two men to live twenty years and two months longer—that is, to the age of eighty-one years and six months—and continue to loan their money. During this period it would double twice.

Thus	$128,750	70
10 years and one month's interest	128,750	70
	257,501	40
2d 10 years and one month's interest	257,501	40
Total accumulation in 60 years and 6 months	$515,002	80
The two men do not labor during the last 20 years and 2 months, and expend for their living during that period	15,002	80
	500,000	00
In 40 years and 4 months, they earn by their labor $24,000, and live twenty years and 2 months on their money without labor		
Subtract money earned by labor	24,200	00
Remainder accumulated by interest on $24,200	$475,800	00

Every dollar of the $475,800 is earned by the labor of others and given to the two men, as the legal interest upon $24,200. These men live laboriously, and work for a very moderate compensation. They take only the legal rate of interest, and do not demand the principal of the money as long as the interest is paid. Neither do they enter into any speculations. It is, therefore, said, that labor earns their large fortunes. Cases similar to this are often brought to prove that an industrious man may, by his labor, accumulate a large property. That this conclusion is erroneous, is manifest from the foregoing table, by which it appears, that more than nineteen out of twenty parts of the large fortunes of these men are earned by others, and paid to them to satisfy the legal interest on their loans of money.

Now let us suppose the interest on money to be one per cent., and, with this difference only, these two men to be placed in the same circumstances in which they have been already described. They earn over and above their expenses a dollar a day, three hundred days in each year, during a period of forty years and four months. They loan their earnings at the legal rate of interest, (one per cent.,) and collect and reloan the interest half-yearly.

TABLE.

INTEREST AT ONE PER CENT. ON $300.

1st half year's labor....	$300 00	Amount brought up··	604 51	
6 month's interest at 1 per cent.,..............	1 50	3d half year's labor...	300 00	
	301 50		904 51	
2d half year's labor....	300 00	6 months' interest.....	4 52	
	601 50		909 03	
6 months' interest.....	3 01	4th half year's labor...	300 00	
	604 51	.	1,209 03	

COMPARED WITH LEGAL INTEREST. 131

Amount brought up	$1,209 03
6 months' interest	6 05
	1,215 08
5th half year's labor	300 00
	1,515 08
6 months' interest	7 58
	1,522 66
6th half year's labor	300 00
	1,822 66
6 months' interest	9 11
	1,831 77
7th half year's labor	300 00
	2,131 77
6 months' interest	10 66
	2,142 43
8th half year's labor	300 00
	2,442 43
6 months' interest	12 21
	2,454 64
9th half year's labor	300 00
	2,754 64
6 months' interest	13 77
	2,768 41
10th half year's labor	300 00
	3,068 41
6 months' interest	15 34
	3,083 75
11th half year's labor	300,00
	3,388 75
6 months' interest	16 92
	3,400 67
12th half year's labor	300 00
	3,700 67

Amount brought up	$3,700 67
6 months' interest	18 50
	3,719 17
13th half year's labor	300 00
	4,019 17
6 months' interest	20 10
	4,039 27
14th half year's labor	300 00
	4,339 27
6 months' interest	21 69
	4,360 96
15th half year's labor	300 00
	4,660 96
6 months' interest	23 30
	4,684 26
16th half year's labor	300 00
	4,984 26
6 months' interest	24 92
	5,009 18
17th half year's labor	300 00
	5,309 18
6 months' interest	26 55
	5,335 73
18th half year's labor	300 00
	5,635 73
6 months' interest	28 18
	5,663 91
19th half year's labor	300 00
	5,963 91
6 months' interest	29 82
	5,993 73
20th half year's labor	300 00
	6,293 73

Amount brought up $6,293 73		Amount brought up $6,299 00	
1 month's interest..... 5 27		1 month's labor 50 00	
6,299 00		6,349 00	

In the first ten years and one month, the two men would earn by their labor the same sum as in the former case, viz:... $6,050 00

Interest during that period at 1 per cent. on the money earned.. 299 00

6,349 00

2d ten years and one month's interest at 1 per cent., re-loaned half yearly............................... 671 73

7,020 73

2d ten years and one month's labor, with interest thereon at 1 per cent..................................... 6,349 00

13,369 73

3d ten years and one month's interest at 1 per cent..... 1,414 53

14,784 26

3d ten years and one month's labor, with interest thereon 6,349 00

21,133 26

4th ten years and one month's interest at 1 per cent..... 2,235 87

23,369 13

4th ten years and one month's labor, with interest thereon 6,349 00

$29,718 13

In the above forty years and four months, the two men earn by their labor the same sum as when interest was at 7 per cent., viz.......................... ... $24,200 00

Interest at 1 per cent. upon this sum during a period of forty-four years and four months.................. 5,518 13

$29,718 13

Brought over.................................. $29,718 13
Interest on this sum at 1 per cent. for twenty years and two months, or until the men arrive at the age of eighty-one years and six months—first ten years and one month's interest................................. 3,144 17
                                                                                        ─────────
                                                                                        32,862 30
2d ten years and one month's interest................ 3,475 80
Total amount of earnings, and interest thereon at 1 per cent. for sixty years and six months................ 36,338 10

As in the former case, suppose the men to live the last twenty years and two months of their lives upon their money, and deduct for their expenses................ 14,995 00
                                                                                        ─────────
                                                                                        $21,343 10

With interest at seven per cent., at the age of eighty-one years and six months they have a fortune of $500,000, while with interest at one per cent. they have but $21,343, making a difference of $478,656. If in the former case they decease at the age of eighty-one years and six months, their fellow-citizens are indebted to their estates or heirs, $500,000, with an annual interest of $35,000; and in the latter, the citizens are indebted to them $21,343 with an annual interest of $213 44. Even at one per cent., the interest legally accumulates for them more than one-half as much as they earn by labor.

Let us now suppose another case, of two men who become of age at the same time as the former two, and who are equally good workmen. They likewise earn a dollar per day over and above their own support; but they marry, and have the expense of supporting their families. Each rents a house at $100 per annum; and thus one-third of their surplus earnings is paid for tenements. Their earnings must also supply their families with food, clothing, fuel, etc. Although these two men work as diligently and as skillfully, and earn as much as the former two, yet, instead of being able to lend money upon interest, they are obliged to pay interest on the houses they occupy. Strict economy is requisite to make one dollar a day, over and above their personal expenses, school their children, pay rent, and furnish necessary supplies. These two men labor as much as the former two, and contribute at least an equal share to the public good. All their earnings are devoted to the payment of artisans, teachers, and others, whose services they require. The former two, without performing more labor than the latter two, live twenty years and two months without labor, and leave fortunes to the amount of $250,000 each. The latter work as long as they are able, but in old age are, perhaps, compelled to seek an asylum in the poor-house.

If the former two men as they earned their money had invested it in farming land, or in houses and stores, and had rented the property at seven per cent. on its cost, they certainly could not have oppressed the producing classes more than they would by lending them money at seven per cent. In either case they would compel others to earn for them more than nineteen out of twenty parts of their fortunes.*

The amount to which nations and individuals are indebted, is a subject of general complaint. The above illustration exhibits the cause. The difference in the amounts due to the estates of these men, under the supposed circumstances, can be traced directly to the difference in the rates of interest. At the rate of seven per

---

* We do not dispute the right of the bachelors to use all the money that they can earn by their labor, and to lend their money on interest to others; but the interest which they have a right to receive from others, should be restricted to the necessary expenses of furnishing and supporting a money representative of value. If a just rate of interest be maintained, landlords and tenants, in voluntary agreements, will naturally fix upon a just rate of rent; because the foundation upon which agreements will then rest will be just.

cent., a sum of $500,000 is due to their estates. It would take the labor of a single man for more than 1,666 years to pay this principal; and it would require, at one dollar per day, the constant toil of more than 116 men to pay the yearly interest of $35,000. From generation to generation, they might continue to pay the interest, and still the burden be undiminished. In the short space of sixty years and six months, two men entail this debt upon this small nation. Not the labor of these two men entails this evil, but the *law* which fixes the unjust rate of interest. It is the natural result of the law, and must be alike disastrous to large and small communities.

SECTION VII.

TWO PER CENT. PER ANNUM, TOO HIGH A RATE OF INTEREST.

However fertile a country may be, interest even at two per cent. per annum will inevitably oppress the producers. In the following table interest is calculated at two per cent., under the same circumstances and for the same period as in the former cases. The interest will be found far to exceed the principal.

TABLE.

INTEREST AT TWO PER CENT. ON $300.

1st half year's labor..	$300 00	Amount brought up.	$609 03
6 months' interest at 2 per cent.	3 00	3d half year's labor....	300 00
	303 00		909 03
2d half year's labor....	300 00	6 months' interest....	9 09
	603 00		918 12
6 months' interest.....	6 03	4th half year's labor...	300 00
	609 03		1.218 12

A RATE OF INTEREST

Amount brought up	$1,218 12	Amount brought up	$3,804 76
6 months' interest	12 18	6 months' interest	38 05
	1,230 30		3,842 81
5th half year's labor	300 00	13th half year's labor	300 00
	1,530 30		4,142 81
6 months' interest	15 30	6 months' interest	41 43
	1,545 60		4,184 24
6th half year's labor	300 00	14th half year's labor	300 00
	1,845 60		4,484 24
6 months' interest	18 46	6 months' interest	44 84
	1,864 06		4,529 08
7th half year's labor	300 00	15th half year's labor	300 00
	2,164 06		4,829 08
6 months' interest	21 64	6 months' interest	48 29
	2,185 70		4,877 37
8th half year's labor	300 00	16th half year's labor	300 00
	2,485 70		5,177 37
6 months' interest	24 86	6 months' interest	51 77
	2,510 56		5,229 14
9th half year's labor	300 00	17th half year's labor	300 00
	2,810 56		5,529 14
6 months' interest	28 11	6 months' interest	55 29
	2,838 67		5,584 43
10th half year's labor	300 00	18th half year's labor	300 00
	3,138 67		5,884 43
6 months' interest	31 39	6 months' interest	58 84
	3,170 06		5,943 27
11th half year's labor	300 00	19th half year's labor	300 00
	3,470 06		6,243 27
6 months' interest	34 70	6 months' interest	62 43
	3,504 76		6,305 70
12th half year's labor	300 00		
	3,804 76		

OF TWO PER CENT. PER ANNUM.   137

Amount brought up	$6,305 70	Amount brought up	$14,815 07
20th half year's labor..	300 00	10 years and 1 month's interest............	3,292 35
	6,605 70		
Add one month's interest..............	11 06		18,107 42
	6,616 76	3d 10 years and 1 month's labor and interest...........	
Add 1 month's labor..	50 00		6,666,76
	6,666 76		
Add 10 years and 1 month's interest at 2 per cent...........			24,774 18
		10 years and 1 month's interest...........	5,505 88
	1,481 55		
	8,148 31		30,280 06
2d 10 years and 1 month's labor and interest...........		4th 10 years and 1 month's labor and interest...........	
	6,666 76		6,666 76
	14,815 07		$36,946 82

Add the interest at two per cent. for twenty years and two months longer, until the men reach the age of eighty-one years and six months.

1st 10 years and one month's interest................	8,210 69
	45,157 51
2d 10 years and 1 month's interest..................	10,035 35
	55,192 86

In forty years and four months the two men earn by their labor	24,200 00
The interest upon this sum for a period of sixty years and six months, even at two per cent., amounts to........	30,992 00
	$55,192 00

This is $6,790 more than they earn by their labor.

When it is considered that this interest or rent is paid for the mere use of money or of capital, every reflecting, honest mind must be convinced that two per cent. is a higher rate of interest than a people can afford to pay. It is surely most unreasonable for the laws to compel producers to pay for the use of the property which a man may acquire by forty or fifty years' labor, twice or thrice the sum of the property so earned. The thing produced is more highly estimated than the power that produces it. If an interest of two per cent. upon a well regulated currency would accumulate the property of a nation in the possession of a few, can it be considered strange that the rates of three, four, five, six, and seven per cent. and even higher rates, which are exacted in different countries, should have concentrated property into so few hands? The only wonder is, that producers have continued to live under this oppression.

A rate of interest of even two per cent. per annum, would put it out of the power of the people to fulfil their contracts. The establishment of this rate of interest would be equivalent to the passing of a law, compelling the laboring classes to double the capital of a nation, in favor of capitalists once in thirty-four and a half years, besides producing their own support. Suppose a foreign nation owned all the real and personal estate in this nation, and a fair estimate were made of the value of all; and then our people were legally obliged to pay two per cent. yearly upon this valuation, besides maintaining themselves, would not a tribute or tax like this keep us forever in poverty? Our laws enforce much higher rates of interest on capital, which are little less oppressive to the great body of our producers, because they are paid to a few capitalists in our own land instead of to foreigners.

It may be objected that some of the illustrations of the accumulative power of interest are based on so long periods as to present exaggerated results; but it must be borne in mind that interest, and rents, at too high rates are continually accruing to the capital of nations, and are producing their evil effects upon the people whether the loans be for longer or for shorter periods.

SECTION VIII.

The reduction of interest would be an equal benefit to the producing classes, whether property should rise or fall in price, in consequence of such reduction.

It may be supposed that if interest were diminished to one per cent., property and labor would rise in the same proportion, and therefore, the producing classes would receive no benefit from the reduction. But whether property should rise, or fall, or maintain its present price, producers would have the same relative advantage; their gain would be from the lessened per centage on capital. If a man borrowed a hundred dollars for a year, he would pay but one dollar for the use of one hundred, instead of paying seven dollars. If he hired a hundred acres of land, he would have to earn only one acre to pay for the use of one hundred, instead of being obliged to earn seven to pay for their use; for the per centage on money governs the rent of land. This principle of the adequate reward of labor, by the decrease of the interest on money, although property and labor in consequence should rise in price, will be illustrated in the following table. The price of labor is calculated at six dollars per day, and the interest on money at one per cent. per annum. The men earn their money, and loan it as in the former cases.

TABLE.

INTEREST AT ONE PER CENT.—LABOR AT $6 PER DAY.

1st 6 months' labor..	$1,800 00	Amount brought up	$1,809 00
6 months' interest at 1 per cent.........	9 00	2d half year's labor...	1,800 00
	1,809 00		3,609 00

140   REDUCED INTEREST A BENEFIT

Amount brought up...	$3,609 00	Amount brought up...	$18,410 44
6 months' interest....	18 04	6 months' interest.....	92 05
	3,627 04		18,502 59
3d half year's labor..	1,800 00	11th half year's labor..	1,800 00
	5,427 04		20,302 59
6 months' interest....	27,14	6 months' interest....	101 51
	5,454 18		20,404 10
4th half year's labor..	1,800 00	12th half year's labor.	1,800 00
	7,254 18		22,204 10
6 months' interest....	36 27	6 months' interest....	111 02
	7,290 45		22,315 12
5th half year's labor..	1,800 00	13th half year's labor..	1,800 00
	9,090 45		24,115 12
6 months' interest....	45 45	6 months' interest	120 58
	9,135 90		24,235 70
6th half year's labor..	1,800 00	14th half year's labor..	1,800 00
	10,935 90		26,035 70
6 months' interest....	54 68	6 months' interest.....	130 18
	10,990 58		26,165 88
7th half year's labor..	1,800 00	15th half year's labor..	1,800 00
	12,790 58		27,965 88
6 months' interest...	63 95	6 months' interest....	139 88
	12,854 53		28,105 76
8th half year's labor..	1,800 00	16th half year's labor..	1,800 00
	14,654 53		29,905 76
6 months' interest....	73 27	6 months' interest.....	149 53
	14,727 80		30,055 29
9th half year's labor..	1,800 00	17th half year's labor..	1,800 00
	16,527 80		31,855 29
6 months' interest....	82 64	6 months' interest.....	159 28
	16,610 44		32,014 57
10th half year's labor..	1,800 00	18th half year's labor..	1,800 00
	18,410 44		33,814 57

WHETHER PRICES RISE OR FALL. 141

Amount brought up..	$33,814 57	Amount brought up..	$35,962 56
6 months' interest	169 07	20th half year's labor .	1,800 00
	33,983 64		37,762 56
19th half year's labor..	1,800 00	1 months' interest....'.	31 47
	35,783 64		37,794 03
months' interest.....	178 92	1 months' labor.......	300 00
	35,962 56		$38,094 03

10 years and 1 month's labor and interest..............	$38,094 03
2d 10 years and 1 month's interest.....................	4,030 44
	42,124 47
10 years and 1 month's labor and interest..............	38,094 03
	80,218 50
3d 10 years and 1 month's interest..	8,487 24
	88,705 74
10 years and 1 month's labor and interest..............	38,094 03
	126,799 77
4th 10 years and 1 month's interest....................	13,415 34
	140,215 11
10 years and 1 month's labor and interest.........	38,094 03
	$178,309 14

In 40 years and 4 months, the two men earn at $6 per day ....'.......	$145,200 00
Interest thereon for 40 years and 4 months at 1 per cent.	33,109 14
	178,309 14
Let the interest on $178,309 14 accumulate 20 years and 2 months, until the men arrive at the age of 81 years and 6 months. Interest on $178,309 14 for 10 years at 1 per cent..	18,865 02
	197,174 16
2d 10 years' interest................................	20,854 80
	218,028 96

```
Amount brought up.....................$218,028 96
The men cease to labor at the age of 61 years and 4
  months, and expend during 20 years and 2 months, six
  times more than when labor was at $1 per day. They
  expend six times $14,995. Deduct................  89,970 00
                                                   _____
                                                   $128,058 96
```

With interest at seven per cent., and labor at $1 per day, (see Sec. VI.,) the two men leave to their heirs $500,000; while with interest at one per cent., and labor at $6 per day, they leave to their heirs $128,058, only a fraction over one-fourth as much as in the former case. The interest on $500,000 at seven per cent., would be $35,000 annually. It would take the labor of one man at $1 per day, one hundred and sixteen years to pay the interest for a year. The interest on $128,058 at one per cent., would be $1,280. The labor of one man for two hundred and thirteen days, at $6 per day, would pay the interest for a year.

SECTION IX.

EFFECTS UPON PRODUCERS OF HIGH AND FLUCTUATING RATES OF INTEREST.

The following illustration, based upon land, will show the effect of high and varying rates of interest upon producers, and the safety with which money could be loaned, if interest were reduced to a just and uniform rate.

Suppose W. owns a thousand acres of land, which he has bought from the Government, and upon which he is paying the taxes. The land will produce no income, unless he cultivates it himself, or sells or rents it to others, who will cultivate it. He sells the land in five tracts, of two hundred acres each, at five dollars per acre. A., B.,

OF VARYING RATES OF INTEREST. 143

C., D., and E., are the purchasers, and move upon and cultivate the land, and pay the taxes. No other payment is to be made for five years, at the expiration of which period, A., B., C., D. and E., are to pay up the interest on their respective tracts of land, and after that to pay the interest annually. All the land sold is of nearly the same quality. Each purchaser agrees to pay a thousand dollars, and gives a bond and mortgage upon his land to secure the payment. W. takes A.'s bond and mortgage, bearing two per cent. interest; B.'s bearing four per cent.; C.'s bearing eight per cent.; D.'s bearing sixteen per cent.; and E.'s bearing thirty-two per cent. interest. At the end of five years, A.'s bond and mortgage will have drawn $100; B.'s $200; C.'s $400; D.'s $800; and E.'s $1,600 interest. Yet W. sells the land to all at the same price, and all the difference in the indebtedness of A. and E. is caused by the difference in the rates of interest that W. charges them. This difference makes E. indebted to W. $1,500 more than A. All the debtors must pay the interest with the products of their respective farms, and W. does none of the labor toward making the production.

Now let X. sell the same land to the parties on a credit of one year, and charge them six per cent. interest. Suppose money to be so scarce, that at the end of the year they clear only the interest, and are compelled to lose their farms by foreclosure, or else to borrow the money and pay off their mortgages. A., B., C., D. and E. borrow on the best terms possible, on mortgage of their farms and stock. A. procures the money at two per cent. interest; B. at four per cent.; C. at eight per cent.; D. at sixteen per cent.; and E. is compelled to pay thirty-two per cent. per annum, or two and two-thirds per cent. a month. This amounts to the same thing as if they had bought their farms of W., agreeing to pay him these rates of interest. The money enables them to keep possession of their farms. From the sales of their products they must pay the different debts and interest. The rate of interest in each case decides what proportion of the products shall go to pay for the use of the farm. When the farmers borrow the money to pay off their mortgages, they do not keep the money. It continues to circulate, and to decide what rents others shall pay for the privilege of keeping the use of property for a given period.

But suppose the rate of interest to be fixed at one per cent., and that money could always be obtained on the offer of good security. Those who had money to lend would ascertain whether the property offered as security would make the interest safe. If so, the security would be deemed good. When interest is liable to rise from six to twelve per cent., the lenders of money require securities that will make their loans safe if the interest should rise to the latter point. But if the supply of money were such that the interest could not rise, a less security would always keep loans safe. Suppose, then, the rate of interest to be at one per cent., and W. to sell the land to A., B., C., D and E., as before. They purchase two hundred acres apiece at $5 per acre, and pay only the taxes until the end of five years, when they pay the interest for the whole period. The interest at one per cent. on $1,000, for five years, amounts to $50 ; and on the whole $5,000, to but $250, instead of $4,100, the amount in the former case, when the money was loaned at the various and higher rates of interest. The tenants have as much the use of the farms to enable them to pay the $250 as to pay the $4,100. If they make any reasonable improvement on them, W. can incur no hazard of losing his money, for each farm would certainly rent for $10 a year. Even if at the close of the five years the farmers should not have paid the interest, and each farm would rent for $10 50 a year, over and above the taxes, each farm would still be as good as $1,050, at interest, at one per cent.; therefore, in either case, the tenants would keep the sale of the land good, or the loan safe for W., without his personal labor. But if W. sell the farms, when interest is at six per cent., at the end of the five years each of the farmers would owe him $300 interest, which, added to the principal, would make $1,300. The interest on this sum, at six per cent., would be $78 annually, and unless each farm would rent for this sum, W.'s debts would not be safe. The per centage rent on the valuation of property must be equal to the rate per cent. interest on money, or the property cannot be good security for the payment of the money.

It is commonly said and supposed that borrowers pay a certain rate of interest for the use of money. But they do not use the money; they part with it in some way for property, and the rate of interest determines what rent they shall pay for the use of the property. A few illustrations will show the effect of increased rates of interest upon the welfare of producers and distributers whose property is in their products. Suppose a planter raises a hundred bags of cotton, in doing which he becomes indebted for bagging, rope, clothing for his workmen, etc. Let him be compelled to realize the money for his crop as soon as he can get it to market, and at a time when money is very scarce, and the price of cotton extremely low. He is obliged either to sell for cash, or to offer a commission to some one to accept his draft on the pledge of the cotton; and is forced to pay for his acceptance, say two and a half per cent. This will take the proceeds of two and a half bales of cotton. If the draft be drawn on three months' time, and the scarcity of money compel the planter to sell the draft at two per cent. a month, six bales more will be taken from his one hundred bales. He must lose eight and a half bales for the privilege of keeping the remainder three months in store, besides the storage, cartage, and the commission on sales. The proceeds of the eight and a half bales of cotton are gained by the capitalist by means of the high rate of interest, and without any adequate labor on his part. Under a true monetary system, the planter would be able to hold his cotton a year without losing even two bales of it for the advance of money.

Again, a manufacturer makes a package of a hundred pieces of cloths, and sends them to market. Six months pass before the goods can be sold, and, with interest at six per cent. per annum, he loses three pieces as the interest on the ninety-seven which he has left. If, at the end of six months, the commission merchant sell them on a credit of eight months, at the above rate of interest the manufacturer must lose four pieces more, in all seven pieces of cloth. But suppose the manufacturer is greatly in need of money, and must have the eight months' note cashed. Let the commission merchant, in consequence of a rise of interest, sell the note in market at two per cent. a month discount, and the manufacturer must lose sixteen pieces of cloth on the note, instead of four pieces, the loss at six per cent. Add these to the first three, and it will make nineteen pieces, paid to others out of the one hundred pieces, to enable him to keep eighty-one pieces, or their proceeds, for fourteen months. These are a total loss to the manufacturer. Besides, he has to pay cartage, storage, commission and transportation. The proceeds of the nineteen pieces of goods go into the hands of the money-lender.

Now let us see the result in the same transaction, with interest on money diminished to one per cent. and maintained at that rate. The manufacturer sends the hundred pieces of cloths to market, and they lie six months unsold. He loses only half a piece of cloth for the six months' interest on his goods. The commission merchant sells them on eight months' credit, as before, and gets the note discounted at the rate of one per cent. per annum. This amounts to two-thirds of a piece of cloth, and added to the half piece, is a loss to the manufacturer of one piece and one-sixth of a piece during the fourteen months, instead of being a loss, as in the former case, of nineteen pieces. This difference is caused solely by the difference in the rate of interest. Although the bales of cotton or the pieces of goods lie unused and uninjured in the storehouse, yet a number of bales of cotton or pieces of goods are taken from their owners by the legal growth of the money, or by the growth or accumulation on the paper obligation given to obtain the money. The rate of interest decides how many bales of cotton shall be owned by the planter—how many pieces of goods shall be owned by the manufacturer; and the proportion of them that shall be given to those who lend the money to represent their value.

SECTION X.

THE OPPRESSION OF LABOR BY A MONOPOLY OF LAND NOT AS GREAT AS THE OPPRESSION BY HIGH RATES OF INTEREST ON MONEY.

It is supposed by many that the monopoly of land is the cause of the centralization of wealth, and that landowners are the greatest oppressors of the laboring classes. They think that if all had access to a certain portion of land, the means of support would be within reach of all. But if the land were equally divided, many persons are not qualified to improve it to good advantage, nor are all, or nearly all, capable of manufacturing the implements which must be used in its cultivation. The mechanical arts are absolutely necessary to the improvement of the land; and men who are engaged in these arts require very little, if any land, to cultivate, because their time is occupied with the various trades by which agriculturists and others are supplied with houses, implements of industry, clothing, and so forth. A monopoly of manufactured articles would be as likely to cause the evil as a monopoly of land; for if all implements of agriculture were held by a few, it would be nearly impossible to cultivate the land; and should all owners of houses refuse to receive tenants, more than three-quarters of the people in our large cities would be turned into the streets. Doubtless it is for the interest of landlords to rent their houses, but it is equally for the interest of landowners to lease or rent out their lands: for, if they keep them in their own possession, neither the houses nor lands can be useful to their owners, except so far as they can cultivate the one, and live in the other. The same is true of all kinds of implements and merchandise. Neither lands nor products have any natural monopolizing power. The monopolizing power is an artificial one, instituted by our national laws, and is in the money which represents the property and products. The monopoly is one of the effects, it is not the cause of the evil. If the land and wealth were now to be equally distributed, the same cause which has thus far centralized them would accumulate them again in the hands of a few. In the illustration of the one hundred families and their descendants, (see Chap. III., Sec. II.,) no land is bought except the two hundred acres for their personal residences; yet they take from the people as large a quantity of their products, by the interest on money, or on their obligations, as if they had invested the twenty millions in farming land, and let the land out to tenants at six per cent. interest on its cost, reinvesting the interest half-yearly in land during the hundred and fifty years. The tenant of leased land pays the rent by the sale of its yearly products. If he cannot support himself well besides paying the rent, it is evident to all that the rent is too high. The landlord and the tenant come in direct contact, and the wrong done by the former to the latter is manifest. But nothing grows upon money with which the borrower can pay the interest. He exchanges it for merchandise or lands, and expects to make a profit on them which will pay the interest on the money. If, however, he be not able to pay the interest, it is set down as bad management on his part, instead of being attributed to the too high rate of interest on the money. The owner of money, by the legal interest, imposes as great hardships upon the borrower, as if he had lent him land or merchandise at the same per centage on its valuation.

The following illustration will show the different estimates put upon the leasing of land at a certain per centage on its value, and the lending of money at the same rate. K. is the owner of $100,000. He expends this sum for well-improved farms, which he leases in perpetuity at six per cent. per annum on their cost. His tenants are, therefore, obliged to pay $6,000 a year for the use of the farms. They would find it very difficult to pay so high a rent; and it would be deemed very oppressive to them and to their heirs who must work the land. If the owner of the land should require from each tenant security for the rent, so that one must become responsible for the payment of another's rent, he would be thought a hard landlord. And if in time of drought or disease, which rendered the tenants unable to pay their rent, the landlord should sell the stock from their farms, he would be deemed very oppressive, although his tenants had voluntarily entered into the engagement.

Now, suppose M. to own $100,000, which he lends on interest at six per cent. per annum payable half-yearly. To secure the loan, he requires double its value in land, so that he is twice as well secured as the landowner. He allows the principal to remain outstanding as long as the interest is regularly paid. He annually receives

$6,000 interest on his money, the same sum that the landowner receives for the rent of his land, and he is much better secured, for in some years the crops may fail; but the mortgage on land of twice the value of the loan, is a double security, and will force the sale of the farm the interest be not paid. It takes as many of the products of labor to pay the interest to the money-lender, as to pay the rent to the land-owner; yet the money-lender is deemed a just and honorable man, because he takes only six per cent. interest for his money. If at any time the scarcity of money and the low price of products prevent the payment of the interest, and the money-lender foreclose some of his mortgages, buying in the property, worth double the amount lent, at half price, no stigma rests upon his character, especially if the legal rate of interest be seven per cent., and he charge but six per cent.* Although these cases are so differently regarded, the oppression by lending money at six per cent. interest greatly exceeds that by leasing property.

The following illustration shows how tenants of land are affected by high rates of interest on money. N. owns a farm which he cultivates. He is, therefore, the rightful owner of the products. If, however, N. lets the farm to O., and O. cultivates it, then N. and O. are joint owners of the products. This principle, that labor and capital are together entitled to the products, is in accordance with the laws of nations, and must continue to be so as long as the rights of property are recognized by civil authority. The question which arises for settlement is, what proportion rightfully belongs to the capital, and what to the labor—what proportion of products N. should receive for the use of the farm, and what proportion O. should receive for his labor in cultivating it. It will be said at once that the proportion which O. is to

---

* People seem to look upon money as a sort of sacred thing, and on labor as a mere tool that is subservient to it.

give to N. is a matter of agreement between them ; and, therefore, whatever N. agrees to take, and O. agrees to pay for the rent of the farm, is the right proportion; and that no laws should interfere in such contracts except to compel their fulfilment. This would be right, and just to both the contracting parties, if the public standard of value on which they are compelled to found the contract were equitable. But if the standard or rate of interest be such that O. is obliged by its legal operation to pay nearly the whole surplus products of the farm to N. as rent, the contract is a manifest wrong to O.; because, although he work diligently all his life, the legal standard will keep him forever poor, while N., by the action of the same standard, without labor, will constantly increase in wealth.

We declare that all men are born free and equal; but N. may be born heir to a dozen farms, while O. may be born without property; and, under present laws, by his labor alone he cannot acquire it. Therefore, N. is actually born to live in luxury without labor, and O. is born to be a servant to N. O.'s children are born servants to N., and to his posterity, and live in perpetual toil and hardship, that N.'s children may be supplied with all the luxuries of life without labor. N. and his children receive these luxuries from the rent that O. and his children pay for the use of the land owned by N. If all men are by nature free and equal, why has legislation reversed the order of nature so as to secure the greatest possible inequality? It is not in the power of man to continue a more effectual method of concentrating property in a few hands, than by high rates of interest. This method works rapidly and securely, because it extorts consent as it operates. If civilization require that property should descend from father to son, it certainly does not require that legislation should do its utmost to magnify the inequalities arising from this right of inheritance. These inequalities only exist because the whole body of producers are obliged to pay an exorbitant price for the yearly rent of every description of property; and why are they obliged to pay this price? Because the rent is determined by the legal interest on money, he standard of value, to which no individual, nor class of individuals, can offer successful resistance. If N., instead of leasing the farm to O., lend him money with which to purchase a farm, O. rents the money from N. instead of renting the farm. But he is as much compelled to pay the interest on the money with the products of the farm, as he is to pay the rent of the farm with the products. If the interest on money were at one per cent., N. could not let his farm to O. at such a rate as to compel O. to give him in rent a sum equal to the principal of the farm in less than about seventy years. But if interest on money be fixed at seven per cent., N. can compel O. to give a rent for the farm which will equal the principal of the farm in about ten years. At this rate, in seventy years O. must give N. the value of one hundred and twenty-seven farms as the legal rent of one. High rates of interest under any form of government will centralize the wealth of the nation, and degrade and impoverish its producers. In fixing the rate of interest, governments determine what proportion of their earnings the producing classes shall pay for the use of capital. Laborers have no means of resisting the overwhelming power of accumulation thus given to capital, except by a change in the monetary system, and the establishment of a just rate of interest. Then the inequalities of birth and condition will be greatly diminished, and no class of laborers can be kept, for any length of time, subservient to capital.

SECTION XI.

THE RATE OF INTEREST DETERMINES THE PRICE OF PROPERTY, AND A RISE OF INTEREST INCREASES THE POWER OF MONEY TO COMMAND PROPERTY.

The value of money is determined by the interest that it will accumulate; and the value of all property is determined by the rent that can be obtained for it. The market value, or price of property must conform to the legal standard.

If the rent of any property be not sufficient to accumulate a sum equal to the estimated value of the property itself, in as short a period as money loaned, the property will fall in price until the rent bears the same proportion to the value of the property that the rate of interest bears to the principal.

It is perfectly right that the interest on money should govern by its own per centage the rent of all property, because money is the legal representative of all property, and the standard by which its value is estimated. This interest is of the same quality as the principal loaned, and each fractional part is of proportional value; and the rents of property must conform to this rule. For example, if the per centage be in the proportion of one to one hundred, the tenant of a hundred acres of poorly cultivated land must pay as rent a sum in money equal to the value of one acre of land of the same quality. If he improve the farm and make it produce double, he must pay the value of one acre of improved land for the use of the improved one hundred. He pays more value, but no greater per centage on the value of the land. Money is the standard; if the per centage interest on it be fixed at a just rate, it will equitably regulate the rent of all property, and also secure to labor its earnings.

The value of property depreciates in proportion to the increase of the value of the dollar that measures it. Whenever the value of money increases by a rise of interest, there is a corresponding decrease in the value of property. The diminution of the market value of property, by a rise of interest, may be compared to the moving of a fulcrum on the beam of a scale. As one end of the beam is lengthened, the other end is shortened, so that a pound weight, on the long end, may balance as many products as three, four, or five pounds would before the fulcrum was moved. So, with the rise of interest on money, property falls in price, and one dollar, in money, balances two, three, four, or five times more property than it did before the rise. Enough property must be added to make the rent equal to the interest on money; for no man will invest his money in property unless he supposes that the property will yield as good an income as the money he pays for it. Therefore, the price of property must fall whenever the interest on money increases, that the incomes from property and from money may be equal. When the power of the dollar to accumulate is increased, no alteration is made in its form, weight, or external appearance, as when the fulcrum is moved no alteration is made in the weight, but the *power* of the weight is increased.*

SECTION XII.

THE RISE OF THE RATE OF INTEREST INCREASES THE LIABILITIES OF ALL DEBTORS.

All obligations for the payment of money are based upon money, and hold the same position, with respect to labor and property, that money does. They are private

* See Appendix, B.

representatives of their amount of money, and, being secured on property, call for the payment of a definite sum of money as principal, and a definite rate of interest. When the interest on money rises, property falls in price, so that the value of the bonds, notes, mortgages, etc., payable in money, is increased with respect to property, for they will purchase more; but their value is diminished, compared with money, for the interest on money is greater than the interest on the obligations. Hence the obligations fall below, and will not sell for their par value, although they continue to bear the same rate of interest, and to call for the same amount of money as at the former period. The value of money has increased above its former value, instead of the value of the obligations being diminished, except relatively. The obligations still demand the same amount of money, which will now draw a higher rate of interest, and command a greater amount of property. But the amount of interest which the obligations at present draw, is not increased, and is less than that on money.

For example, if interest rise from six to twelve per cent., a State bond, bearing the former rate, will fall below its par value, but will continue to bear the same rate of interest that it did previously to the rise of interest on money; yet the bond can be exchanged for more property than before the rise of interest. Hence the liabilities of all debtors whose means of payment are in their property, or in their ability to labor, are increased in proportion to the increase of interest upon money, because the full amount of all debts must be paid in money, of which the power to purchase property has thus much increased—or, in other words, the rise of interest has decreased the market value of property and labor, so that two, three, four, or five times the quantity formerly required, must be sold to procure money to cancel debts. Labor, however low its price, is no tender for debts, and must be disposed of for money before it can be a legal equivalent in payment for anything. When goods are sold on time, the property of the purchaser, both real and personal, is legally bound for the payment of the debt; and although the purchase of the goods caused the debt to exist, no kind of property is legally competent to pay it. The debtor must convert his property into money for this purpose, or the creditor can legally enforce the sale of a sufficient amount of the debtor's property to satisfy his claim and pay the costs of suit. The debtor's property is collateral security to the money, and is made subject to its power, but the property has no legal authority over the money.

The injustice done to debtors by increasing the value of the measure by which their debts were contracted, is evident. It has already been shown that the dollar is the measure of more or less property, according to the rate of interest. Therefore, debts contracted when interest was low, and falling due when interest is high, will require a much larger quantity of property to pay them than was understood in the contract. The following is a familiar illustration of this principle. A man agrees to make and deliver to another nine yards of cloth. He brings the usual amount of cloth to fulfil the contract, but in the meantime, the length of the yard-stick is increased to four and a half feet, and the cloth falls a third short of the required length. The debtor weaves a third more on the end of the piece, and presents it. The length of the yard-stick is again increased to six feet, and the cloth again falls short. The construction of the yard-stick may allow its length to be increased without additional labor, but the debtor is obliged to add both labor and material to produce the required length of cloth. The additional cloth is fraudulently taken from him by the increase of the length of the measure.

To exemplify the principle with respect to money, the

measure of value. The rise of interest on money increases the liabilities of all debtors. A man lends on mortgage of a house and three vacant lots, $1,000 at six per cent. interest. The interest on the money for a year is $60, and the house of the borrower rents for $60 a year. The rate of interest increases to nine per cent., consequently the interest on the $1,000 increases to $90. To make the loan safe at the advanced interest, the borrower is required to erect another house on one of the lots covered by the mortgage. He builds one costing $500, and lets it for $30. The two houses now bring $90 a year, just the interest on $1,000. Interest rises to twelve per cent., and the holder of the mortgage requires the borrower to erect a second house, costing $500, on another vacant lot covered by the mortgage. This house is likewise let for $30. The three houses rent for $120, and the mortgage for $1,000 draws twelve per cent. The mortgage now brings in as much income as the three houses. The $1,000 as much balance the value of the three houses now, as they did that of the one house when the money was loaned; for it now takes the rent of three houses, as it then did that of one house, to pay the interest on the mortgage. Two houses are added by material and labor, and no material or labor is added to the mortgage or money; yet the mortgage or money at twelve per cent. interest, is worth as much to the holder as the whole property.

As the value of money increases, the market value of the things to be measured by it decreases, so that it works in a double ratio against producers, for rents of property diminish as interest on money increases. But in the foregoing example, this feature has not been exhibited, no diminution of rent being supposed to take place in consequence of the rise of interest, although experience proves that this is the invariable result.

SECTION XIII.

RENTS, WHETHER HIGH OR LOW, BEAR THE SAME RELATIVE VALUE TO THEIR PRINCIPAL; BUT, WHEN THE PER CENTAGE INTEREST ON MONEY IS INCREASED, NOT ONLY IS ITS RELATIVE PROPORTION TO THE PRINCIPAL INCREASED, BUT EACH FRACTIONAL PART HAS INCREASED VALUE.

It is proposed to show that there is a wide difference between renting property and lending money, and that the rent and market value of property decrease in proportion to the rise of interest, whereas the market value of money, and of the interest upon it, increases in direct proportion to the rise of interest.

If the rent of a farm, store, or house rise to double, the price of the farm, store or house is doubled. If the rent of the farm before the rise be $300 over repairs, etc., and money be at six per cent. interest, the farm is worth $5,000. But if the rent rise to $600, the price of the farm will be increased to $10,000. Therefore, if the owner invest the income or rent in other land before the rise of rent, he can buy as much land with the $300, as he can buy after the rise with $600. If the rent fall again to $300, the price of the farm will fall again to $5,000; but the $300 will buy twice as much land as it would if the rent had been maintained at $600. Neither the rise nor the fall of the rent alters the actual value of the farm, for its productiveness is neither increased nor diminished by either. The nutritive properties of its wheat and corn cannot be altered by the rise or fall of its rent. But the *dollar* received when the rent is $600, is worth only one-half as much as the dollar when the rent is but $300; for when rents are low, one dollar will buy as much land as two will when rents are double. The intrinsic value of the property undergoes no material change, but the standard changes by which its market value is estimated. Now note the different effects of the rise of the rent on property, and the rise of the interest on money. Let the rate of interest on money rise from six to twelve per cent., and the rent on property will inevitably fall in about the same ratio. The price of property will of course fall in proportion to the fall of its rent. When the interest on money is doubled, the value of every dollar received as interest is doubled; for each dollar of interest will buy double the property that it would before the rise. But when the rent on property is doubled the dollar is worth but half as much as it was before, for it will not purchase more than half as much property as it would before the rise of rent.

If the rent on land rise to double, the land itself will sell for double its former price; therefore, the rent will not double its principal of land in any shorter time in consequence of the rise. But when interest on money rises to double, the interest will double the principal in half the time that it would before the rise of interest. When the rent on land rises, the rent continues to hold the same relative value to its principal of land that it did previous to the rise. But when the interest on money rises to double, the relative proportion of the interest to the principal is doubled.

For example: P. lends to Q. for a year $20,000 at six per cent. interest. The interest amounts to $1,200. P. invests this income in a farm at the then market price of land. At the commencement of the following year, there is a scarcity of money, and P. reloans to Q. the same $20,000 at twelve per cent. interest. At the end of the year, Q. must pay to P. as the interest on the $20,000, $2,400, twice the sum that he paid the previous year. Scarcity of money and high rates of interest invariably depreciate the price of property. Its price falls one-half, so that each dollar of the $2,400 received as the interest on the money when interest is high, will purchase twice as much property as it would before the rise of interest. Hence, if the interest at six per cent. on $20,000 will buy a farm worth $1,200, when the interest on the $20,000 rises to twelve per cent.—*i. e.*, to $2,400,—and the price of the farm falls one-half, the $2,400 will buy four farms, all as good as the first bought at $1,200. The income from the $20,000 will be worth four times as much as it was before the rise of interest.

Making the calculation in dollars and cents, we shall arrive at the same result. The interest on $20,000 at six per cent. is $1,200. Loan the $1,200 at six per cent. and it will accumulate in the ensuing year $72. Now loan the $20,000 at twelve per cent. and we have $2,400 as its interest for the year. Loan the $2,400 at twelve per cent. and it will accumulate in the ensuing year $288, just four times $72. Thus the value of the income at twelve per cent. is four times greater than at six per cent. whether it be invested in land, or whether it be reloaned on interest. With interest at twelve per cent. per annum the capitalist possesses power to monopolize property four times greater than with interest at six per cent. per annum. The centralizing power of money increases in geometrical proportion to the rate of interest. This is a practical as well as a mathematical truth or law; which is constantly operating to centralize wealth in the hands of a few at the expense of the producers.

SECTION XIV.

TO CHEAPEN PRICES BY AN UNJUST RATE OF INTEREST AND A SCARCITY OF MONEY, IS BUT TO CHEAPEN THE LABOR OF ALL PRODUCERS, AND GIVE THEIR EARNINGS TO CAPITALISTS WITHOUT AN EQUITABLE EQUIVALENT.

When low prices are paid for labor, the prices of products are proportionally low. It is, therefore, generally supposed that the laborer can as readily procure all needful supplies when labor is at a low price, as when it is at a high one. But the articles whose price is diminished by the lowering of labor, are the productions of labor; and the producing classes suffer great injury from this depression of both their labor and products.

The following illustration will exhibit the advantage of high prices for labor. A man raises a hundred bales of cotton, sends them to market, and receives three and a half cents per pound. A laborer in New York receives fifty cents a day for his labor; with a day's work he can purchase fourteen pounds of cotton. If labor be at a dollar per day, and cotton at seven cents per pound, with a day's labor he can purchase the same quantity. If labor rise to a dollar and fifty cents a day, and cotton to ten and a half cents per pound, a day's labor will still purchase fourteen pounds of cotton. Thus far we do not observe the difference of price to have any influence upon the ability of the laborer to purchase; but we have yet to notice the condition of that class of producers who raise the cotton at the first price, three and a half cents per pound. After paying for the use or rent of the plantation one-half the price at which a loan of money can be obtained, say three or four per cent. interest on the cost of the plantation, they do not earn fifty cents a day, but, in fact, receive little or no compensation for their labor. The same labor and land are required to produce cotton when it brings three and a half cents, as when it brings fourteen cents per pound. Suppose a workman in New York to buy cotton at fourteen cents per pound; a barrel of flour at $8; wheat at $1 50 per bushel; potatoes at 40 cents; corn and rye at 80 cents; brown sugar at 10 cents; coffee at 12 cents; boots at $3 a pair; shoes at $1; a fur hat at $3; brown sheeting at 10 cents per yard; and good calico at 12 cents per yard. If labor fall to 50 cents per day, and he have full employment, to be as well off as when labor was at $2 per day, he must buy flour at $2 per barrel; wheat at $37\frac{1}{2}$ cents per bushel; potatoes at 10 cents; corn and rye at 20 cents; brown sugar at $2\frac{1}{2}$ cents per pound; coffee at 3 cents; boots at 75 cents per pair; shoes at 25 cents; a hat at 75 cents; brown sheeting at $2\frac{1}{2}$ cents per yard; good calico at 3 cents; and everything else in proportion. Travelling expenses, rents and taxes, must be diminished three-quarters. All the necessaries of life must be reduced in price three-quarters, or the laborer who is out of debt will not be as well off when labor is at fifty cents per day, as when it is at two dollars per day.

But suppose one class of the laborers to buy at these low prices, what will the producers of wheat, rye, corn, etc., receive for their labor? The reason that the laborer can buy as much cotton when labor is at fifty cents per day, as when it is at two dollars, is, that he buys a fellow-laborer's products at a price which will not pay a cent a day for the toil of producing them. So when the prices of labor are reduced in this ratio, laborers, as a body, are unable to provide themselves with the necessaries of life. The reduction of the prices of labor and products, consequent upon a scarcity of money and a rise of interest, forces producers and merchants to suffer great losses, because the diminution of the prices of products does not diminish the amount of their debts, nor their legal obligations to pay them; while the capitalists who own these debts will compel laborers and owners of land and products to sell double, treble, and quadruple the quantity of these, to obtain money to satisfy the debts. Thus wealth passes with great rapidity into the hands of a few capitalists. If the merchant has bought goods at as low a price as they can be afforded by the manufacturer, it is no safeguard against loss by the fall of goods in the market, because the market price of the goods does not depend upon the labor necessary to their production, but upon the ever-varying value of the dollar. Our laws make the dollar the real value, and producers and all kinds of property are controlled by its power.

The objection is often urged, that to make money plenty would destroy the value of products. But how would or could it destroy their value, to allow the needy to earn the means to purchase them? Will not a starving people buy products? Does any one suppose that the people of Ireland would live upon their present scanty food, if their labor would afford them the means of purchasing more and better? Was there ever a bad market for products when labor was receiving what are called high prices, or a good market when labor was at a low price? The market is made poor by the inability of the laboring community to earn enough to make purchases. If labor were well paid, the market would always be good, and the laborer, assured of a just reward, would work cheerfully.

Large production, at a fair price, gives a better compensation to producers, than half production at double price. The families of producers require as many products for their own consumption when the crops are diminished one-half, and their price is doubled, as when products are abundant. The producers cannot then spare a sufficient quantity to sell for their usual profits, even at the increased price, and capital makes the same requisition upon their labor for rent or interest as if their crops were abundant.

SECTION XV.

VOLUNTARY AGREEMENT NO TEST OF A JUST RATE OF INTEREST.

The laws do and ought to restrict some contracts and give freedom in others. Restrictions should apply to transactions upon a wrong basis, and those made upon a right one should be entirely free. Agreements founded upon a just basis would naturally be mutually beneficial to the parties contracting them, but no agreements founded upon a wrong one can ever do equal justice.

Lotteries and various kinds of gambling are rightly prohibited by law, although the buying and selling of lottery tickets, and betting on games of cards, are voluntary transactions. If mere voluntary agreement makes contracts just, why do the laws annul those made in gambling, while they enforce the fulfilment of other less voluntary agreements? A man without property must become a pauper unless he agree to work for others, or have the property of others to work upon. He is not as free in his contracts as the gambler, in whose case there is no such necessity; for the latter must have money or property to stake, or others will not bet with him. The only reason for making gambling contracts void in law, is, that no equivalent is rendered to losers for what is gained by winners. If, then, wealth is the product of labor, and it passes into the hands of a few capitalists by agreements less voluntary than betting and buying lottery tickets, is not the former even more contrary to justice than the latter? Wrongs of this kind to the laboring classes are surely as greatly to be deprecated as those to gamblers; and as no mutual agreements will ever make gambling just, so no mutual agreements founded on a wrong money standard can ever be fair and equal.

If R. be a hatter, and T. a shoemaker, the products of their labor must be exchanged, in order to supply both their families with hats and shoes. If X. hold the medium by which this exchange must be effected, and by its power and use can obtain without labor more hats and shoes from R. and T. than they can together retain as the reward of their labor, X. evidently holds an unjust power over them and their products. R. and T. are not only obliged to exchange their hats and shoes with each other, but are also obliged to exchange them for every necessary of life, and even for the materials out of which the hats and shoes are manufactured. They cannot make these exchanges without an agreement with X. for the use of the legal medium. Neither the shoemaker nor the hatter can refrain from the use of money as a man can from gambling; and, under the operation of the present monetary system, by using it they are certain to lose the greater share of their surplus hats and shoes. They do not even stand the same chance for winning by their labor that the gambler does by gambling, for the dice may turn in his favor, but a rapidly accumulating power will never turn in favor of producers. When money shall be rightly instituted, and a just rate per cent. interest maintained, agreements among R., T. and X. will naturally award to each his equitable share of products; but until this medium of exchange is rectified, the legal rights of property must continue at variance with actual justice. The income power will absorb what the producing power earns, and no voluntary agreements according to demand and supply, can prevent this result; for the suffering is caused by injustice in the laws, and not by faults in the agreements.

Public opinion appears to lean toward less legal restraint upon trade. This would be well, if the foundation of trade were made just. But first to fix upon an unjust money basis, and then to make laws enforcing the fulfilment of voluntary agreements made upon it, is first to establish an evil, and then trust to a competition in doing the evil to produce a good. It makes the grossest corruption legal and gives it the greatest freedom. But financiers assert that laws cannot be enacted which will regulate the rate per cent. interest, and thus keep money at a uniform value; and that the rate per cent., like the market value of commodities, can only be regulated by supply and demand. Under this law of supply and demand, agreements according to the necessity of the borrower and the avarice of the lender, are considered tests of a just rate of interest, and must regulate the standard by which all values are determined. Under this system, directors and the favored few borrow money from banks at five, six, or seven per cent. per annum, and lend it at three, four or five per cent. a month; and if mutual agreement makes justice, all these rates are equally just; although one class pays from six to ten times more than the other, and the favored class gains the difference by a mere exchange of paper, without in any way benefiting the sufferers. A broker borrows money from a bank at the rate of six per cent. per annum, and lends it on the same day to a merchant who is "cornered" at one per cent. a day—just sixty times as much—and according to this great law of supply and demand, as it is often called, each party pays exactly the right and just rate per cent. interest. The broker demands the money from the bank, and the bank supplies him at the rate of six per cent. per annum: but the merchant demands the money from the broker, and the broker supplies him at the rate of 365 per cent. per annum. If a man fall into the water and demand help to get out, the person who supplies assistance has a perfect right, according to this law of supply and demand, to take all the property a man may own; for who but a miser would not give all his wealth to save his life? In Europe, laborers, by voluntary agreement, work for ten or fifteen cents a day, and are often thankful to get work at these rates to save themselves and their children from starvation. If mere freedom of agreement, or supply and demand, constitute the justice of contracts, independently of their basis, these prices must be a standard whereby to estimate the true value of labor, which, therefore, would depend on the price the capitalist would pay for it, and not on its utility.

This wrong basis of contracts also causes a competition among laborers themselves according to their necessities; the tendency of which, under present systems, is to reduce the price of labor to the mere subsistence of the laborer. But the reverse of this is true of competition in lending money. Whenever a strife occurs in the money market, and one bank begins to run upon another, and capitalists strive for the highest rate per cent. for the use of their money, the tendency is at once to increase the rates of interest. The greater the strife the higher the interest rises, until the whole business of the country is paralyzed; for the rise of interest increases indebtedness, destroys credit, diminishes the wages of labor, and throws it out of employment.

It is probable that every man, woman, and even every child over five years old, in this nation, has seen and handled more or less gold, silver or copper money. If we tell the public that the legal power of money is the greatest, the most controlling and influential of all earthly powers; that it determines the rate per cent. that shall be paid for the use of all property; that it decides who shall be born in the lap of wealth, and live in luxury, and who shall be born in poverty and want, and be subjected to a life of the severest toil and servitude in order to subsist; that it also rules governments and the destinies of nations, and that its present power is directly opposed to virtue and in favor of vice; if we tell the people all this, we shall only tell them the truth. But will they believe us? Will they not say, "We, and our children, and our fathers before us, have seen and handled more or less money all our lives, and we have never seen in it any such power." It is true they have no more seen this power than they have seen the law of gravitation, because it is just as invisible; yet they have as sensibly felt the effects of the centralizing power of money as they ever have the effects of the law of gravitation. People work hard all their lives, without considering by what laws the products of their labor are governed, and they are taught to believe that as the mining and coining of the gold and silver are the products of labor, that this labor performed is what constitutes the value of the money. These coins are only the material of money, they are not its power. The power of money is to collect a per centage income, and this is a legal power, and not a material thing. This power is the product of law, and not the product of labor. Yet this invisible, legal power of money as much controls and centralizes the productions of labor, as the mind directs what the physical man shall perform. By its unjust power the wealthy few govern the destinies of man. When they lend money liberally to the public, at what is called a low rate of interest, it sets the multitude at active production, so that they are as busy as bees in a warm summer morning. But when the few call in their loans, and raise the rate of interest, the producing classes are paralyzed, like the bees when the thermometer is at zero. The financial skill of a few Rothschilds, wielding the power of money, as much determines where the wealth of a nation shall be centralized, as the captain and pilot of a steamship direct at what point or wharf the passengers shall be landed. Not only the producing public, but the government itself, is about as much directed by a few money-lenders as the crew of the ship by the captain and pilot. If the commanders of the ship run her upon the breakers, they endanger their own property and lives as well as those of the passengers; but the managers of this financial power, by calling in their money and reloaning it at higher rates of interest, not only cripple the government, and compel it to sell its own credit at usurious rates of interest, but they also paralyze the business of the producing classes, deprive them of the means of subsistence, drive multitudes of them into distressing poverty, despondency and suicide, and by thus wrecking the public they gather large gains out of the spoils. Money, as now instituted, is the most deceitful power that ever has been or can be established. The groundwork for its first institution is false, and subsequent laws for the regulation of such money can no more remedy its evil power, than a good house can be built on a foundation previously laid upon a quicksand, where every tide of the ocean would cause some part of the foundation to change its position.

SECTION XVI.

THE LAW OF INTEREST ON MONEY AN ACCUMULATIVE, NOT A PRODUCING POWER.

Money loaned is universally spoken of as bearing interest; but this is a mistaken idea. It is the borrower's obligation, and not the lender's money, that bears interest. It is generally believed that borrowers have the use of money for the time that they hire it, just as a tenant has the use of a farm for the time that he rents it. This also is a mistaken idea, for the farm is usable in the tenant's hands, but money is not usable in the borrower's hands. If a man borrow $10,000, and give to the lender his note payable in one year, with seven per cent. interest, at the end of the year he will owe to the lender the principal and $700 interest. Now what does he have to use during the year out of which he is to gain the interest? It certainly cannot be the $10,000; for if he keep the money in his own pocket, there can be no increase in quantity, and at the end of the year, he will not have enough by $700 to pay the debt. But the borrower's obligation in the lender's pocket has increased the debt $700. The $10,000 must enable the borrower to have something else to use for the year, or certainly he would not borrow the money, and agree to pay the interest. As soon as he has the money in his possession, he either pays a debt previously contracted, or buys land, or some kind of goods, wares or merchandise with it. If he buys land, he has the use of it for the year by paying $700 rent. If he is a manufacturer, and has been disappointed in the sale of his goods, and owes $10,000 that has become due, he pays the debt, and this enables him to keep $10,000 worth of his goods for the year. It gives him a year's time to sell these goods, and turn them into money to pay the debt. Thus the so-called interest on money is the rent that he pays for the use of the goods for a year: it is not paid for the use of the money. The money and the interest are both representatives of value. The value is in the goods, or land, and the labor that makes the property productive. The money is always dead, and strictly speaking, people never pay a fraction of interest for its use. The practical effect of the per centage called interest, is simply to determine the per centage rent of property.

A tree bears fruit, because the fruit grows out from the vitality of the tree. But money is authorized and organized by human laws, and human laws do not organize or create vitality, therefore money is of necessity a dead power, and has no vital energy to produce other money. Money loaned accumulates by interest, but the money produces no interest. All the money in this nation will be kept over from to-day until to-morrow, and will bear no interest to those who keep it; it will gain nothing by interest for him who may keep it a week, month, year, or any other longer or shorter time. All the money in the country is barren of interest in the hands of somebody to-day, and will be barren of interest in the hands of somebody to-morrow. It may change owners a hundred times, but it is always a dead power in the hands of somebody. Borrowers, whether for a longer or shorter period, always pay out the money as soon as possible; they do not keep it. The money is not usable as property, it is not susceptible of being improved by labor, nor is it competent in itself to supply any want of man, or to make any improvement. It is dead in their hands, and they at once part with it for something which is usable, such as materials that can be improved, or houses that will shelter themselves and their families, or lands upon which they can raise crops, or goods, wares and merchandise which they can use, or can exchange for a profit.

As we have said, the per centage interest that borrowers agree to pay for the use of money, simply determines what per centage rent they shall pay for the actual use of a certain amount of property for a given period. Borrowers use the property, not the money; and from the property they must produce or gain the means to pay the interest. If F. be a farmer, and borrow from A. $1,000 at seven per cent., F. must raise one hundred and forty bushels of corn, and sell it at fifty cents a bushel to pay the yearly interest of seventy dollars. It is then the productiveness of F.'s farm coupled with F.'s labor, that produces the money to pay the interest. The thousand dollars lent by A. to F. do not produce anything: but the money, by a legal, arbitrary power, takes one hundred and forty bushels of corn from F., and appropriates them to A.'s use. If A.'s thousand dollars possessed vital instead of legal power, and could hire land, buy the seed, plant, cultivate, gather, shell and sell the corn, it would then actually produce for A. what the money now legally compels F. to produce for him. But as no human law can make the dollar a naturally productive thing, it is impossible to gain wealth by finance, unless the labor of others produces what is gained by the financiers.

Money, then, earns for its owner by an accumulative power; by a power to gather things already produced, and not by a natural power of growth, like that contained in the germ of wheat or grain. Where this power to accumulate by interest is made greater and more rapid, than the natural power of production by labor, this law of interest becomes a most powerful engine of evil. It gathers into the hands of a few capitalists the productions of labor, and often deprives the producers of the necessaries of life.

All nations have considered money to be wealth, because it possesses this power to accumulate; but whether made of gold or of paper, it really contains a very small amount of actual wealth. The laws make money a legal equivalent for all property, and give it the power to accumulate by interest. They make $100,000, loaned at six per cent. interest, earn for the owner $6,000 a year, without labor on his part, while the labor of twenty men, for three hundred days in the year, at a dollar a day, will earn no greater sum. The labor of twenty men, for a year, would make a visible improvement on a farm; but the interest makes no visible improvement on the money loaned.

Nothing has prevented, nor now prevents, the full employment, and adequate compensation of labor, but the monopoly of money, and unjust rates of interest. All nations and all political parties profess to legislate for the protection of industry, but in reality, they have from time immemorial legislated to support exorbitant interest on money. And since the interest on money governs the rent or use of all property, legislation, by fixing high rates of interest, has always supported and increased capital, and depressed labor. This enormous per centage interest on money has reversed the true order of nature; for the increase of the earth is the natural reward of labor, but the too great income power gives the reward to those who neither plant nor water, and often starves the laborers on the soil which their own hands have cultivated. By this exorbitant interest, the bounties of God are made a sacrifice on the altar of Mammon, and the poor are oppressed because they are poor, and in their toil there is little salvation from want and misery. This income power, established by the laws of nations, has not in the least altered the laws of production. Production has always been made by labor upon the soil, and by mechanics and artisans; but the unjust income power is a mere human contrivance, by which actual producers are made slaves to non-producing capital, and by which the few monopolize what the many produce by their labor.

It is impossible for the producers of a nation to pay three, four, or five per cent., or more, for the yearly use of property, and also furnish themselves with the comforts and conveniences of life. All the per centage collected for the rent on property, or as the interest on money, must be paid by sales of the yearly productions of labor, which remain over and above the support of the producers. If a very few rich men, in any civilized nation, should live frugally, and their posterity should do the same, in the course of a few generations they would reduce to poverty nearly every other individual in the country. Consequently, under present monetary laws, extravagance in the rich, and the frequent inefficiency and imbecility of their children, are great advantages to producers. The second evil is necessary to modify the overwhelming power of the first.

The income or interest, legally fixed and maintained upon money, governs not only the rent of property, and the dividends on stocks, but also the entire general income on all other things, because the interest on money is the standard. This income is a yearly tax levied upon producers, which at the present rates is enormous and oppressive. Laws may be made to prevent the entailment of property, to compel banks to divide yearly or half-yearly their earnings, and various other laws may be made to prevent the unjust accumulation of property in the hands of the few, and to give the laborer what he really earns; but all these will be of little avail to ameliorate the wrong. But as the per centage interest is diminished, producers will be benefited; and when it is reduced and maintained at the just rate, the laboring classes will receive the chief part of their own products. The currency is the national standard by which the value of the labor and products of all citizens is estimated, and all are obliged to use it and found their contracts upon it. If a fundamental law, like that of the rate of interest on money, be made just, it will be easily supported by other just laws; but if it be made unjust, it will be difficult to support it, for all the laws which sustain it must necessarily be unjust. A man who utters a falsehood must support it by other false assertions. A hundred lies may be required to give the first the semblance of truth. So if a nation fix an unjust standard of value, every law which sustains that standard must be unjust. An unjust standard has been used from the earliest ages of which we have a record; but the long use of it will never make it just, more than the long use of a falsehood with a hundred lies to support it, will make the falsehood truth; or the long use of evil make the evil good. When governments make money unlimited in quantity, at a just rate of interest, laws will be simple, debts paid, labor rewarded, and peace and happiness will pervade the country. Money will be easily obtained in exchange for labor, instead of labor being superabundant, and money scarce. Non-producing capital—*i. e.*, anything which requires the expenditure of labor to make it produce—should bear a low interest. Actual production will then receive a suitable reward.

SECTION XVII.

ESTIMATE OF A JUST RATE OF INTEREST.

From what has been said of unjust and fluctuating rates of interest, it must not be inferred that money loaned should bear no interest; for the accumulative power of money is as essential to its existence as food to the support of life. Without this power money would not represent production, and, consequently, could not be made an equivalent in payment either for labor or productive property, and therefore could not be maintained as a medium of exchange. We are, then, seeking no extreme measures, but that just rate of interest which shall secure to the whole people the greatest good. We do not advocate the annihilation of interest, but we urge that the amount should not be so great as to oppress the laborer whose toil produces every necessary of life, and even the material for the medium of exchange.

The rate of interest fixed upon money determines what proportion of the value produced by labor shall be awarded to the capitalist for the use of his capital, and what proportion the laborer shall receive for his toil in making the production. It is, therefore, important to ascertain what per centage the people of a nation can pay to capital, and still receive a due reward for their labor. To arrive at a just conclusion, we must form an estimate on a large scale, and for a term of years. Take the following as such an estimate: Suppose a country lay off our coast equal in every respect to that of the United States, but in its primitive wildness. Allow those classes of people whose labor makes all improvements to have the use of the United States in their present condition, with their cities, railroads, canals, farms, goods, wares and merchandise, bank, State, and other stocks, money, etc., for the term of seventy years. At the close of this period, they are to return the property uninjured by use, perishable articles replaced by new ones, and decayed buildings and machinery repaired and renewed. And for the use or rent of all these, they are meanwhile to make in the adjoining new country every improvement already in this; cities, railroads, canals, shipping, improve farms, make money, stocks, etc., etc., and render the country in every respect equal to the United States. At the end of seventy years they must give up the United States, together with the new country and all its improvements, and this would only be paying for the use of the property an interest half-yearly, at the rate of one per cent per annum. We will repeat the length of time in which money doubles at certain different rates of interest, the interest being paid and reloaned half-yearly. At two per cent. per annum, it will double in about thirty-fiv years; at three per cent., in less than twenty-four years at six per cent., in a little less than twelve years; and at seven per cent., in a little more than ten years. If the laboring classes can make as many improvements in a new country as now exist in this, and can afford to give the whole improvement for the use or rent of this country for ten years, seven per cent. would be a just rate o:

interest. If the people require twenty-three and a half years to perform this labor, beside making a comfortable provision for themselves, three per cent. would be the just rate; if thirty-five years, two per cent.; and if sixty-nine and a half years, one per cent. should be the rate.

Take the same estimate under a different form. Suppose all species of property in the country to receive a fair valuation, and its owners sell it on a credit of one hundred years, the interest or rent to be paid half-yearly, at the rate of seven per cent. on the amount of valuation. At this rate, the purchasers must pay every ten years to the sellers a value in interest equal in amount to the value of the whole property of the nation. If, however, the property were sold upon the same credit, bearing an interest of one per cent., nearly seventy years would elapse before the purchasers must pay to the sellers an amount in interest equal to the value of the principal.

If the distinctions between the value of gold and of paper disappear when both are used as money, it follows that the value of gold and silver money cannot be regulated by the quantity of metal in each piece, any more than the value of paper money could be regulated by the quantity of paper in each bank-note. The power of money over property and labor is increased or diminished just in proportion to its accumulative power, hence the only possible way to affix a true value to money, is to regulate a right rate per cent. interest for its use. A nation should not allow any money to circulate that is not perfectly good, and at par, and also a legal tender in payment for debts in every part of the country. Good money is a representative of value, and must be permanently secured by property that possesses intrinsic value; for if the property which formed the basis for the issue of the money, should cease to be valuable, the money of course would cease to represent value, and would be worthless, except for the actual value of the material out of which it was made. Money to be good must also represent production, hence it must always be susceptible of being loaned for a rate per cent. interest. Now, as labor in any useful occupation should be justly compensated, so also the necessary labor to furnish and issue the money of a nation should be fairly remunerated; and the per centage interest on the money furnished and loaned by an Institution established by the Government for that purpose, should be equivalent to pay for the material and labor employed in producing and loaning it. Thus the borrowers of the money would pay the cost of the production and issue (see *Part II., A True Monetary System*), and this would form the rate per cent. interest to be charged by any subsequent owners of the money when they should reloan it. Money thus organized would always pay for its own support, without aid from the Government.*

SECTION XVIII.

BENEFICIAL RESULTS TO LABORERS AND MERCHANTS FROM THE REDUCTION OF THE RATE OF INTEREST.

It may be said that the reduction of the interest on money would cause property to rise in price in proportion to the decrease of interest, and, therefore, the condition of the laborer would not be improved. It will be supposed that if the market value of property should rise in proportion to the decrease of interest, speculators and owners of property would be the gainers by the reduc-

---

* The two modes of estimating the just rate of interest, set forth in this chapter, do not differ in their result; but the author considered the latter (which is taken from his more recent writings) the final criterion; and spoke of it repeatedly, during the last winter of his life, as a point to which he attached great importance.—[M. K. P.]

tion; that interest being reduced from seven to one per cent., V.'s four farms (see Section I.) would rise in their market value from $10,000 to $70,000, and a rent of one per cent. on the $70,000 would be $700—precisely the same sum as seven per cent. on $10,000—and thus the tenants would gain nothing by the lessening of the interest, but V. would gain by the rise in the market value of his farms. By looking a little deeper into this matter, we shall see that such would not be the fact. For, if V.'s farms rise to $70,000 each, and A., B., C. and D., hire them at one per cent. on this valuation, that is, at $700 a year for each, which V. on its receipt, loans out at one per cent., yearly collecting and reloaning the interest, it would be seventy years before the rent and its accruing interest would buy four other farms. Hence the relative gain of the laborers by lowering the rate per cent. interest, would not be altered by any rise in the market value of the farms. To show this yet more clearly, suppose the market value of each farm increase from $10,000 to $70,000, and let V. instead of renting sell them, and loan out their proceeds on bond and mortgage at one per cent. per annum, yearly collecting and reloaning the interest, it would still be seventy years before the interest would equal the principal, and amount to $280,000; and the $280,000 gained by interest, would buy for V. only four farms worth $70,000 each; whereas, with interest at seven per cent., if V. should sell the same four farms at $10,000 each, loaning out the $40,000 proceeds at seven per cent., and yearly collecting and reloaning the interest at the same rate, in seventy-one years and nine months he would gain $5,080,000, which would buy five hundred and eight farms.

Whether property rise or fall, or maintain its present price, the reward of labor would be equally increased by the diminution of interest. Suppose H. has a lot that cost him in cash $1,000, and builds a house upon it costing $1,000—together worth $2,000. Interest on money is at six per cent. per annum; therefore to make the property worth the money it cost, H. must let the house for $120 a year, clear of insurance, repairs, and taxes. Labor is then at one dollar per day. Reduce the interest on money to one per cent., and, in consequence of this reduction, let the lot and house rise to six times their former price—that is, from $2,000 to $12,000. The interest on $12,000 at one per cent. would be $120, the same as when the property would sell for but $2,000. The house could not rise from $2,000 to $12,000, unless labor should rise proportionally—that is from one dollar a day to six dollars a day. The same amount of labor would as readily build the house at one time as another. With labor at six dollars per day, the tenant could pay the $120 rent with twenty days' work; whereas, with interest at six per cent., and labor at one dollar per day, it would take one hundred and twenty days' labor to pay the rent, six times more than when the interest on money was at one per cent. Now suppose the change in interest to produce no effect upon property, and the house and lot to continue worth only $2,000. The interest on the $2,000 at one per cent. would be $20. If property did not rise, labor would not rise, because it would require the same number of days' labor to build the house, and it would take twenty days' labor to pay the rent—the same number of days that it would if the property should rise to $12,000.

A just per centage on money being established, the rise or the fall of property would not affect the relative positions of labor and capital. If property should rise in price, the tenant would not be obliged to build another house for the use of one, any sooner than if property should fall in price. He could pay the rent in the one case as easily as in the other, and with the same amount of labor; but a change in the rate of interest would immediately affect him.

The amount of products required as the rent of land would be diminished by reducing the rate of interest. Suppose G. owns a farm of one hundred acres of well improved land worth $100 per acre. H. rents this farm at seven per cent. interest on its cost, and consequently must pay to G. $700 a year. If the land produce twenty-five bushels of wheat to the acre, and wheat be worth $1 per bushel, H. must sow, reap, and sell the products of twenty-eight acres, and pay the whole proceeds to G. as the rent of one hundred acres for the year. If interest were at one per cent. instead of at seven, the rent of the farm, or of the $10,000 for the year would be $100, instead of $700; and H. would be obliged to cultivate and sell the products of four acres only to procure one hundred bushels of wheat, or $100 to pay the rent. If he performed the same labor when interest was at one as when it was at seven per cent., he would retain the products of twenty-four acres—*i. e.*, six hundred bushels of wheat as the surplus earnings of his labor, instead of paying them to G. for the use of capital. The reduction of the rate of interest would not lessen the quantity of products, nor decrease their value; it would only give a larger proportion to producers. If G. should cultivate his own farm, he would receive the whole of its products as the earnings of his labor, whether interest were at one or at seven per cent. But if interest were at one per cent., and H. should rent the second farm, G. could exact but a small proportion of the products of the farm as rent. G. would receive a more just sum for the use of the farm, and H. would likewise receive a more just reward for his labor upon it.

A low and uniform rate of interest would have a most beneficial effect on trade; and of this the following is a practical illustration. Suppose a merchant in the city now pays $2,000 rent for his store, and $800 for his house. His rents must be paid from the profits on his goods before he can gain anything for his own support. Reduce the rate of interest to one per cent., and his rents would be reduced to $400. The interest on his stock of goods would also be but one-seventh its present amount. Estimate his stock at $40,000 and the interest upon it at seven per cent. would be $2,800 a year. But reduced to one per cent., the interest would amount to but $400. The saving of interest on the goods, and of rents on the house and store, would amount to $4,800. Suppose the merchant to sell $250,000 worth of goods in a year, he must calculate at least two and a half per cent. for guarantee of bad debts. This per centage would be $6,250. Reduce interest to one per cent., and probably it would not be worth a tenth of one per cent., to guarantee the debts. In this item, there would be a clear saving of $6,150. Add the $4,800; there would be saved $10,950. The cost of the transportation of products from one part of the country to another would be greatly reduced; because the per centage to be paid for the use of capital to make internal improvements would be reduced to one per cent. All this difference of interest would be gained and saved by producers and distributers.

That a low rate of interest would drive specie from the country, is a false supposition. Do the lower rates of interest in England drain that country of its specie? Does six per cent. interest in the New England States drive their specie into the southern and western States, in which the legal interest is eight per cent. per annum? Such is not the fact. Where interest is the lowest, money and specie are the most abundant. If *products* pay a profit by shipment to England, they go forward rapidly to meet the demand. Not so with money. In England, money is often lent for months together at from two to three per cent. per annum, while the New York banks lend at six and seven per cent. per annum. For years past, the people of the United States have paid, nearly or quite, double the per centage for the use of money that has been paid in England. Why does not money from England flow in and supply the market, so as to equalize the rates of interest of the two nations? Why do the States which pay the highest rates of interest go abroad most frequently to borrow money, and still have not enough? It is because the rates are so high that the people of these States cannot produce a sufficient surplus to pay the interest to capitalists among themselves, and to other States where the interest, though lower, is still oppressive, to procure the money required to carry on their business. Money is a legal representative, and serves to fix an income, but not to produce wealth. Loan it twenty or thirty times where the interest is high, and every time it is lent it makes an income for the lenders for a longer or shorter period, which impoverishes the borrowers, because they must sell their products to pay the interest. The principal borrowed must soon be returned to the lenders in interest, and the interest is reloaned to the people. These high rates of interest serve to make the people paying them tributary to a few money-lenders among themselves, and in other States. For a few years previous to 1851, the State of Wisconsin made all rates of interest legal; that is, the rate of interest was a matter of agreement between borrower and lender. The consequence was, that the rate of interest varied from 12 up to 100 per cent. per annum. We are credibly informed that the highest rate was, in many instances, exacted, and good landed security obtained for its payment. Let us see what effect certain rates of interest on money borrowed abroad must have upon the circulating medium of the State. If the rate of interest were at one per cent., and T., living in New York, should lend $10,000 in Wisconsin at that rate, the borrower, at the close of the year, must send T. $100. The people of Wisconsin would have $9,900 of the money borrowed remaining among them as a circulating medium. But if T. lend his money at twelve per cent., the borrower must send T. at the close of the year $1,200, and but $8,800 would be left circulating in Wisconsin. If he lend at fifty per cent., the borrower must duly send T. $5,000 to pay the interest, so that one-half of the borrowed money is returned to T. in New York, and only $5,000 are left in Wisconsin. But if T. lends the $10,000 at a hundred per cent. per annum, the borrower must send T. at the end of the year $10,000, and not one dollar of it is left in Wisconsin. Still the borrower would be indebted to T. for the principal of $10,000 and in another year would owe T. $10,000 more in interest. It would not take a very large amount of money lent at this and approximate rates by the citizens of New York to those of Wisconsin, to throw the balance of trade against Wisconsin and in favor of New York: nor, in such a case, would it be strange that money should be scarce in Wisconsin while it was plenty in New York.

In the United States, if interest were reduced to one, or to one and one-tenth per cent., useful productions would probably increase from twenty-five to fifty per cent. The wealth, instead of being accumulated in a few hands, would be distributed among producers. A large proportion of the labor employed in building up cities would be expended in cultivating and beautifying the country. Internal improvements would be made to an extent, and in a perfection unexampled in the history of nations. Agriculture, manufactures, and the arts would flourish in every part of the country. Those who are now non-producers would naturally become producers. The production would be owned by those who per formed the labor, because the standard of distribution would nearly conform to the natural rights of man.

SECTION XIX.

THE LOW PRICES OF LABOR IN EUROPEAN COUNTRIES NOT CAUSED BY THEIR LOW RATES OF INTEREST.

In answer to the principle advanced, that the establishment of a low rate of interest will secure a better compensation to labor, it will be said that money is plenty in all old countries, at a low rate of interest, and that labor is very poorly paid; whereas, in new countries, in which interest is always high, high prices are paid for labor. In England, France, and Germany, money is loaned at two, three, four, and five per cent. per annum, and in all these countries the prices of labor are very low; while in the United States of America, in which the lowest legal rate of interest is six per cent., and the average rate double that of European nations, the prices of labor are also double. In former ages, the rates of interest in these now old countries were very high, and by this means the property was early accumulated in the possession of a few. These few owning the property, and letting it to those who were destitute of the means of paying the rent or interest except by the products of their labor on the property, the lenders could no longer collect the high rates; and a reduction of interest necessarily followed, because the laws could not enforce the collection of the higher rates, where the ability to pay them did not exist.

As a general thing, emigrants to new countries are industrious and enterprising persons, who have little property, and seek a new home because they have not the means of purchasing farms, etc., in old settlements. If these pioneers hire laborers to assist them in clearing and preparing their lands for use, they must pay higher

wages than are usual in older countries, for the laborers have many hardships to encounter. The first settlers import their provisions until they can raise a crop. The new soil produces largely. All fresh emigrants being compelled to buy provisions until they can raise their own,
 constant market is afforded for the surplus products of earlier settlers, and they are, consequently, able to pay good prices for labor. Emigrants to new countries raise the principal part of their provisions, but depend, in a great measure, on older countries for clothing, implements of husbandry, etc. Their products are consumed among themselves; and they have few, if any, to send to cities or manufacturing towns, to exchange for necessary articles. They must send money to buy them; or, if they purchase on credit, the money must be had at the maturity of the debts. This drains off their money. Although they make great improvements, add immensely to the value of their land, and the wealth of the country rapidly increases, yet money is very scarce, and the people are compelled to contract debts for clothing, implements of husbandry, etc. Any one who has money to lend can obtain exorbitant interest, and those who are in debt will offer high rates to their friends in older countries, to induce them to lend their money in the settlement. The scarcity of money is so great, that capitalists require the best security that can be offered, to quadruple the amount of their loans. Interest is maintained at ten twenty, or a higher rate per cent. per annum, and this rapidly draws property into the possession of capitalists. Every money-lender thinks himself justified in demanding as high a rate of interest as his neighbor. When mortgages become due, property, in many cases, is sold for less than half the cost of the labor to make the improvements upon it. The holder of money can buy property at one-fourth of its actual value, and another who has not the money to pay, will perhaps repurchase it at

a large advance, paying a small portion down, and agreeing to give a high rate of interest on the remainder. He makes what is termed a good bargain in the purchase. In this way interest is maintained at enormous rates, and lands and improvements pass rapidly into he hands of capitalists.

In new and thinly settled countries, where fertile lands are at low prices, the people do not starve, even when they are charged ten, twenty, or even thirty per cent. per annum on borrowed money and property; but these rates of interest concentrate the property rapidly into the hands of a few, and break up and keep hundreds of thousands of laborers poor. They can, however, generally find employment by which they may obtain their food. But as countries grow older, the population more dense, lands higher in price, and concentrated in fewer hands, the mechanical arts begin to flourish, and manufactories are established, in which hundreds of workmen labor for their daily support. The manufactories are carried on by individuals, by firms, or by incorporated companies. If money become scarce, and interest increase to double, treble, or quadruple the ordinary rate, the prices of goods inevitably fall, the wages of the workmen are reduced, and great numbers are thrown out of employment. The demand for goods rapidly decreases, for producers generally have become impoverished, and are unable to purchase their usual supplies, and many of them must subsist on charity. If the scarcity of money and the high rates of interest continue, the manufacturers too must break; for to pay the same amount of debt, they must sell twenty-five or fifty per cent. more of their goods than when interest was at the lower rate.

Although the rates of interest in all old countries are much lower than in newer countries, yet they are sufficiently high continually to centralize the wealth, and to increase more and more the number of the poor. In all the old countries the established rates of interest are high enough to concentrate the wealth in a few hands, even in a *new* country; not, however, so rapidly as the higher rates of interest which are usually paid in newer countries. In consequence of our higher rates of interest the property of the United States is accumulating in the hands of a few men much more rapidly than in the older countries. This accumulation will continue until the rates of interest are reduced below the rates obtained in the older countries.

The fluctuations of the rates of interest, in all countries, render it difficult to offer any very clear illustrations of their bearing upon labor, except upon general principles. In England, the rates of interest vary according to the necessity of the borrower, from one, two, or three per cent. per annum, to four, five, six, seven, eight, nine, ten, eleven, and twelve per cent.; and similar variations of interest, though at much higher rates, occur in our own large cities, and to a considerable extent in our towns and villages. But let twelve nations fix twelve different rates of interest, maintaining the rates uniform, the first at one per cent., the second at two per cent., and so on to twelve per cent., and the concentration of wealth in few hands, in the different nations, would increase in nearly the same ratio with the rates of interest. The ratio would be almost exact, except for the profligacy and extravagance of many of the rich, and the benevolence of others. This general principle will hold good, whether the country be new, rich and fertile, or whether it be old, or poor, because the accumulation is according to the rate per cent. A copper cent, loaned at six per cent. interest per annum, will double its principal in precisely the same time that a gold eagle, at the same rate of interest, would double its principal. It is a mistaken idea, that it is right to pay a higher rate of interest in a new and fertile country, because production is more easily made. If labor will produce a greater quantity of products, capital has no right, through an unjust standard of accumulation, to take them without rendering a fair equivalent; but if the rate of interest be too high, it will inevitably do so. There is no more justice in increasing the rate of interest, on account of facility in production, than there would be in increasing the size of the bushel, because labor would produce more bushels of grain.

In all ages and nations, the rates of interest maintained have been so high as continually to concentrate the wealth in a few hands. When the wealth of a nation becomes thus centralized, the producers and distributers who are destitute of property, are compelled to borrow money, and rent property from its holders. Suppose the whole property of a nation to be accumulated in the possession of one man (for this shows the principle more strongly), then all other individuals would be compelled either to buy the property on credit, or to rent it. If he should charge three per cent. per annum on the money or property, it could hardly fail to keep nineteen-twentieths of the people in perpetual poverty. For a few years they might appear to be prosperous, but their prosperity could not possibly be permanent, because the rent, or interest, would certainly absorb more than the people could earn. A rate of interest of even two per cent. would produce the same results, but in a less degree, because there would be many more owners of property, and the general indebtedness of the people would not be nearly so great, as it is at the higher rates of interest. It cannot then be true, that the low rates of interest maintained in the old countries, are the cause of the low prices of labor, and the poverty of the producers, but on the contrary, the former high rates of interest accumulated the property in a few hands, and the present rates of interest are sufficiently high to continue the accumulation and prevent the reward of labor. High rates of interest have been, and are, the cause of the poverty of producers in all nations.

In England, where the average rate of interest is three per cent. per annum, the labor is compelled to double the entire capital of the nation, in the hands of its holders, in twenty-three and a half years, besides which, the laborers must furnish their own support. But this is not the only cause of the depression of labor in Britain. An enormous sum of money was borrowed by the government of its wealthy citizens, and expended in wars. This National Debt amounts to about $4,000,000,000, the annual interest on which, at an average of three per cent., is $120,000,000, which the people must pay by an annual taxation of their products. Labor receives no benefit from it. The money is not invested in land, nor in anything else of which the labor has the use by the annual payment of the interest. This interest on the National Debt is additional to the too high rate of interest already charged on all the capital actually employed.

It is commonly supposed that the land owners of England are the oppressors of the toiling multitude. The power to lease land, at the present rates, is given by the law, fixing the rate of interest on money. The oppression by lending money, however, is greater than that by leasing land, because the rates of interest on money are continually fluctuating, and the oppression of the producing classes by its power, being indirect, can be made greater. The income of the holder of English government securities is earned by the operatives in the mines and factories, and by the seamstresses and various workwomen in the cities. But the bondholder comes in direct contact with none of these. His income is paid by the government, which gathers it from every branch of industry in the country by grievous taxations. Does it not beggar the producing classes to pay the interest to the money-owner, as much as to pay the rent to the land owner? Are the operatives in the manufactories and mines any better provided for than the laborers on the soil? Overgrown landed estates have generally been acquired through exorbitant interest on money. The only way to eradicate the oppression caused by holding them at high rents, is to reduce the interest upon money to such a rate that the products of labor will legally go to those who perform the labor, instead of going to the owners of capital. Every dollar that passes into the hands of the receiver of interest, is representative of products, and all the excess, above a just rate of interest, is taken from the rightful earnings of the laborer. Without the intervention of the government, which collects the interest by various taxations, so that the means of oppression are somewhat concealed, the people would refuse to submit to the injustice, and revolution in this system would naturally follow.

If the national rate of interest, in Great Britain, on all bank and private loans, and on the National Debt, were reduced to one per cent., and the interest were regularly paid, the bonds of the government would always be at par. A hundred pounds of the National Debt would be worth as much as a hundred pounds in coin, or a hundred pound note of the Bank of England. Now this Bank and private bankers continually vary the rates of interest. At some periods they charge two, three, or four times more than others, while the bonds of the government bear a regular rate of interest. Therefore, when the Bank and its Branches lend at a low rate, the government securities rise in price; and when they lend at very high rates, the government bonds depreciate.

Suppose the interest on the National Debt were reduced from three to one per cent. per annum. This simple procedure would save to the laboring classes eighty millions of dollars' worth of their products. If the interest on loans of money by the Bank of England, and by capitalists, and brokers, were also reduced to one per cent., it would increase the saving to the laboring classes to some two or three hundred millions annually. The per centage income upon capital can only be paid with the proceeds of labor; therefore this reduction of the per centage income would be equivalent to the distribution of several hundred millions of dollars among the producing classes, according to the labor performed. The effect of so large an annual distribution among this class would be to diffuse, in a few years, competence and happiness where now exist only poverty and misery.

The maintenance of the interest on money at one, or at some other rate per cent. lower than this, would soon and forever end the periodical depressions of trade, labor, and the prices of products, and the general oppression of the laboring classes.

CHAPTER IV.

THE BANKING SYSTEM.

SECTION I.

THE NATURE OF BANKS, THEIR INSTITUTION, AND THE PRINCIPLES BY WHICH THEY ARE GOVERNED.

BANKS, like other incorporated companies, receive their chartered powers by legislative enactments. These charters make it incumbent upon the banks to divide their gains in dividends to their stockholders, and to report to the legislature yearly, or oftener, their situation and standing. It is presumed that the publishing of these dividends and reports will keep the people informed of the doings and utility of the banks. Yet the practical operations of banking, and their special and general influences for good or for evil, are hidden from the public view. Causes are felt to be in operation which the people cannot comprehend—the changes in the market value of property, and in the prices of labor, are accounted for by the abundance and scarcity of money; but why money is scarce at one time, and abundant at another, is to the great body of the people utterly unknown.

It is the intention of the author to place the institution and operation of our banking system fairly before the producers of the nation, that they may clearly understand its effects upon their interests. The producers themselves will then determine whether they will change the system for one to be established on right principles, and that will act for the good of all, or continue the present one, the effect of which, for ages, in this and other countries, has been to accumulate wealth in the hands of a few, to the constant injury and hopeless poverty of the many.

The Constitution of the United States declares, Art. I. Sec. X., " No State shall emit bills of credit, make anything but gold and silver coin a tender in payment of debts." A bill of credit is a representative of property. A bank bill is a bill of credit; it is taken for the amount of value, or property, set forth upon its face, and if it does not actually represent that value, the owner must suffer loss.

The General Government has reserved to itself the right to coin money and emit bills of credit. It has, at least impliedly, assumed the obligation to provide a representative of property to the extent required. It has, however, neglected to supply the necessary kind and quantity of money to effect the exchanges essential to the interest and welfare of all civilized communities. The consequence has been an attempt of the State governments to supply the deficiency by the establishment of banks. The mode of instituting banks has been various, but however instituted, experience has shown their unfitness to fulfil the *public purposes* of their institution, and also their unequalled power as instruments for gathering the earnings of labor to capital, without any adequate return.

The nature of banks is sometimes said to be similar to that of manufacturing companies. The chief point of resemblance in their constitutions is, that the stockholders, both in manufacturing companies and in banks, are bound only for the amount paid in as capital stock, and are not liable for any further debts of the institutions.

THE NATURE OF BANKS.

In this particular they are on the same footing. But in other respects they differ widely. Banks are chartered in order to furnish the people with a public representative of value, that is, with a currency by which their soil and products may be exchanged. Manufacturing companies are chartered in order to facilitate the production of useful articles for the support and comfort of man. Banks deal in representatives of property, and the interest on these representatives is the source of their gains. Manufacturers gain by increasing the amount of actual production, for combinations of machinery diminish the expense of producing useful articles. Still, although manufacturing companies may have an equal amount of capital with banks, say from $100,000 to $2,000,000, yet any man may manufacture articles made by companies, or any number of men may combine for the same purpose, without a charter or any other legislative authority; and they have as much right to sell their articles in market as chartered companies. If banking institutions and manufacturing companies be of the same nature, why do not legislatures allow individuals, however small their capital, to manufacture and circulate their notes as money, as well as to manufacture goods and sell them to any one who will purchase them? Why, too, do they limit the amount of business that banks may transact, and leave manufacturing companies to be governed by the discretion of their directors? If bank-notes be merchandise, why not allow banks to sell their notes for other merchandise, instead of lending them for an interest in money? Why do legislatures limit the interest that banks may charge for the use of their bank notes, more than they limit the price of goods manufactured by chartered companies? It is because the notes issued by the banks are made a public medium of exchange for all property, even for the goods of chartered manufacturing companies, that their quantity, and the interest upon them, are legally re stricted. It is true that legislative action has thus far accomplished very little toward the regulation of a currency; but these restrictions upon it, and the necessity for legal authority to create it, prove that it is not regarded as merchandise.

The business of the public generally is made greatly dependent on that of a comparatively few individuals and corporations, who are empowered to issue bank-notes; for all the debts of the people must be founded upon and paid in money, most of which these individuals and corporations are alone authorized to furnish. It is generally understood that the banks provide a very large amount of capital for public use, and it is therefore thought just that they should receive large amounts of interest. But if it be found that the public furnish all the security to make the bank-notes a safe currency, and that the banks gain immense sums in interest merely for their labor in manufacturing the bank-notes, and exchanging them for indorsed notes of the people, it will be evident that the public is suffering a great and unnecessary loss, and could have this labor performed, and the same results accomplished, or rather a far more equitable currency maintained, at a comparatively small expense.

Formerly, all our banks were conducted under special charters, granted to each; and their capital was professedly all specie. More recently, several of the States have passed General Banking Laws, under which United States and State stocks, and bonds and mortgages are substituted as part of capital stocks. To establish a bank under the first system the persons desirous of banking petition their State government for a charter granting them the privilege. The petition states that the bank is needed by the public, yet we shall see presently that it is not only for private purposes, but that it is to be conducted solely for the benefit of the stockholders. The charter, according to law, requires the parties, or the tockholders, to furnish a certain amount of money, which constitutes the capital stock. When this is paid in, the bank becomes an office of discount and deposit, and is authorized by its charter to issue and lend bank-notes to circulate as money. The chartered banks in the State of New York are authorized to discount two and a half times the amount of their capital: that is, a bank that has, say one million of dollars paid in as capital stock, is at liberty to discount or lend to the people two and a half millions of dollars. Without a bank charter, the men who own the million of money which constitutes this capital, could lend only one million of dollars. In granting the charter, the legislature grants to these few individuals the privilege of charging the people seven per cent. interest on one and a half millions of dollars never owned by the stockholders. The bank issues bank-notes bearing no interest, and exchanges them for the indorsed notes of the people, bearing interest.*

The bank pays no interest upon deposits, and charges interest on all the indorsed notes given in exchange for its bank-notes. The interest upon one and a half millions of dollars' worth of indorsed notes, at seven per cent., amounts to one hundred and five thousand dollars a year. This interest is paid on a capital which is entirely fictitious, so far as the bank is concerned. If there be any capital underlying this one and a half millions of dollars, it is furnished in the indorsed notes given by the people in exchange for the bank-notes. The solvency of the bank for one and a half millions, depends upon the goodness of the indorsed notes received from the people, and not upon its own capital; for however safely its one mill-

---

* Money is popularly said to *bear such a rate of interest*, as if the money itself bore the interest. But, in fact, money bears no interest; the *obligations given for the use of money bear the interest*; for when money circulates in making cash purchases of commodities and property, in which no obligations are given, no interest is paid.

ion of capital may be loaned, it can redeem but one million of liabilities. If the bank should lose a million of dollars, by bad debts, or otherwise, the entire loss would fall upon the stockholders, for this amount is comprised in the capital of the bank; and, by the charter, is made first liable for the losses which may be sustained. But the remaining $1,500,000 of bank-notes loaned could not be redeemed unless the indorsed notes received in exchange for the bank-notes were against responsible persons. If the drawers and indorsers were able to pay only a part of these notes, then only a part or a certain per centage of the bank-notes could be paid; and, if no part of the indorsed notes could be collected, the million and a half of bank-notes would be a total loss to the holders.

The original $1,000,000 of capital has little basis of specie, and the surplus $1,500,000, issued over and above the capital, has none. The latter is based upon a privilege granted by the government to a company of men to make bank-notes bearing no interest, and exchange them for the indorsed notes of the people bearing interest. True, all bank-notes are made payable on demand in specie, and if banks refuse to pay specie they are liable to forfeit their charters. But all obligations between individuals, even to book-accounts, are also legally payable in specie; and all debtors are liable to prosecution if they refuse to pay their debts in specie. The law which requires the banks to redeem their notes on demand in specie, no more furnishes them with specie for that purpose than it furnishes individuals with specie to redeem their notes and pay their debts. Nearly three times the whole amount of specie in the banks in the State of New York, from 1835 to 1845, would have been required to pay their deposits, at any one time during that period, and this without redeeming in specie a dollar of their circulation. If specie should be generally demanded, the laws could not enable the banks to pay their notes and deposits in coins, nor individuals to pay their notes and debts in coins.

The principle upon which the contracts between the banks and the people are made, may be illustrated by supposing the government to fix a value upon ten silver spoons belonging to John Doe, and make them a tender in payment of debts. As they are not sufficient in amount to form a currency, John Doe is empowered to make twelve paper spoons on the credit of each silver one, all of which paper spoons he is to redeem on demand with silver spoons. He retains the ten silver spoons, and loans at seven per cent. interest the one hundred and twenty paper spoons, charging interest on them at seven per cent., and receiving in exchange for them good indorsed notes payable in two, three, or four months in silver spoons. All the paper spoons loaned to the people are payable in silver spoons on demand at John Doe's office, who has but ten silver spoons to pay the one hundred and twenty paper ones. If the holder of ten paper spoons, should demand and take the ten silver spoons, John Doe would be obliged to make the indorsed notes which he had received from his customers for paper spoons redeem the remaining one hundred and ten paper spoons which he had issued. All these were based upon paper, and must be paid again in paper if they are paid at all. Still, he would receive from the people interest upon a hundred and ten silver spoons which he never owned, and this by means of a legislative charter granted to him because he was the owner of ten silver spoons. If the legislature would not sanction the balancing of these debts with paper, the people could never pay Doe in silver spoons the indorsed notes they owed him; nor would Doe be able to redeem his paper spoons with silver spoons. The drawer of the ten silver spoons would have engrossed the whole tender upon which all the contracts were founded.

In general, debts are contracted for land, labor, and products; but none of these is a tender in payment of debts. Debts are payable in a tender established by law, but are generally paid in bank-notes which are used as a substitute for the tender. Admitting, then a silver dollar to possess intrinsic value equal to its nominal amount, how is it possible for it to make twelve representatives of itself, and make each one of the twelve as valuable as itself, when at the same time any one of the twelve has power to demand and take the silver dollar, and thus to leave eleven destitute of any basis of silver, and incapable of being paid in it? If paper money be allowed to pass as representative of specie, there should be a silver dollar for every paper dollar. Otherwise, the paper money cannot represent specie. A silver dollar cannot be represented by two paper dollars, each of which would be as valuable as itself, more than the owner of one acre of land can give two deeds, each for the one acre, to different individuals, and make both deeds good. The first deed must take the entire acre. If the second be of any value, it must be made so by offsetting the consideration given in payment for the deed, and not the land which the deed purports to secure. If paper money be allowed to circulate, it should not be under the pretence that it represents what it does not and cannot represent.

In April, 1838, the State of New York passed a General Banking Law, allowing any number of individuals to associate together and establish a bank, provided they furnish a capital of not less than $100,000. To secure the public from loss by the issue of bank-bills under this law, the banks deposit with the Comptroller an amount in bonds and mortgages, or State stocks, equal to the amount of bank-bills which they are authorized to issue. The bills are then countersigned by the Comptroller. If any bank fail to redeem its bills, the Comptroller is em powered to sell the bonds, and redeem the bills with the proceeds.

This mode of supplying the public with money is deemed by many a very safe one. Still, during the first six or seven years in which this new system was in operation, thirty-four banks failed, and did not redeem their notes at par. Some paid only twenty-five or thirty cents on the dollar. Others paid a per centage varying from thirty to ninety-four cents. Of forty banks closed by the Comptroller, only six redeemed their circulation at par. At the time of the Comptroller's sale of the securities given for the redemption of their bank-notes, the forty banks had a circulation of $1,233,374. The circulation of the six banks of which the notes were finally redeemed at par by the Comptroller amounted to $120,729, leaving a balance of circulation of $1,112,645, which was compromised at rates varying from twenty-five to ninety-four cents on the dollar. Doubtless a large amount of these notes was bought up by brokers at a much greater discount than that at which they were eventually redeemed by the Comptroller, so that the public lost probably from $700,000 to $800,000, besides the losses of depositors which do not appear.

It may be said that the securities placed with the Comptroller were not the bonds of the State of New York, but those of other States; that these States failed to pay their interest, and consequently their bonds depreciated greatly below their par value, and were not good security. True; but at the time they were taken by the Comptroller they were deemed good security for the redemption of the bank-notes. It must be remembered, too, that in 1837 the bonds of the State of New York, bearing an interest of six per cent., sold at about thirty per cent. below their par value. The securities pledged with the Comptroller at the present time are of the same nature as those then pledged. If the interest on money should now rise as high as then obtained on loans of bank-notes, the bonds of the State would again depreciate as much as in 1837. The same loss of confidence in the ability of the State to pay its debts would exist, because rates of interest at two, three, and four per cent. a month so rapidly increase the indebtedness of the people, that their wealth is soon transferred to a few capitalists, who are enabled to control the rate of interest, and consequently the market value of State bonds and property. As long as money can be obtained on good securities at six or seven per cent. interest per annum, the bonds of the State, bearing six per cent. interest, will command at least their par value. But only so long as banks and capitalists choose to keep the rate of interest as low as six or seven per cent., will these State bonds continue safe for the redemption of the bank-bills.

We will now see by whom the security of this banking capital is furnished, and by whom the interest upon it is paid. In order to provide capital for a bank, the individual who desires to establish the institution must buy State bonds to secure the bank-notes which he intends to issue. He invests $100,000 in bonds, on which the people pay him six per cent. interest. Although his money is invested, yet he receives $100,000 in bank-notes, countersigned by the Comptroller, upon which he is authorized to bank. Adding a few thousand dollars in specie to his bank-notes, he opens an office of discount and deposit, loans out the $100,000 in bank-notes, which he received from the Comptroller, and perhaps $100,000, or $150,000 more received from the people in deposit, on which he pays no interest. He charges interest on all the money he lends. If the people should call upon him to redeem his bank-notes, and pay their deposits in specie, he would probably not have more than $10,000, $20,000, or $30,000 in specie; and if there should be a run upon the bank, this would not meet the demand for a single day. The banker would be compelled to suspend specie payments. What would then secure the remaining indebtedness of the bank except the indorsed notes of the people, and the State bonds, for which the people are responsible ? The banker is not liable beyond the capital invested. He lends his money on securities furnished by the property of others. The object of this Banking Law was the security of the bank-notes. This object, as we have shown, has not been realized. The people have not only lost $700,000 or $800,000 by the failure of the banks to redeem their notes, but the depositors also have lost large amounts. Deposits in a public banking institution, ought to be as secure as the bank-notes circulated; but for this no provision is made by the law. Bankers, under the sanction of the General Banking Law, obtain interest from the people on two or three times more property than they actually own. This law, as also all other laws granting banking privileges, creates a fictitious capital for which the people are compelled to pay interest five or six times greater than they can afford to pay for *real* capital and at the same time justly reward labor. It has operated to enrich bankers and capitalists, instead of operating for the benefit of the people.

SECTION II.

THE AMOUNT OF SPECIE OWNED BY THE BANKS, AND THE INTEREST PAID BY THE PEOPLE ON BANK LOANS.

The chartered banks profess to transact their business entirely on a specie basis. If, to show the actual amount of their specie, we take that of the banks of Connecticut, which have been conducted with as much safety to the public, and credit to themselves, as those of any other State in the Union, and far more than the average, it will be not only a fair but a favorable criterion of the specie capital of the banks in the other States. The following table, extracted from the "Merchant's Magazine," vol. xvii., page 209, is an abstract of the Commissioners' Report for eleven years, from 1837 to 1847 inclusive; to which is added from the same work, vol. xxii., page 320, the Commissioners' Report for the year 1849. Thus we have the following statement of the condition of the banks during twelve years.

Year.	Capital.	Circulation.	Total Liabilities.	Specie.	Loans and Discounts.
1837	$8,744,697 50	$3,998.325 80	$15,715,964 59	$415,386 10	$13,246,495 03
1838	8,754,467 50	1,920,552 45	12,802,631 11	585,447 86	9,769,286 80
1839	8,832,223 00	3,987,815 45	14,942,779 81	502,180 15	12,286,946 97
1840	8,878,245 00	2,325,589 95	12,950,572 40	499,032 52	10,428,630 87
1841	8,878,927 50	2,734,721 45	13,866,878 45	454,298 61	10,944,673 85
1842	8,876,317 57	2,555,638 33	13,465,052 32	471,238 08	10,683,413 37
1843	8,580,393 50	5,379,947 02	12,914,124 66	438,752 92	9,798,892 27
1844	8,292,238 00	8,490,963 06	14,472,681 82	455,480 80	10,842,955 85
1845	8,359,748 00	4,102,444 00	15,248,235 79	453,658 79	12,477,196 06
1846	8,475,630 00	3,565,947 06	15,892,685 25	481,367 09	13,032,600 78
1847	8,6-5,742 00	4,437,631 06	15,784,772 04	462,165 53	12,781,857 43
	95,273,629 57	88,549,575 18	$157,550,872 44	5,168,957 95	126,292,898 38
1849	8,955,917 00	4,511,571 00		575,676 00	13,740,591 00
	$104,259,546 57			$5,744,633 95	$140,033,489 83

```
Average Capital..................................................$8,688,295 55
Average Liabilities..............................................13,129,239 87
Average Specie....................................................478,719 50
Average Loans and Discounts..................................11,669,457 44
```

By the foregoing table it will be seen that the average amount of the specie held by the banks in the State of Connecticut, for the twelve years, was $478,719, while the average amount of their loans to the public, during the same period, was $11,669,457—more than twenty-four and one third times as much money as the banks had specie. The annual interest on $11,669,457 was $700,167. If they could have loaned only their specie, the interest would have amounted to but $28,723. The banks gained from the public annually, $671,444 above the interest on their specie; and, in the twelve years,

$6,057,328. They collected this interest in advance, and made their dividends half yearly to their stockholders; therefore, it is proper to compound this interest half yearly, which would swell their gains to nearly $12,000,000, that is to say, $1,000,000 interest annually. These were actual gains, as much realized by these banks as if they had produced and sold annually $700,167 worth of agricultural products.

These banks were chartered with a professed specie capital, averaging for the twelve years, $8,679,962; while the average of the specie actually held by them was less than one-eighteenth part of this sum. How was this excess of capital above the average $478,719 in specie made up, and was it furnished by the stockholders or by the public? The specie held by these banks, as we have said, did not constitute one-eighteenth part of their professed capital; hence there must have been other capital to make up the seventeen parts we find wanting, otherwise their bank-notes could not have been safe; for, one thousand dollars' worth of land is as good security for the payment of eighteen thousand dollars in money, as one thousand dollars in specie for the payment of eighteen thousand dollars in bank-notes. But the banks, instead of eighteen lent over twenty-four dollars for each dollar in specie, so that the specie held by the banks was but a fraction over four per cent. of their loans. The specie was, then, a very small item in the security of the bank-notes, and was not essential to their safety. If the banks in other States have, in proportion to their loans, double the amount of specie owned by the Connecticut banks, it is no evidence that they are more safe, because their safety cannot depend upon four or eight per cent. of specie. No bank-notes can be safe money unless secured for their full amount.

Let us see how the specie capital of banks is generally made up. Suppose one bank to be chartered with a specie capital of $500,000, all paid in, and to lend $750,000 for approved indorsed notes. A second bank is likewise chartered with a capital of $500,000; to make up which, $400,000 of the notes of the first bank and $100,000 in specie, also drawn from it, are paid in. The notes of the first and second banks, together with a small sum in specie, form the capital of a third; and thus bank after bank is formed, say to the number of eighteen, each with a professed specie capital; while, in reality, all of them together own only $500,000 in specie. How is this excess over the $500,000 secured? The loans of the first bank for $500,000 were secured by the same sum in specie; but when it had lent $250,000 more, the excess was secured by the indorsed notes offered by the people for discount. When the second bank had discounted $750,000, the two banks had under discount a million and a half of dollars, one million of which was secured by indorsed notes, and but half a million by specie. A third, fourth, and finally eighteen banks having discounted $750,000 each of indorsed notes, the aggregate amount would be $13,500,000, of which $500,000 only would be secured by specie, and the sole security for $13,000,000 would be the indorsed notes held by the banks against the public. Some of these discounted indorsed notes might be against stockholders in the banks; but all of them, whether against stockholders or others, are secured by the property of their drawers and indorsers, and not by the capital of the banks. If thirteen, out of thirteen and a half millions of dollars, are made safe for the public use by these indorsed notes, evidently the remaining half million could be made safe in the same manner; and we could thus dispense with specie altogether. If ninety-six per cent. of the money is now secured by indorsed promissory notes, certainly the other four per cent. can be secured by similar means.

The people furnish the security for the bank-notes, and

pay the interest, which is the source of all the gains of the banks. R. and S. are men of property. R. draws his note at six months for $10,000, gets S. to indorse it, and then has it discounted at bank. If interest be at seven per cent., R. will receive only $9,650 in bank-notes, and at the maturity of the note must pay $10,000 to take it up: the bank thus gains $350 as the interest or rent of the bank-notes for six months. Under no circumstances would the bank discount the note unless it were deemed perfect security for the return of the money and the payment of the interest. R.'s note, indorsed by S., and held by the bank, is secured by the property of these men; and the bank-notes secured by the indorsed notes are also secured by the same property of R. and S. If the bank-notes circulate for six months, R.'s indorsed note also secures to the bank the return of $350 more than it gave for the note.

A similar illustration may be made on a more extended scale, say on $5,000,000; about the sum kept under discount by some of the larger banks in New York. Suppose a bank to discount notes, drawn and indorsed by various individuals in good credit, for $5,000,000, having (to simplify the process, and bring the gains under one item) twelve months to run. It would pay to these individuals $4,650,000 in bank-notes: and the $350,000 deducted as discount would be clear gain, less the labor to make and exchange the bank-notes. If the public need the $4,650,000 to meet their business obligations for the year, the money will continue to circulate, and the bank will not be called upon to redeem it, during that period. At the close of the year, when the indorsed notes become due, if the drawers should collect every dollar of the bank-notes issued, $350,000 would still be wanting to pay the bank the indorsed notes for $5,000,000; and the people would be dependent on the bank for a further discount of notes to obtain the money due as the year's interest. If one bank furnished all the money of the nation, the people would be dependent on that one for money to fulfil all their obligations. Increase the number of banks to a thousand, and the indorsed notes in proportion, and the transactions will be more numerous and appear more complicated, as they actually are; but it will not alter in the least the principles upon which the banks gain the interest out of the earnings of the public, while the public furnishes all the security necessary to make the bank-notes safe to circulate as money.

The people furnish double the security to make the bank-notes safe that they give to each other in the ordinary purchase and sale of products. The farmer sells his produce to the miller or merchant on credit; the miller sells his flour, the wool-grower his wool, and the manufacturer his goods mostly on two, four, six, eight, ten and twelve months' credits to city merchants, who resell them on like credits to other city or country merchants, and these dispose of them chiefly on credit, to farmers, mechanics and other consumers. Farmers, mechanics and merchants, in ordinarily good credit, can buy goods on their own responsibility; and their purchases are generally limited only by their own discretion. But they cannot take book accounts to the banks, and get bank-notes in exchange on the responsibility of the man who owes the money. Notes offered for discount must have only a certain time to run, must be drawn by men known to the directors to be responsible, and indorsed by one or two others in equally good credit. Thus the people do give at least double the security to make the bank-notes safe to circulate as money that they do to secure themselves against loss in the sale of the products of their own labor. Yet they pay to the banks five or six times more than a fair equivalent for the material and labor to make and exchange the bank-notes for the indorsed notes; and this is a total loss to the producing classes, and a clear gain to the banks.

We will now estimate the proportion of capital stock furnished in specie by the stockholders of the banks in the State of New York, and the proportion furnished by the balancing power of paper against paper. The following table, taken from the State Register, shows how much of the State currency, in 1844 and 1845, was based upon specie, and how much was based upon paper notes:

BANK REPORTS FOR 1844-45.

COMPARISON OF THE PRINCIPAL ITEMS, AT QUARTERLY PERIODS, FROM FEBRUARY, 1844, TO FEBRUARY, 1845, INCLUSIVE.

	February 1, 1844.	May 1, 1844.	August 1, 1844.	Nov. 1, 1844.	February 1, 1845.
Capital	$43,649,897	$43,462,311	$43,443,005	$43,618,607	$43,674,140
Circulation	16,835,401	18,365,031	18,091,324	20,152,219	18,513,402
Canal Fund	1,483,843	1,506,167	1,210,794	1,584,553	1,607,572
Deposits	29,026,415	30,742,289	28,757,112	30,391,622	25,976,246
Due Banks	15,610,554	15,467,494	16,102,922	14,431,103	11,501,102
Loans and Discourse	$70,025,734	$74,527,858	$75,546,592	$77,847,718	$70,888,578
Stocks and promissory notes	11,052,458	10,362,330	10,648,211	10,773,678	10,244,048
Specie	10,086,542	9,455,161	10,191,974	8,968,092	6,893,236
Cash items	4,502,479	5,999,952	4,916,862	6,047,528	4,839,886
Bank-notes	2,275,172	3,148,421	2,511,826	2,368,467	2,387,408
Due from Banks	10,267,207	8,817,179	8,359,328	8,767,513	7,684,308

From the foregoing table, it will be perceived that the banks were indebted at the above period to the amount of from $101,272,468, up to $110,128,104. Their average indebtedness, including the refunding of the capital stock to the stockholders, was $106,931,004. The average amount of their specie at the different periods as above, was $9,119,001. Deduct the specie from the indebtedness—*i. e.*, $9,119,001 from $106,931,004—and we have left $97,812,003, which sum must have been cancelled by paper. Our banks have specie enough to redeem only about one-fifth part of their capital stock. The balance of their capital stock, the redemption of the bank-notes in circulation, and the payment of the deposits, are secured by the indorsed notes of the people, binding the property of the drawers and indorsers. Their property as much secures the bank-notes, as it does their own notes. The bank-notes are representatives of the property of the people, and not representatives of the property of the banks. Not a single dollar of the paper issued over and above the actual amount of specie, is secured by their capital stock, because, if none of these indorsed notes and bonds of the State were ever paid, not a single dollar of the indebtedness of the banks, either for bank-notes or deposits, above their actual specie, would ever be paid. The $97,812,003 would be a total loss to the holders of the bank-notes, to the depositors, and to the stockholders.

The interest collected on the indorsed notes and State bonds supports the banks, and pays all their extravagant expenditures in granite buildings, salaries of officers, etc. They can pay their presidents and cashiers from $3,000 to $5,000 each, and other expenses, house-rent, etc., in proportion, to the amount of $40,000 or $50,000 yearly. They can also pay to the stockholders from three to five, six, or seven per cent. in dividends every six months. The banks under legislative authority make the public furnish the capital, and then pay interest on this capital. But although the industry of the people supports the whole, they have no voice in the management. The directors in the banks can at any time call upon them to pay off their notes and cancel the bank-notes; and if they fail, they are blamed for over-production and over-trading. When the banks contract their loans rapidly, and distress the people, the directors are said to be prudent and judicious managers. Yet if the people should demand specie, the banks could not pay it, unless they could collect it out of the indorsed notes of the people. But these indorsed notes were never founded upon specie, and could not be paid in it, because the drawing and indorsing of the notes by the people, and the engraving of the bank-notes by the banks, and the exchange of the bank-notes for the indorsed notes, do not create gold and silver coins to pay either the bank-notes or the indorsed notes. There has never been a time when the banks could have paid specie for a week, for their average deposits are more than three times their whole amount of specie.

The table shows that the average amount of the capital of the banks in the State of New York, during the period mentioned, was $43,569,591; and their average indebtedness was $106,931,004. The difference of these two sums is $63,361,413. The annual interest upon $63,361,413, at seven per cent., was $4,435,333, which the people of the State paid to the stockholders and officers of the banks for furnishing bank-notes above the amount of their professed specie capital. The people wrote their own notes, had them indorsed, and took them to the banks to be discounted. The banks engraved their bank-notes, and gave them in exchange for the indorsed notes. For engraving these notes, and making these exchanges, the people of the State paid to the banks annually $4,435,333, or as much as the farmers of the State receive for four millions four hundred and thirty-five thousand three hundred and thirty-three bushels of wheat, at $1 per bushel. The labor of producing such an amount of wheat was great; the labor of producing the bank-notes was very small, yet the interest paid on these bank-notes would have bought this quantity of wheat. At the end of the year the people of the State returned all the bank-notes to the banks, together with the value of this large amount of wheat to pay the year's interest. The same amount of interest accrued every year, and called for the same amount of their products. They sold their products in market, and paid the interest to the banks with the proceeds of the sales, the same to them as if they had carried their wheat and products directly to the banks to pay the interest. If the entire capital of the banks had been specie, the people would have paid the same amount for the use of the bank-notes which would have been issued over and above the specie.

The interest yearly paid for the use of $63,361,413, in bank-notes, was a legal equivalent for the four millions four hundred and thirty-five thousand three hundred and thirty-three bushels of wheat yearly raised upon a certain quantity of land; and the legal value of the $63,361,413, in bank-notes, was equal to the actual value of the land and labor necessary to produce the wheat. The power of the bank-notes was an exact balance against these products and the land upon which they were produced. If the quantity of money was at any time diminished, and the rate of interest increased, a larger amount of products was required to balance the smaller amount of money, and a larger amount of products to balance the interest on the smaller amount of money. Still this money must have been used to balance products, for it was the only public representative of value, and must have been employed as a tender, or as a substitute for a tender, in payment of debts. The promise of the banks to pay specie for their bank-notes on demand, does not enable them to pay the specie, nor does it alter the monopolizing power of the interest on the money over products.

If our bank-notes are good for the purchase of property by the people, certainly they should be equally good for the purchase of property by the banks. Let us reverse the relative positions of the banks and the people. Suppose instead of lending their money to the people to buy property, the banks should buy property with their bank-notes, and let it out to the people. This would put the bank-notes into circulation, and the banks would be the landlords of the property, instead of being the owners and lenders of the money. Let the people then call upon the banks for the redemption of the bank-notes in specie, and in default of payment sue them; and if they wish to borrow bank-notes to save their property from sheriff's sale, charge them one, two, or three per cent. a month for the use of the bank-notes. Let the banks try to rent their property so as to make the rents pay these rates of interest. This would only place the stockholders in a position similar to that in which they now often, though indirectly, place the people. It is evident that it would be impossible for them to redeem their bank-notes in specie, or to redeem them in any way except by selling their property and taking these bank-notes in payment, as the people now give their notes to the banks and pay the discount, and when their notes become due, collect these bank-notes together, and take them to the banks to redeem their indorsed notes. If the banks should buy the property with their bank-notes, and their friends should guarantee the property worth the price paid, the property and the guarantee would secure the bank-notes. It would only place the banks under the necessity of cultivating their property, and selling the products to pay the interest. It would be as possible to redeem the bank-notes with specie, under the supposed circumstances, as it now is. If the banks were called upon to redeem them now, they would crowd the people, and sell their property, and in the supposed circumstances, the people would crowd the banks, and sell their property. In both cases the debts must be cancelled by offsetting the property against them, for they could not be redeemed with specie.

It is perfectly obvious that our legislative bodies have founded our banking system on false pretences—upon promises the banks do not even expect to fulfil. The only reason why the banks can exist upon such a basis is, that the people do not demand the specie for their notes and deposits. The government enacts a law binding all debtors to make their payments in specie, when it is perfectly well known that specie does not exist in sufficient quantities to enable them to fulfil the requirement. More than eleven-twelfths of the debts between the banks and the people are contracted with a paper balance, and have no reference to specie. Of course, the only means of paying them is by balancing one paper note with another. If the banks, or the people, or the government should in every case exact what the laws require, it would be impossible to meet the demand. If the three should exact specie in payment for their obligations, it would inevitably bankrupt them all, and almost certainly cause starvation in the midst of abundance, if not civil war. If the governments of the States as well as the General Government should refuse to take bank-notes in collecting and disbursing their revenues, probably the people could not pay their duties and taxes. The necessary withdrawal of specie to meet these engagements would at once cause the banks throughout the Union to suspend specie payments. The need of money would then compel the people to petition the legislatures of their respective States to sanction this suspension, and allow the banks to continue to discount without paying specie on demand. They would, however, still be allowed to charge interest upon all the indorsed notes of the people received in exchange for the bank-notes, which would then be avowedly destitute of any basis of specie.

Can anything be more directly opposed to every principle of justice, than laws requiring the performance of impossibilities? Laws which, if the people should attempt to execute them, instead of promoting peace and happiness, would cause the greatest calamities that could possibly befall a nation. It is essential to good government that the interest and welfare of the people should require the execution of its laws, and whenever their violation becomes necessary to the public good, it is self-evident that there is something radically wrong in the government itself. A government should never allow anything to pass as a substitute for money; the tender itself should be equal in amount to the wants of business. The law making gold and silver the only tender in payment of debts is well adapted to build up and sustain monarchical governments, because it must infallibly accumulate property in the hands of a few, constituting aristocracies, which are essential to this form of government; but the same reason that qualifies it so admirably for this purpose, renders it incompatible with a government having for its sole object the welfare and happiness of the people.

SECTION III.

BASIS OF THE BANK OF ENGLAND.

The Bank of England is established upon a basis similar to that of the banks of the United States. Indorsed notes secure the bank-notes, and not specie. The bank-notes are not representatives of specie. The bullion in the bank seldom much exceeds the amount of the deposits. Should the depositors draw the specie, the only way in which the bank could redeem its bank-notes would be to take them in payment for the indorsed notes it holds against individuals. If these indorsed notes were not good, the bank-notes would be worthless. These indorsed notes are secured by the property of their drawers and indorsers; their property, and not the property of the bank, secures the bank-notes.

The Bank of England first issues £14,000,000, on government securities. This is making paper balance paper. It gives to the bank no ability to pay the £14,000,000 in bullion. If two individuals should exchange obligations for £14,000,000, this exchange would not produce bullion to pay either obligation. The bank-notes for £14,000,000 have not a fraction of value, except in so far as they are secured by the government bonds, and these bonds are secured not by the bank, but by the property and productive industry of the people of England.

All the gains of the bank by the recent * rise of interest, were unfairly taken from the industry of the people, and appropriated to the stockholders of the bank. The idea was given out that the bank was compelled to raise the rate of interest in order to be able to pay specie for its obligations. If the bank had been established upon a proper basis, and had loaned its money to aid the productive industry of the nation, at a low and uniform rate of interest, instead of making its loans to stock-jobbers and brokers to reloan at high rates, the recent crisis, or any former crisis in the monetary affairs of the country could not have happened. But the bank is established upon a false basis, promising to pay specie which it has not and cannot have. Therefore, in the recent crisis, it was compelled to lend its money to brokers and stock-jobbers, otherwise they would probably have drawn its specie, and compelled it to suspend specie payments. The bank and this class of citizens work for one another's interest, and extort the last penny from the producers of the wealth, under the pretence that the money, or the bullion, is the real wealth of the nation, and they keep the people constantly toiling for the bullion without ever possessing it, while the owners of the bullion contrive to live in luxury upon what the labor of the people produces.

To show that the bank is sustained in its specie payments by its reciprocal operations with capitalists, and

---

* This was written previous to 1849.—[M. K. P.]

that the bank-notes are secured by the indorsed notes of the people, and not by the bullion in the vaults, it will only be necessary to refer to the weekly reports of the bank. October 23, 1847, bullion, £8,312,691. Deposits, £8,588,509. Net circulation, £20,318,175. The bullion amounted to £275,818 less than the deposits: and if the deposits had been called for in specie, there would not have been a shilling in bullion toward paying the £20,318,175 of bank-notes. These, if paid at all, must have been paid by balancing them off against the indorsed notes of the people, held by the bank. Again, January 22, 1848, the bullion had increased to £13,176,812, the deposits had increased to £10,774,870, and the circulation had diminished to £19,111,880. Deduct the deposits from the bullion, and there remained £2,401,942 in bullion to pay £19,111,880. Deducting the bullion there remained £16,709,938, which, if it had been paid at all, must have been paid by balancing off the bank-notes against the indorsed notes held by the bank; as if two individuals should exchange notes, and agree to pay them in specie, but as neither has the specie to pay, agree to exchange notes again, and thus close the transaction. The exchange of the bank-notes, for the indorsed notes of the people, is different in this respect; the bank pays no interest to the people, but it makes the people pay interest on the bank-notes, and this interest absorbs the productions of labor.

SECTION IV.

THE BALANCING POWER OF BANK-NOTES AND DEPOSITS.

It has been already stated that if the banks become indebted for a larger sum than the amount of specie in their vaults, the surplus above the specie must be paid by balancing paper notes with paper notes, until the amount of specie in their vaults is exactly equal to the amount of paper for which they are liable. This statement was made taking into consideration only the indorsed notes discounted by the banks, and the bank-notes issued by them as their proceeds. The bank-notes are, however, not only the balancing power for the indorsed notes discounted, but are also the balancing power for all individual notes given in payment for sales of merchandise. Although these business notes be not discounted at bank, nor put into bank for collection, the bank-notes are the balancing power with which all these debts must be paid, as well as all State bonds issued, all bonds and mortgages given by individuals, and all debts contracted for lands, goods, wares and merchandise sold on credit or for cash. All these debts must be paid either with bank-notes, or with specie. Taking an average of the whole amount of contracts, it is probable that not one dollar in a hundred is paid in specie.

A small amount of money is always capable of balancing or paying a large amount of notes, bonds and mortgages, and also of purchasing many times its own amount of property. The money which pays for one farm may also pay for a second, third, and fourth, the same day.

The banks gain as much by the deposits left with them, as they would by the circulation of an equal amount of bank-notes. They pay no interest on deposits, and they lend their deposits to depositors and others, and charge interest on them. In cities, every man who has a large business, keeps an account, and deposits his ready money in some bank. Suppose a thousand merchants and mechanics keep deposit accounts of a thousand dollars each in the same bank, the sum will amount to a million of dollars. The bank can lend this sum to the depositors themselves, and make them pay interest on it. The money may be paid out many times during the day;

but before three o'clock, when the banks close, it will return in deposit, and be ready for use the next day. Some of the deposit accounts may be drawn down to a hundred, and some even to five dollars, while others may be increased to five, ten, or twenty thousand dollars, yet the average balance in bank will vary but little. It appears from the Report of the Bank Commissioners, that the deposit accounts in cities are always very large, whereas in country banks they are generally small. When farmers have money, they usually keep it in their own possession until they have occasion to pay it out. The inhabitants of large cities deposit their ready money in banks, and pay it out by giving checks on the banks. Most of the contracts in large cities are paid in this way. The money is kept on deposit for convenience and safety; and the owners can draw checks for larger or smaller amounts, and thus avoid counting the money. The holder of a check has as good a right to draw specie as the holder of bank-notes. He can draw the money or he can deposit the check as if it were money.

SECTION V.

THE MANAGEMENT OF THE BANKS AND THE EFFECTS OF THEIR OPERATIONS UPON THE PROSPERITY OF TRADE AND PRODUCTIVE INDUSTRY.

Our present banking system, and the present legal rates of interest, even with the fairest and best management, are a powerful means for the unjust accumulation of wealth. But looking a little deeper into the subject, and observing how the business of the banks is conducted, we shall find that their unavoidable evil tendencies are greatly augmented by the manner in which they are controlled and directed.

The banks are empowered to lend two and a half times their capital. They have no legal right to exceed this sum, but they may expand and contract their loans as much as they please within this limit. They can discount notes at longer or at shorter dates. They sometimes discount notes having six, eight, ten and twelve months to run, and then suddenly stop discounting any having over ninety days to run. They can make money very abundant, or very scarce. The banks can make good indorsed notes sell in Wall street at a discount of one, two, or three per cent. a month; or they can make money so plenty, that the same quality of paper will sell at less than a half per cent. a month. They can make the business of the nation prosperous, and make labor command good prices, or they can so greatly curtail business that the industrious laborer will be compelled to beg his living.

When a bank is extending its discounts, it will hold out inducements to merchants and mechanics to open accounts with it, being glad to discount for them to any reasonable amount. The merchant and the mechanic open accounts, and perhaps for a considerable time the paper which they offer is discounted at the legal interest of seven per cent. They are well satisfied, although the bank discounts for brokers and large capitalists at four, five, and six per cent. per annum, while it charges them seven per cent. But suddenly there is an apparent scarcity of money, and the bank declines discounting the paper of merchants and mechanics at long dates. The applicants inquire of the officers the reason of this refusal. They are answered, that money is becoming scarce, and that the bank discounts but one-half the paper offered. In reality the amount of money is not in the least diminished, nor the amount of discounts required increased but the banks and the capitalists keep it in their own possession to make the money-market tighter, that they may reloan to the business community at higher rates.

If for two days they discount only one-half their usual amount of paper, it is felt in the money-market. Those who are disappointed in obtaining discounts, must procure money elsewhere. They are driven to brokers and large capitalists, and are obliged to pay perhaps twelve per cent. per annum for money which has been borrowed by favored brokers and capitalists at seven per cent. per annum.

The merchant and the mechanic again offer at bank for discounts, and are a second time disappointed. Upon inquiry they are again informed that money is becoming very scarce, and that, besides, in looking over their deposit accounts, the officers find theirs small, and that others who keep much larger accounts are now asking for discounts. The merchant and the mechanic reply that they have heretofore kept good balances, and should be glad to continue them, if the bank would discount for them. But they are told that their balances were never as large as those kept by certain capitalists and brokers, who, although they kept large balances, seldom asked for discounts. Now, as money is scarce in the market, and they need discounts, the bank must favor them, for it is bound to attend to its own interest, and merchants and mechanics must attend to theirs. In these hard times the banks must discount for those who keep the largest deposits, and offer the best secured paper, as merchants and mechanics will sell their wares, or goods, to those customers who serve their interests best. It is as much the duty of the banks to consult their interest, and the interest of the stockholders, as it is that of merchants and mechanics to consult their interests, and the interests of their families. This reasoning sounds plausible enough, and seems to satisfy the people. If the articles dealt in by both parties were the actual productions of labor, and neither of them was created by law, these arguments would have some force. Or if any man who had a pack age of calicoes could issue paper-money bearing no interest, and pay his debts with it, and the mechanic could make a paper representative of his steam engine pass as money as easily as a bank can engrave and sign bank-notes, and make them pass as money, this reasoning might be sound. But when the article traded in by banks is a legal tender for debts, or is of necessity used as such, and the articles dealt in by others are the products of labor, and not a tender, nor used as a tender in payment of debts, then such arguments are false and ought to be powerless. They do not bear upon the facts; for the holders of the products of labor, or of their avails, are dependent upon the banks who make and possess the money which is a product of law. It requires little labor to create millions of dollars. The labor to make a five thousand dollar bank-note is the same as to make a one dollar note. But the difference of labor between raising five thousand bushels of wheat, and one bushel, is very great. Yet the bank-note for five thousand dollars is as much legally worth five thousand times more than the one dollar bill, either to lend upon interest, or to purchase products, as the five thousand bushels of wheat are actually worth five thousand times more than one bushel.

But to return. The applications of the merchant and the mechanic, at bank, for discounts are refused. The paper they had discounted when money was plenty is maturing, and must be paid. Meanwhile, in Wall street interest rises from one to two per cent. a month. Capitalists and brokers find it very profitable to get the notes which they buy at two per cent. a month discounted at seven per cent. per annum. The bank considers this paper far preferable to that of the mechanic and the merchant, because the capitalist or the broker, who bought the paper, was careful to have it secured by good indorsers before the purchase, and offers, besides, to leave a certain portion of the proceeds on deposit, which the bank can lend to others. The refused applicants at bank have no alternative but to pay the two per cent. a month to the broker or to the capitalist. Capitalists generally buy notes through a broker, and the broker receives a quarter per cent. on the amount, for brokerage. This, too, must be paid by the borrowers, in addition to the two per cent. a month.

As money becomes more and more scarce, and the offerings increase, the paper of large capitalists, and of the richest merchants and brokers, is often thrown out, and not discounted. If the more humble applicant, the merchant or the mechanic, should again inquire why his paper could not be discounted, the officers of the bank would mention the names of some of the most wealthy men, whose paper they were obliged to throw out for want of means to discount it. In Wall street money is loaned for from two to four per cent. a month, and even at these rates, the best paper can be obtained, with bonds and mortgages, or bank and State stocks as security for the prompt payment of notes. Directors in banks who are allowed by law to borrow an amount equal to one-third of the bank capital, have an opportunity to borrow money at the usual rates, and purchase State bonds and other securities, at a great discount from their par value. Capitalists who lent out money when it was abundant, at six or seven per cent. per annum, call it in, and invest it in State stocks, or in bonds and mortgages, which can be purchased at ten, fifteen, or twenty per cent. discount.*

---

* All who become rich by speculations in bank, State and other stocks, gain their wealth at the expense of the producing classes; for no increased production is made by the changing market value of these stocks. It is clear, that when the rate of interest is increased, the gains of money-lenders are augmented, and the money gained will buy a greater quantity of property and labor. The increased gains

The apparent scarcity of money soon spreads in every direction throughout the country. The banks in all the cities and towns shorten their discounts, and prepare for the approaching crisis. Their officers look over their paper, and collect that of the men whom they think least able to pay their notes. Not that the ability of these men to meet their engagements would be doubtful if money were plenty, and at the ordinary rates of interest; but it is not certain they could maintain their payments during a long pressure. The officers, therefore, if possible, collect all paper of this description, and from time to time obtain more security upon such as cannot be realized in money. They now lend money upon such paper only as they consider very strong and well secured, and which they think will be paid in full at maturity. The mechan-

of the lenders must be paid by the borrowers by the productions of their own or of others' labor. The increased transfer of money as interest from borrowers to lenders produces no increase of property, nor does the rise or depression of stocks by speculation, add a fraction to the wealth of the nation; yet a few may become rich by their rise, while many will be made poor by their fall. The market value of stocks is governed by the market value of money: if money can be loaned for a higher per cent. interest than the stocks are paying dividends, they will fall below their par value; but if money be loaned at a lower rate than the dividends on well secured stocks, the stocks will rise above their par value. If money could be supplied at all times, and safely loaned at a uniform rate per cent. interest, all well secured stocks paying like per centage dividends would be uniformly at par, because they would bring in precisely the same income as loans of money. The value of money is the standard by which the market value of stocks is governed; hence if the National Government would provide a means of supplying the public with the necessary amount of money at a uniform rate of interest, the State Bonds and all other securities would be of uniform value; consequently there would be no inducement to make a sacrifice of one class of securities to invest in another, because no advantage could be gained; and all these speculations in borrowing money at banks at lower, and reloaning it at higher rates of interest, and in the rise and fall of stocks, would at once and forever cease.

ics and the merchants who have sold their wares or goods to the country, are compelled to pay. not only one, two, three or four per cent. a month upon the money they have to borrow, but the scarcity prevents the collection of the debts due by their country customers; and if they have had any of their notes discounted before the pressure, they come back upon them to pay in addition to their other payments. The payment of these exorbitant rates of interest for the use of money, is sufficient to account for all our commercial revulsions.

When a scarcity of money commences in Wall street, the offerings of paper to be discounted at the banks are greatly increased, sometimes fifty, sometimes a hundred per cent. The reason is this: when banks stop discounting long paper, and confine their loans to paper having thirty, sixty, or ninety days to run, in order to maintain their circulations, the discounts must be increased just in proportion to the shortening of the paper. If the banks discount paper having only sixty days to run, then in the sixty days they will collect in the whole amount under discount. If their loans have on an average only ten days, then in ten days they will collect all their loans, and will not have a dollar under discount unless they lend out as well as collect in daily. If they should discount no paper having more than one day to run, they would collect in all their loans every day, and must reloan the same amount daily to maintain their circulations. Therefore, it is evident that if the banks maintain their lines of discount they must be increased exactly in proportion to the shortness of the paper that is discounted. Suppose a merchant has $1,000 to pay, and holds a business note for $1,000, payable in six months. To obtain a discount he is compelled to procure another note, having not more than sixty days to run. At the end of sixty days he must procure a second discount for a thousand dollars to pay the first, and in sixty days more a third to pay the second. In six months he is obliged to procure three loans of a thousand dollars each, and pay three thousand dollars, whereas, if the bank had discounted the six months' note he would have procured but one discount for a thousand dollars. Consequently, during the six months he would have offered but one-third as much paper at bank, and but one-third as much money would have been required to make his payments.

The interest on money will sometimes rise in a few months from six or seven per cent. per annum, to two or three per cent. a month. In 1837, a broker in Wall street sold the post-notes of the Delaware and Hudson Canal Bank, having four months to run, at a discount of five per cent. a month; and sold more notes the next day, for the same person, at six and a quarter per cent. a month. Six and a quarter per cent. a month, for four months, would take one-fourth from the principal of the note. This is equivalent to compelling a tenant to pay in advance one-fourth of the value of a house, or farm, for the use or rent of three-fourths during a period of four months, at the end of which he is responsible for the return of the whole; for the return of the fourth of which he had not the use, as well as of the three-fourths which were in his possession. The borrower of the money received but three-fourths of the par value of the notes. If at the end of the four months, when the post-notes became due, the bank had not paid them, the borrower would have been bound to pay their par value. As well might the tenant pay as exorbitant a rent for a house or a farm, as the borrower of money so high a rate of interest. These high rates of interest are not paid by all. Doubtless, favorites at bank could and did borrow money the same day in Wall street at seven per cent. per annum. The Delaware and Hudson Bank was solvent and good at the period named, and has so continued. At their maturity, if not before, the post-notes were paid. The money lent at six and a quarter per cent. a month was no better than that lent at seven per cent. per annum. Take from a $1,000 post-note $250, and there remains $750, of which the borrower had the use for four months, by paying the lender $250. The favored one who borrowed at bank $750 at seven per cent. interest per annum, paid for its use for four months $18 40. The first borrower paid thirteen times more than the second for the use of the same article, in the same street, and on the same day. Neither bought anything but the use of the principal, for at the end of the period the principal was returned to its owner. A man who was obliged to borrow money was charged thirteen times more than one who had no use for it except to gain the difference in interest. This procedure was as unjust as it would have been to charge men suffering for food $6 50 a bushel for potatoes, and to charge those who possessed an abundance only fifty cents. Such exactions do not occur in sales of products, but it is no uncommon thing in Wall street for money to be lent to the needy at a quarter per cent. a day, or ninety per cent. a year, which is fourteen times more than the banks are allowed to charge for discounting short paper. If a government agent should be directed to sell a quantity of flour to a needy people at six dollars per barrel, but for *certain* considerations, should sell it all to a capitalist, knowing that he would compel the people to pay $90 a barrel or starve, it would be similar to the abuse of the power conferred on the banks, and wielded by them in favor of capital.

Some of the large capitalists in the city of New York, during the years included between 1836 and 1840, bought up bonds and mortgages perfectly well secured, and bearing six and seven per cent. interest, at from ten to thirty-three and a third per cent. discount from their par value. They also bought millions of dollars' worth of well indorsed notes at from one and a half to five per cent. a month from the face of the notes. Some will say that the paper sold at these rates was of doubtful character, but such was not generally the fact. Individuals of known wealth, extensively engaged in business, and in want of money, sold large amounts of their paper indorsed by men in equally good standing, at three per cent. a month discount. These notes were, to say the least, quite as safe as the bank-notes for which they were exchanged.

The following illustration will show the bearings of these speculations in money upon the welfare of the producing classes. H. is a wealthy broker, and a bank director. His income, as also the income of the bank, depends upon the interest on money. He is worth $100,000, $20,000 of which are in bank stock. He uses $80,000 as a broker in buying mercantile paper. Suppose him to be able to effect a change in the rate of interest, from six per cent. per annum, to two per cent. a month, and the interest on his $80,000 will be increased from $4,800, to $19,200, making a clear gain of $14,400. At the bank in which he is a director, and at other banks he obtains discount for $80,000, at six per cent. interest per annum, on short paper, and pledge of his bank stock. Loaning this at two per cent. a month, he makes a clear gain of $14,400 more, making with the former, in one year, a clear gain of $28,800 over the six per cent. interest. By the rise of interest from six per cent. per annum to two per cent. a month, H. increases his income from $6,000 to $34,800. This increase is paid to him by merchants for money to meet their engagements, and, consequently, their debts are increased this sum. If interest had remained at six per cent., the broker would not have borrowed of the banks, for there would have been no inducement to borrow money which he could not reloan at a higher rate of interest. The money would, therefore, have been loaned by the banks directly to the merchants at six per cent. per annum, and the merchants would have saved $28,800, which they paid to the broker.

When the banks curtail their discounts, numerous contracts depending on their loans must lie over unpaid. Those who are desirous of meeting their engagements will suffer themselves to be defrauded in the rate of interest, rather than have their paper protested; for in a large city, if their paper lies over, their credit is gone, and their business ruined. They are compelled to pay these exorbitant rates of interest, however sensible they may be of the injustice. Good and evil are not set before them to choose between; but two evils are placed before them, and they must choose one or the other. If they wish to do right, they will choose the one which they think will do the least injury to themselves and their neighbors; but to one or the other of the evils, to usurious interest or to bankruptcy, they are compelled to submit.

Such are, however, by no means all the evil consequences of speculations in money. Money is the standard of value, by which the products of the soil, all merchandise, and the labor of the people are estimated. The incomes from labor and products diminish in proportion to the increase of the income from money. The change of the rate of interest compels the producers to labor four times more to clear $100, than before the rise of interest. Each sum of $100 contained in the $28,800 gained by the broker, will purchase as many products of labor, as the $100 gained by the four-fold toil of the producers; and yet the broker has done nothing to aid production or distribution, but has retarded both. City merchants sell goods to country merchants, and country merchants sell them to farmers and mechanics, from whom they must collect the money. But the diminished price of products puts it out of the power of the mechanics and farmers to pay, and thus the merchants are bankrupted. Meanwhile brokers and capitalists, who are neither engaged in productive labor, nor in the distribution of products, grow rich on the spoils. They are reverenced for their wealth, while mechanics, farmers and merchants, who have become correspondingly poor, are despised for their poverty, and blamed for being unable to fulfil their engagements.

The nature of money is not understood by the public, nor by the farmers, mechanics, and the great masses of the laboring classes; for if they did understand it, they certainly never would submit to its overwhelming and oppressive power. The newspapers in the City of New York devote several columns daily to giving the state of the money market, the prices of various stocks, and their fluctuations from day to day, according to the state of the money market. Now if money were properly instituted and regulated, there would never be such a thing as a money market. There would be a market for the productions of labor; and these would doubtless vary more or less in their market value or price, but there would be no variation in the market value of money. It is as unreasonable for people to gain great wealth by fluctuations in the market value of money. as it would be for them to gain great wealth by fluctuations in the length of the yard. Money is as much a standard of value as the yard is of length; and deviations in the market value of money are as much a fraud upon the public as deviations in the length, weight and size of other measures. No matter how long this gross wrong has been practised upon all nations, it is no less an evil; and it has shown itself to be such by the centralization of wealth in every nation, and the poverty of the people whose labor has produced the wealth.

It is now quite generally admitted that money is only a representative of value; and we presume many of the writers of the money articles in our daily papers would acknowledge that its value is only representative. Yet in the next breath they will tell you, that the country is rich in all the productions of labor, but what the people need is capital to get their products to market: that the manufacturers have plenty of goods, but there is a great want of capital to buy them, and therefore there is no market for the goods—just as if the money was the actual capital, and the labor and the productions of labor, merely represented the value of the money. The reason why money thus appears to be the real capital is, that all agreements for the sale or the exchange of property are founded upon it, and it must be had to meet the payment of these debts, for nothing else is legally competent to pay them. When money has been made by law a standard of value and a tender in payment of debts, it has the entire control over the value of the labor and property of the nation. The money has legal value, but property and labor have no legal value, and are solely dependent upon the value and power of the money. Hence we often see a nation in great prosperity, the labor busily employed, and all branches of business remunerative. But suddenly there comes up a crisis in the money market, and the business of the nation is prostrated. The power of money has brought a blight upon trade and industry. Money has suddenly become worth everything, and the laborers have suddenly become beggars in the streets of our cities, and the products of labor almost worthless in the market.

The following illustration shows the effect of differing rates of interest in different sections of the country. A merchant in New York for goods sold, holds a $1,000 note against a merchant in Alabama, which note he indorses and has discounted at bank. The southern merchant is not able to take it up when due, and it is returned to the New York merchant, who, to preserve his credit as indorser, must raise the money and pay it. Money is so scarce that he is obliged to sell a note hav-

21

ing six months to run, at a discount of three per cent. a month. The Alabama customer had abundant means to pay his debts, but the scarcity of money made it impossible for him to pay the note when it was due. Some time elapses, and the New York merchant sends out the note for $1,000 to Alabama for collection. Meanwhile, until the note is collected, he must borrow the money at three per cent. a month. He raises the money, and pays the returned notes by selling other notes having six months to run at a discount of three per cent. a month. Discounts thus:

Note at six months.................................. $1,219 51
Three per cent. a month off for six months is eighteen per
 cent... 219 51
                                                     ———————
                                                     $1,000 00

The note for $1,219 51 falls due, and he sells another note having six months to run at three per cent., and with the proceeds takes up the first note.

Note.. $1,487 20
Three per cent. a month for six months=eighteen per
 cent... 267 69
                                                     ———————
                                                     $1,219 51

This note falls due, and he sells another six months' note at three per cent., and with the proceeds takes up the second note for $1,487 20.

Note.. $1,813 55
Three per cent. a month for six months=eighteen per
 cent... 326 35
                                                     ———————
                                                     $1,487 20

This note falls due, and he sells another six months' note at three per cent., and with the proceeds takes up the third note for $1,813 55.

MANAGEMENT OF THE BANKS.

Note..	$2,211 64
Three per cent. a month for six months=eighteen per cent..	398 09
	$1,813 55

This note falls due, and he sells another six months' note at three per cent., and with the proceeds takes up the fourth note for $2,211 64.

Note..	$2,697 11
Three per cent. a month for six months=eighteen per cent..	485 47
	$2,211 64

Two and a half years have elapsed since the note in Alabama fell due. Being disappointed in its collection, the New York merchant, to save his credit, has raised and paid the money for two and a half years. From this has grown the note now due for $2,697 11. The Alabama merchant pays every dollar of this note with interest and costs in New York current funds. Thus:

Note..	$1,000 00
Two and a half years' interest at seven per cent..	175 00
	$1,175 00
From the increased note of the New York merchant..	$2,697 11
Deduct the note and interest received from the Alabama merchant..	1,175 00
Balance due by New York merchant..	$1,522 11

The difference of interest on $1,000 for two and a half years, causes a loss to the New York merchant of $1,522 11. The interest amounts to more than one and a half times the principal. The dollar is said to be the product of labor; but is this difference of interest the product of labor, or is it a change in the measure of value? Certainly, if the Alabama measure and the New York measure were the same, the debts would balance each other. They balanced each other two and a half years before, but in this period the thousand dollars in New York have increased $1,697 11, while $1,000 in Alabama, during the same time, have increased but $175. One has accumulated nine and a half times more than the other. The Alabama merchant pays all he owes the New York merchant, and the latter appropriates it to the payment of the $1,000 which he raised to take up the note of the southern merchant; but he still owes on this transaction $1,522. The third person who gets the $1,522, gains it without producing or distributing any products.

The following table exhibits the discounts on six months' notes for a term of sixty years. A thousand dollars in money are taken, and with this sum a note payable at six months is discounted. When the first note is paid, a second note having six months to run is discounted with its proceeds, and a third note with the proceeds of the second. This calculation is continued on six months' notes for sixty years. The table shows the accumulation on $1,000 for sixty years, at the various rates of 1, 2, 3, 4, 5, 6, 7, 8, 12, 18, 24, and 30 per cent. per annum, taking off the discount, as is always done by banks and brokers. The highest rate calculated is thirty per cent. per annum, or two and a half per cent. a month, a rate not nearly so high as is often paid in Wall street.

TABLE OF DISCOUNTS.

SHOWING THE ACCUMULATION ON $1,000 FOR A PERIOD OF SIXTY YEARS BY DISCOUNTING NOTES HAVING SIX MONTHS TO RUN, AT 1, 2, 3, 4, 5, 6, 7, 8, 12, 18, 24, AND 30 PER CENT. PER ANNUM.

1 PER CENT.	5 PER CENT.	12 PER CENT.
10 years $1,105 45	10 years $1,659 24	10 years $3,447 18
20 " 1,222 02	20 " 2,758 06	20 " 11,881 90
30 " 1,350 87	30 " 4,567 97	30 " 40,957 07
40 " 1,498 83	40 " 7,579 83	40 " 141,177 95
50 " 1,650 78	50 " 12,575 87	50 " 486,644 91
60 " 1,824 87	60 " 20,866 85	60 " 1,677,481 45

2 PER CENT.	6 PER CENT.	18 PER CENT.
10 years $1,222 64	10 years $1,838 93	10 years $6,594 85
20 " 1,494 88	20 " 3,381 06	20 " 43,485 48
30 " 1,827 63	30 " 6,218 65	30 " 286,755 62
40 " 2,234 52	40 " 11,485 67	40 " 1,890,988 71
50 " 2,732 00	50 " 21,029 39	50 " 12,469,831 63
60 " 3,340 23	60 " 38,671 58	60 " 82,280,496 79

3 PER CENT.	7 PER CENT.	24 PER CENT.
10 years $1,352 93	10 years $2,689 17	10 years $12,692 78
20 " 1,830 46	20 " 4,153 22	20 " 166,228 76
30 " 2,476 48	30 " 8,479 82	30 " 2,143,086 89
40 " 3,350 44	40 " 17,290 79	40 " 27,680,338 24
50 " 4,532 91	50 " 35,258 90	50 " 356,281,914 13
60 " 6,132 73	60 " 71,898 92	60 " 4,592,819,817 86

4 PER CENT.	8 PER CENT.	30 PER CENT.
10 years $1,497 89	10 years $2,262 43	10 years $25,800 11
20 " 2,243 66	20 " 5,118 59	20 " 665,645 68
30 " 3,360 75	30 " 11,580 46	30 " 17,173,731 66
40 " 5,034 01	40 " 26,199 97	40 " 448,084,165 99
50 " 7,540 36	50 " 59,275 70	50 " 11,431,620,222 06
60 " 11,294 60	60 " 134,107 05	60 " 294,936,059,207 87

In the foregoing table it appears that interest at one per cent. would transfer $824 worth of the products of labor to the capitalists to pay for the use of $1,000 for sixty years; at six per cent., $37,671 58; at seven per cent., $70,898 92; and at thirty per cent., $294,-936,058,207 37. In any community the rise of the rate of interest on all the money used, whether for a longer or a shorter period, transfers from producers to capitalists a sum proportioned to the increase of the rate per cent., as demonstrated in this table.

When money becomes scarce, and interest rises to exorbitant rates, the rates of exchange between one city and another, and between one State and another, always increase. These exchanges are merely a cover under which the banks obtain a higher rate of interest than the one allowed by law, and a means to enable them greatly to increase their dividends. In 1836, the banks in New York began to do a business of considerable amount, by collecting notes on the South and West, and charging various rates of exchange, from one to three or four per cent. The discount at seven per cent. on a note having three months to run, would be one and three-quarters per cent.; and by charging three per cent. exchange on Georgia or other southern States, it would amount in the three months, to four and three-quarters per cent. If their money was returned free of expense, these exchanges were much more profitable to the banks than lending money at seven per cent. interest per annum. To secure the return of the money without loss or trouble, when another person applied for a discount of a note payable in New York, it was very easy to tell him that the bank could not discount, that its funds were locked up in Georgia or elsewhere, and that if he were willing to take a draft on a Georgia bank, it would discount his note. Being compelled to have the money or break, the applicant would take the draft on Georgia, and through a broker sell it in market. If the bank did not then buy the draft back at a discount of three or four per cent., at all events by the two transactions it would have made its funds payable in New York. It would have saved the exchange of three per cent. on the first note discounted and this would have amounted to about double the legal rate of interest. The banks sometimes made seven or eight times more in this way than by interest. This mode of exchanging spread through the Union; and in the spring of 1837, when the New York banks and the banks generally suspended specie payments, the rates of exchange still increased.*

To show that the banks profited largely by the embarrassments and fluctuations in 1836 and 1837, we have only to notice the per centage profit gained by them in the State of New York at different periods. The published statements in the New York Assembly documents show that the average dividends of the Bank of America, for ten years, from 1818 to 1828, were 5.30 per cent annually. But in the years 1836 and 1837, money was very scarce, and the difficulties of the community proportionably great. During these years the profits of the bank averaged more than 16.14 per cent. annually. More in one year of embarrassment than in three years of general prosperity. The same published statements of the following six banks, viz., Bank of America, City Bank, Mechanics' Bank, Merchants' Bank, Bank of New York, and Union Bank, show a result as follows. During the same ten years, from 1818 to 1828, their average dividends were 5.70 per cent. per annum. But in the two years 1836 and 1837, their profits were 13.35 per cent. annually. The same statements rendered by fifty-nine country banks in this State, show that in the same two years, their average profits were 11.36 per cent. per annum.

To effect a rise of interest, it is not necessary for the banks to allow their money to lie dormant any length of time. Let the New York banks for one week refuse to

---

* I know of other instances where paper has been discounted for ninety days and drafts given on Philadelphia at par, when the exchange on that city was over thirteen per cent. discount. The parties borrowing had to sell the Philadelphia funds and lose this exchange, besides the interest; and banks have discounted paper, paying in Philadelphia funds when at as large discount as the above mentioned; if they have not done this in New York, it has been done in a neighboring State.—*Currency, the Evil and the Remedy.*

discount a single note, and the want of money would probably be as great, and as severely felt, as during the most difficult periods in 1837. By this refusal the banks would only lose the interest on the amount collected for half the week. But by the end of the week those who needed money would be obliged to sell paper having three, six, nine, and twelve months to run, at a discount of two or three per cent. a month, and would be subjected to a great loss. The banks in the city of New York keep an average of about $50,000,000 loaned. If the notes thus discounted have an average of fifty-six days to run, the citizens pay into the banks six and a quarter millions of dollars every week. If for one week the banks should refuse to discount, and draw in the six and a quarter millions, they would lose the interest on this sum for an average of three and a half days. This interest at six per cent. would amount to $3,557 69. If this curtailment of the circulation for one week should compel merchants and mechanics to sell their business paper, having but sixty days to run, at two per cent. a month discount, they would lose four per cent. on the $6,250,000, *i. e.*, $250,000. The merchants and the mechanics would sustain a total loss of $187,500 over and above interest for sixty days, at the rate of six per cent. per annum on $6,250,000. Let us extend this calculation, and suppose the banks to stop their discounts for two weeks, and collect in their dues. In the course of two weeks, they would collect in $12,500,000. They would lose the interest upon this sum for an average of one week, in which time the interest would amount to $14,230 77. These curtailments would produce an extreme scarcity of money. Suppose the merchants and the mechanics to be compelled to sell their business paper having six months to run at a discount of two per cent. a month for that period. They would lose twelve per cent. on $12,500,000, *i. e.*, $1,500,000. Their actual loss over and above the interest, at the rate of six per cent. per annum, for six months, would be $1,125,000, while the banks would lose only $14,230 77. If, instead of curtailing their discounts, the banks should refuse to loan to merchants and mechanics, and lend their money to brokers and capitalists, who should reloan it at the above rates to the people, the same results would be produced without any loss of interest by the banks, or any curtailment of their discounts. The $1,125,000 would be lost to business men and gained by brokers and capitalists.

The banks can curtail their discounts as much and as rapidly as they please without violating the laws. In 1837 and 1838, there were not only twelve and a half millions of dollars loaned at two per cent. a month, but probably some hundreds of millions were loaned at much higher rates. One or two per cent. a day was often extorted from the needy. Many merchants and mechanics in New York might be mentioned, who paid from $10,000 to $50,000 in extra interest, that is, interest over seven per cent. before they were compelled to suspend payment. Besides, when collections were made for them in the various States by banks and otherwise, they were subjected to great losses in exchanges on their drafts. Millions of dollars' worth of the best paper was sold at a discount of three per cent. a month. Take the discount off in advance, at this rate, from six months' paper, and $1,000 will buy a note for $1,219 50. At the maturity of this note, its proceeds, *i. e.*, $1,219 50 will buy a second note having six months to run for $1,487 18. Thus it is seen that the indebtedness of those paying this rate of interest was increased, in one year, almost fifty per cent. on all the money they borrowed to meet their engagements.

Curtailments of bank discounts, made under pretence of getting the people out of debt, serve only to increase their indebtedness. They inevitably retard the sale of products, and destroy the regularity of business. If the inhabitants of the State of New York ordinarily pay interest on four hundred millions of dollars, and one-half this sum, *i. e.*, two hundred millions, were loaned at two per cent. a month, their indebtedness would be increased on this one item thirty-six millions of dollars above the interest at six per cent. per annum; and this, too, without taking the interest in advance, which is usually done in cases of this nature. In all these transactions, by which thirty-six millions of dollars would be taken from producers and distributers, and transferred to capitalists, there would be no exchange of products, and the people would receive no consideration for their money. Besides the suffering caused by the increase of indebtedness upon loans of money, the prices of products would be greatly diminished. Those sold would not, perhaps, cancel more than one-half the debts that they would if the rate of interest had not increased. Therefore, the money engrossed by the capitalist would be worth to him double the same sum at the usual interest, for he could purchase with it nearly double the quantity of products that he could under ordinary rates.

A man who owns a farm cannot rent it for thirty or sixty days, and force its return, and keep constantly re-letting it, so as to inconvenience his tenants; because, in these short periods the farm would not produce a crop; but money will gather an income when it is loaned for thirty or sixty days, or for one, two or three days. Many men now devote their time to the loaning of money for one-eighth, one-quarter, one-half, and one per cent. a day, fixing a higher or a lower rate, according to the necessity of the borrower. In this way they extort the largest possible interest. This they say they do "to keep people from breaking." * Doubtless many of those engaged

---

* We feel confident in saying that no intelligent business man in the city of New York will doubt, that there have been many millions of dollars loaned the past week (Sept. 9th, 1854) by the banks in this

in brokerage are ignorant of the effects of their stock-jobbing and loaning operations upon the welfare of their fellow-men, and not any of them fully appreciate the evils they occasion, or, it is to be hoped, they would cease to pursue an employment so blighting to their own moral characters, and so pernicious to the welfare of others.*

In 1837, rents on stores fell to one-half or one-quarter of their former prices, and many stood untenanted. At the same time, bank-notes which a year or two before could be rented at but six or seven per cent. per annum, were rented at from three to ten times more than before, although at the former time the bank-notes were professedly based on specie, and at the latter, no pretension of this sort was made. Was the rise of interest on the bank-notes, or money, caused by an increase of labor to

city, at the rates of six and seven per cent. per annum. Nor will any intelligent business man doubt, that several millions of this same money have been reloaned during the week by brokers and other financiers at one, two and three per cent. a month, and from this rate to a quarter per cent. a day. A quarter per cent. a day is seven and a half per cent. a month, while six per cent. per annum, is but a half per cent. a month. It makes a very wide difference in the rent of property, if one pay seven and a half times more than another. Whether money be loaned at a high rate per cent. interest for one day, one month or for ten years, the loans are all governed by the same principle; it is a certain rate per. cent. to be paid just in proportion to the time for which the money is borrowed. Therefore if it be just at any time to loan for a quarter per cent. a day, it would be equally just to loan at the same rate per cent., for a month or for ten years. It is such a notorious fact that money is loaned at usurious rates of interest, that these impositions are daily published in the newspapers as a constant practice, and the man who can obtain the highest rate is looked up to as a first rate man of business. Financiers talk of the borrowing and lending of money at usurious rates of interest, as if they were buying and selling commodities at a profit or loss. Yet the borrowing and lending money is not buying and selling money, any more than renting and hiring a house is buying and selling the house.

* See Appendix, C.

engrave and secure the notes, or was the fall of rent on stores caused by a diminution of the number of bricks, or the amount of labor necessary to build them? No! it was an arbitrary rise of interest to increase the gains of banks, brokers, and capitalists. Our producers were not idle: we had a superabundance of products for our market: yet, strange as it may seem, thousands in our midst were suffering for the very things of which the abundance was the subject of lamentation. One had raised a surplus of some products, and was in need of surplus products owned by others. But it was nearly impossible to effect any exchange of these products, on account of the scarcity of money. At this juncture, the situation of the producers in Europe was similar to that of the producers in the United States. The Bank of England was openly authorized to increase the rate of interest on its loans in order to check *over-production* and *over-trading*. *

---

* Financial power is instituted by governments; and when a money crisis occurs and prostrates business, governments, to be consistent, must sustain the power they have established, and, consequently the financiers who wield it. But the revulsion must be attributed to some cause in order to satisfy the public mind, and financiers are always ready with hosts of reasons for it. They will tell you that the people one year produced too many agricultural products, and next year too few; that another year they manufactured too many goods, and another year too few: that another year they built too many railroads; another year they imported too many goods; etc., etc., etc. There is no end to the subterfuges resorted to in the endeavor to show that these crises in the money market are caused by the laboring classes, either by not producing enough, or else by over-production, over-trading, etc. Yet all these have never really satisfied the public on this subject; for their common sense tells them, that labor is the producer of wealth, and that there can be no great surplus of products unless this surplus remains after supplying every man, woman and child with all the necessaries of life. It is no proof of a surplus, that the merchants have their stores filled with unsold goods when thousands of the laboring community around them are suffering for the want of these very goods, but cannot sell

How different would have been the condition of the producing classes if the banks had pursued an opposite course. If, instead of raising the interest on their loans, and increasing their dividends to double their amount in previous years, they had lowered the rate of interest so as to diminish their dividends to one-half their previous amount, the prosperity of the producing classes would have as greatly exceeded their prosperity in former years, as it was by the rise of interest diminished below their former prosperity. The amount of bank loans would have been less. Probably money would have circulated with more than double its former rapidity. One million of dollars circulating rapidly will accomplish as much in a given time as two millions will if the latter circulate but half as fast. If in January, 1836, the banks throughout the Union had reduced their rate of interest to four per cent., and had lent their money to business men for good indorsed notes, if they had made no loans on pledge of stocks as security, or to any one who they knew desired to lend the money again at an advanced rate of interest, business would have been attended with increased prosperity; country products would have maintained good prices; the State bonds of every State in the Union, bearing an interest of five per cent. per annum, would have been above par; every State would have paid the interest on its bonds promptly, and in January, 1837, the people would not have owed as much by a very large amount as they were compelled to owe under the actual circumstances. The producing classes would have been comparatively well off, and large capitalists would not

their labor to pay for them. So long as labor commands a fair price in money, there is a ready market for the products of labor; and it is only high rates of interest and a scarcity of money that make labor and the products of labor unsalable. Revulsions in trade are caused by the money power, by financiers, and not by the producing classes.

have become so immensely rich. State stocks would not have been crowded upon the market, nor would capitalists have become competitors with the business community for loans at banks. The producing classes cannot afford to pay even four per cent. per annum, but there would be less distress among them at this rate, than at six per cent., or a higher rate. Their subsistence will always become scanty in proportion to the increase of the rates of interest.*

If the English government should raise the interest on its debt to four per cent. the taxes of the producers would be increased in the same proportion. But if it should lower the interest on its debt to one per cent., and compel the Bank of England and all bankers to take only one per cent. on the indorsed notes of individuals, and to make no loans on pledges of stocks as security, the producing classes of England would be elevated, and their share of their own surplus products would be increased in proportion to the diminution of the rate of interest.

The curtailments of bank discounts seem to be made that producers may know and consider the great value of money, and the comparative worthlessness of the productions of labor. It would seem that the principal wealth of a nation may be dug out of some obscure place in the earth, collected into a very small compass, and placed in the vaults of banks. It there remains as inactive as it was in the mines before it was excavated. This gold and silver money gives power to the banks, the Board of Brokers and a few large capitalists, to compel the people to cultivate the earth, and to gather and market its productions mainly for their use, reserving for themselves of the poorer kinds a bare subsistence.

Do the farmers, mechanics, and the laboring classes in general, believe that the majority of the surplus wealth

---

* See Appendix, D.

which their labor yearly produces, ought in justice to be owned at the end of the year by a few financiers? Does their common sense teach them that a few, for the use of the money necessary to exchange the commodities produced, ought to gain double, treble or quadruple as much of the surplus production as those who furnish the skill and perform the labor to make the production? Does it accord with their sense of justice, that the bankers, brokers, and financial stockjobbers in the city of New York, should realize each year more clear gain in wealth than all the agriculturists and mechanics in the State can gain by their year's toil? Do our producers and the public generally really believe that the principal wealth of the nation is stowed away in the vaults of the banks in our large cities, and that the prosperity of this great nation ought to depend on the quantity of specie in the vaults of these banks? If the people from the highest to the lowest do really believe this, who can wonder that the Babylonians believed that the golden image set up by Nebuchadnezzar was the true God, and that Daniel deserved to be cast into the lions' den for his unbelief; for there was in that golden image as much of the life-giving spirit of God, and ability to provide for the temporal and spiritual necessities of its worshippers, as there is now in our gold and silver money images to provide for our temporal and spiritual support. The law of Babylon which attributed to this image the power of God, and commanded the people to bow down in adoration before it, was hardly a greater imposition upon their credulity and rights than is now practised upon nations by legally authorizing certain gold and silver images to be set up, and attributing to them an innate value equivalent to that of all other things.*

Every man's common sense must tell him, that the

---

* See Appendix, E.

present distribution of wealth is radically unjust. But as similar wrongs have existed in every civilized nation, from the earliest ages, it seems to be taken for granted that they are necessary evils—in other words, that there can be no remedy for them. Yet their continued existence only proves that an evil cause continuing to act will continually produce its evil effects, and that this cause must be removed before the evils will cease. Although the effects produced are exceedingly complicated, these enormous evils of unjust distribution originate in every civilized nation from one and the same fundamental cause, namely, the unjust and uncontrolled power of money. If it be possible to institute money with only a just power, and that power such as can be controlled and regulated by national laws, the fundamental cause of these evils can be easily removed. But if it be impossible thus to institute and govern money, the fundamental cause cannot be removed, and the consequent evils are entailed upon us.

Nations have assumed that the value of gold and silver money is innate, and have established their monetary laws upon this false assumption. Thus, according to law, *all* innate value is in gold and silver money, and there is no innate value in anything else; for the laws have made this money a legal balance in payment for everything that is bought and sold, while no other thing is any tender or legal balance in payment for money. Neither is any other thing a tender in payment for anything that is bought or sold; hence if a value be attached to anything besides money, it is this innate value of money which must determine what that market value shall be; for other things have no legal value except by the permission and determination of this innate value of money. This innate value, assumed by law for gold and silver money, is not like that of any created thing in the mineral, vegetable, or animal kingdom, for it overrules and controls the value of all these things. According to our laws, it is an independent, uncreated power, having an inherent right to govern and settle the value of all things.*

This money power is not only the most governing and influential, but it is also the most unjust and deceitful of all earthly powers. It entails upon millions excessive toil, poverty and want, while it keeps them ignorant of the cause of their sufferings; for, with their tacit consent, it silently transfers a large share of their earnings into the hands of others, who have never lifted a finger to perform any productive labor. The same power has grossly deceived our public teachers; for not being able rationally to account for the great inequalities of wealth and condition existing in society, and being expected to furnish a satisfactory explanation in some way, they tell the people that these great wrongs are providential, that they are the mysterious workings of the providence of God: that all these evils are governed and controlled by His power and goodness. This method of accounting for the gross political wrongs in society has covered up and hidden from view a multitude of heinous sins. Notwithstanding the number of those who now live in luxurious idleness, performing little, if any useful labor, and the great number of those who remain idle because the scarcity of money renders it impossible for them to obtain work, yet with all these impediments, there is generally enough produced each year in each nation to give to every man, woman and child a comfortable living.† Every person of common sense must see, that

---

* See Appendix, F.

† A nation in which each individual should devote four or five hours daily to labor in useful production, would probably be better supplied with the comforts and luxuries of life than any people now on the globe. Not only is a moderate amount of manual labor necessary to the full development and health of the body, but

God in his providence has bountifully provided for man
and that there is some other power working against him,
and diametrically opposed to the righteous distribution
of his bounties. It is the providence of the national
laws, establishing this unjust power of money, which
obs the producing classes of their rights. As the bounties of God are abundant, so must the money for their
distribution be abundant, or they can never be justly
distributed. If the scarcity of money or its centralizing
power retard the production and the distribution of the
products of labor, the power of the money is unjust
and oppressive, and instead of being in unison with
the providence of God, it is the most powerful opponent
of his righteous laws, as well as the most powerful and
bitter opponent of justice and beneficence among men.
It would be as reasonable to expect sweet waters to flow
from a bitter fountain, as to expect just distributions of
property if the standard by which it is valued is unjust.
We are not depicting an unknown evil. Legislators,
financiers and the producing classes all know that money
is possessed of some mysterious evil power, which has
never been clearly explained and defined. We have intended to remove this mystery concerning the nature and
operations of money, and to show what laws must be annulled, and we shall proceed to show what other laws
must be enacted, in order to establish money that will be
endowed with an equitable power. The evil power of
money has been politically established, and it must be
politically annulled. It is a public wrong, and the public
must administer the remedy.

it contributes in no slight degree, to the most ennobling exercise of
the moral and mental capabilities.

SECTION VI.

REMARKS ON THE REPEAL OF THE USURY LAWS.

In the course of the few past years, numerous petitions have been presented to the legislature of the State of New York, praying for the repeal of the Usury Laws. It is proposed that in loaning money the rate of interest should be agreed upon between borrowers and lenders, as the prices of merchandise are agreed upon between buyers and sellers. The position assumed by those in favor of abolishing the Usury Laws is, that the competition between the lenders of money would be so great as to reduce the rate of interest below seven per cent. But such would not be the result. There is now no law against competition at, or below, seven per cent.; therefore the competition at seven per cent. and under this rate, could not be increased by annulling the restriction.

Another argument for the abolition of a legal rate of interest is, that the laws against usury are continually violated. In large cities, money is often loaned at from one to three per cent. a month, at a quarter and a half per cent. a day, and sometimes even at one or two per cent. a day, and the legal rate of seven per cent. per annum does not govern the money-market; it is, therefore argued that the law must be wrong; and that if the price to be paid for the use of money were left open to competition, the demand and supply would equitably regulate the rate of interest.

The idea commonly held out is, that the rates of interest would be lower if the Usury Laws were abolished; and anticipating this result, many are induced to sign the petitions. There is reason to believe that the principal originators of these petitions are those who are now in fringing the laws by exacting extra rates of interest, and who would like to have their extortions legalized. They do not advocate the chartering of banks without restrictions upon their rates of interest. *Banks* should lend money at the legal rates. Then a few capitalists would borrow large sums from them, and discounts would be refused to business men, who would be compelled to borrow money from these capitalists at the rates of interest for which they would agree to lend it. The necessity of the borrower, and the avarice of the lender, would fix the rate of interest. If a capitalist could borrow from a bank $10,000 for ninety days, at six per cent. per annum, and reloan it at three per cent. a month to a man who must have the money or break, he would make by the operation a clear gain of $750. Annul the laws against usury, and this kind of business would be far more extensive than it now is; but under the existing laws, more of it is done than is for the benefit of the public.

Other arguments advanced in favor of abolishing the Usury Laws, are such as these. It is said when goods are sold on a credit, a greater difference is made in their price than the interest at seven per cent. per annum for the time of the credit, and it is therefore right that lenders should receive higher rates of interest for their money. People are not aware that the high and fluctuating rates of interest on money are the cause of the extra prices charged for credits on sales of goods. Suppose a merchant is obliged to turn his goods into money to pay a debt. He sells them on six months' credit, taking the purchaser's note, on which he pays two and a half per cent. a month discount to obtain the cash. He could as well afford to take fifteen per cent. from the goods as fifteen per cent from the note. The purchaser of the goods who cannot pay the money even when offered this large discount off his note, is not as safe for the payment of his note as he would be if others could not get so large a discount by paying cash. It gives a man who can pay the money great advantage over one who cannot, for if the latter pay fifteen per cent. on the cost of his goods for six months' possession, the buyer for cash can undersell him. If money could be always easily borrowed at a uniform and low rate of interest, the difference between sales for cash and credit would vary but little from the rate of interest; for if interest were at a just rate, there would be few bad debts, and a very small per centage on goods would guard against all losses from this cause.

Another proposition is, that the Usury Laws should be taken off from all four months' paper, and the rates of interest on longer loans restricted, as if four months' paper were governed by different principles from that having six or eight months to run. It would be hard to show how selling four months' notes at exorbitant rates of interest would save the credit and property of business men. If, at the end of the first four months, the merchant be obliged to sell a second four months' note at the same rate, is he any better off than if he had at first sold one of eight months, instead of the two four months' notes? If it were legal to demand as high rates of interest as could be obtained on paper not having more than four months to run, paper for longer dates would be unsalable whenever interest on the short paper was high. Usurers now say that they take a higher rate of interest on account of the risk they incur by lending at a rate not allowed by law. Hence, if they could legally demand two, three, or four per cent. a month discount on four months' paper, they would ask still higher rates for discounting six months' paper, to pay for the hazard of the illegal act. Besides, if any rate of interest which people would agree to pay for money for four months were made legal, whenever the rate of interest was high those who owed money on bond and mortgage would probably be called upon for payment. If they could not pay, the holders of the mortgages would give them four months' time, and take a new bond, very likely at two or three per cent. interest a month. In the city of New York there is probably a larger amount loaned on bond and mortgage, that is now due, than the amount of all the capitals of banks in the city. Nearly all our Insurance Companies loan their money thus on one year's time, but do not expect to call for it so long as the interest is regularly paid, unless they meet with great losses. A large proportion of these mortgages is due. Many millions are loaned by individuals and executors of estates, and perhaps a very large proportion of these would be called for, in order to obtain the higher rates of interest. The people would be obliged to pay almost any rates that the owners of the mortgages chose to exact; otherwise their property would be sold to satisfy the debts. Either course would break up a large proportion of the debtors, and their property would pass over to their creditors for half, or less than half, its value.

Another proposed modification of the law is, that if the money-lender obtain from the borrower an agreement to pay more than seven per cent. interest per annum, and prosecute his claim for the recovery of the debt, he shall be allowed to collect no more than the sum loaned and seven per cent. interest. Could any *honest* man propose a law for the prevention of theft, the only penalty of which, in case of detection, should be the restoration of the goods?

If the people desire a more rapid centralization of wealth and power, and to increase the depression and poverty of the producers, let them annul all Usury Laws, and they will be sure of success. But if they wish to perpetuate a democratic government, and elevate the producing classes, they must reduce the present power of money, or it will surely make this nation a practical aristocracy, even though we professedly continue to be a democracy. A righteous government must rule over money, instead of allowing the money to over-rule the government. To do this, it must furnish a sufficient supply of money, and regulate a right rate per cent. interest.*

* See Appendix, G.

CHAPTER V.

THE AMOUNT OF A CURRENCY SHOULD BE LIMITED ONLY BY THE WANTS OF BUSINESS.

It is indispensable to the regulation of the currency that *the amount of money should be limited only by the wants of business.* It has been already shown that the value of money is determined by its income, or rate of interest. This proposition being established, it follows, that if the interest be regularly maintained, the amount of money may be unrestricted without decreasing its value.

The following illustration will show, that no laws against usury can prevent the oppression and evil consequent upon a limited amount of money.

Suppose one hundred thousand persons forming a nation to frame their own government and laws. They make gold and silver coins the legal currency, and fix the rate of interest at six per cent. Severe penalties are affixed to the exaction of a higher rate, and to the exportation of money from the country. This nation has in coin $12 to each inhabitant; probably as much as any people, however wealthy, can keep in active circulation. The specie in the nation amounts to $1,200,000. Twenty men become worth $100,000 each, together $2,000,000. One million is loaned on bond and mortgage and business notes at the legal rate. When all the money of the nation is in active use, the twenty men determine to call in thirty per cent. of their loans, and hold the money for a week or a month in order to make a more profitable reinvestment. This takes out of circulation $300,000, one-fourth of the whole circulating medium, and causes a great scarcity of money. One-fourth of the debts in the nation lie over unpaid, for all the money was before required to meet contracts. The twenty men hold only their own money, and no law can, or should compel them to use it. They do not take more than the legal rate of interest. Let these men hold their money for six months, until the unpaid debts are mostly collected by suits at law, and the twenty men and other owners of money can buy the property of debtors at less than half its value. All securities depreciate, and confidence is lost in the value of property, and in the ability of debtors to discharge their obligations. Yet no money leaves the country, nor is any change made in the rate of interest.

Twelve hundred thousand dollars is an abundance of money for a population of a hundred thousand persons. If we allow it to pass from one individual to another three times a week, (and money passes much oftener in cities,) the $1,200,000 would pay $3,600,000 of debts every week, and in a year $187,200,000. Notwithstanding this abundance, these few individuals can easily affect the money market, and greatly increase their wealth by purchasing property at reduced rates, and selling it when the depression ceases. If the amount of money for each inhabitant were increased to $20, the aggregate amount would be but $2,000,000, and the twenty men would be worth as much as the whole currency of the nation, and could easily keep enough in their own possession to effect the same results. The government is powerless to prevent these evils, for the amount of money is limited, and a few individuals have the control of it.

In the United States within a few years, in times of scarcity of money, cows were sold at sheriff's sale at from $2 to $5 ; good horses at from $3 to $10 ; and cui tivated lands for a few cents an acre, when they cost their owners nearly as many dollars. When money became plenty again, these cows, horses, and lands rose to perhaps quite their former price. No nation should fix upon a standard of value of limited amount. For a limited amount of money, even at a uniform interest, will enable the owners of money to monopolize the property of the nation.

The State of New York has a population of 3,500,000. Multiply this by 12, and we have $42,000,000, a much larger sum, doubtless, than is kept in active circulation in our State. Still, there are probably two men in the State who are worth more than this sum; and who can, whenever they choose, affect not only the money market of this State, but also that of every State in the Union. Neither the State government, nor the General Government has power to prevent it, nor to relieve the people.

A comparatively small sum of money must pay all the debts now existing in the country. It must also pay for the year's crops. When the crops arrive in market they are no more money than while they were in the hands of the farmers, and if they will not sell for money the debts cannot be paid with them. Neither labor nor the products of labor are any salvation from a money crisis. A power is given to money that is totally different from all other powers, and this does not seem to be at all understood. There is not a particle more natural power in the gold, silver and paper out of which money is made, than there is in iron, tin and wood. Consequently the power of money is not in its material substance, but in its immaterial legal authority, which constitutes both its power and market value. The material part of the money only represents the immaterial, and this immaterial power is exerted to an enormous extent where there is nothing in the shape of money to represent it. Hence this power is wofully oppressive; it calls for a material substance, and there is no material substance in existence to meet its demands; and the labor and property must be diminished in their market value so as to conform to the material quantity of the money. Money has legal authority to crush the value of labor and property, but property and labor have not a particle of legal authority over money.

When a national government has established money as a standard of value, so far as the jurisdiction of the laws extend, the money is clothed with an omnipresent power, such as no other earthly thing possesses. This omnipresent power of money is used a hundred times more in the entire absence of its material substance than it is when and where the material substance is present. Manufacturing companies, in this country, mostly send their goods to commission merchants in the city. These goods are credited to the manufacturers, who draw upon the merchants at such dates and times, and for such amounts as are agreed upon between the parties. These goods are sold on four, six, eight and ten months' credit to jobbers in the city, who sell them again to merchants in the country, upon perhaps equally long credits. All these sales are founded upon money, and yet all these agreements are made without any use of the material substance of the money. The material substance is not necessary in making these sales. In running accounts at stores, the goods are extended, summed up, and the amount is a balance against the debtor of so much money: but not the labor of the debtor nor any product of labor has legal authority to pay this balance. There is a certain amount of *money* due, which the creditor can force the debtor to pay, no matter how much the latter may have to sacrifice, of his labor or products in market in order to exchange them for money. Yet in incurring the indebtedness, not a penny of the material substance of money may have been used. It is simply the legal authority and power of money which are used in making all these obligations and agreements; but in order to pay these debts money must be had in its material form.

It is obvious that all agreements for the sale of property and labor are founded upon money, and that no price could be fixed upon any property or labor without first having a standard of value. When this standard is established, it is not a matter of choice but of necessity that the people use it in all business transactions. If individuals barter one kind of property for another, they fix a price for each kind of property, and they must use the power of money in order to estimate the value, so that even in a barter, where not a dollar of the material substance of money is present, its power is used; and the balance may be adjusted by the addition of more property on one side or the substitution of less on the other; but if a balance be left unsettled, the creditor can compel the debtor to pay it in money.

Again, the banks in the city of New York publish weekly statements of the amount under discount, the amount of specie on hand, of money on deposit, and of bank-notes in circulation. These weekly statements are given under oath of the officers of the banks, and the people suppose there is actually so much money deposited in the banks belonging to depositors. Now, are these deposits all money? If they are, the power of money is not in its material substance, for all the specie and all the bank-notes held by the banks would not, in ordinary times, pay even one-half of these deposits as reported. Then in what does the other half consist? It consists in a mere balance of accounts; and if these balances are money, it follows that the power of money is not in its material substance. But this power has the ability to call for the material substance to satisfy its requirements. Let the banks in the city of New York curtail their discounts, so that they shall not exceed the actual amount of their specie and the bank-notes which they have received from the Comptroller, and it would paralyze the business of the nation, and make a far more ruinous crisis than that of 1837, or the one of 1857. The property and labor of the country would sink into insignificance before this overwhelming power of money. The usurers would get almost any price they chose to charge for the use of money, and thus monopolize the great wealth of the nation without even lifting their hands in any productive labor. Under our present monetary laws the people would be compelled to submit to these extortions; for the money has the legal power, but property and labor have no legal authority over the money. The holder of a mortgage for $1,000 on property worth $50,000, if the mortgagor could not pay the money, might buy in the property worth $50,000 for even $100, and enter up a judgment against his debtor for $900. A debtor placed in these circumstances would doubtless try his best to borrow the $1,000, even if he had to pay one or two per cent. a day, in order to prevent this great sacrifice of his property, and in the hope that there would be more ease in the money market. This endowment of money with an immaterial, omnipresent power, which can be, and is, used to any extent without the presence of the material substance, and this immaterial power having the legal right to call for money in its material form to fulfil its requirements and satisfy its demands, when the government has neglected to provide the necessary material substance, is a gross outrage upon the rights of the people.

 A certain amount of money is required to fulfil the business engagements of a nation. If one-fourth of that amount be withheld from circulation, one-fourth of the contracts must remain unpaid. A high price charged for the remaining three-fourths, will not enable them to supply the place of the absent one-fourth, which is indispensable to the prosperity of business. No country can be prosperous, while capitalists can cause a scarcity of money. Their legal right to withdraw their money from circulation cannot be denied; but the exercise of this right should not operate to the injury of others. Some public means must be devised whereby the requisite amount of money for the people may always be supplied, at the legal rate of interest. No government should make a currency of a material of which it cannot supply a quantity adequate to the wants of the people, for it cannot be necessary to have a representative of value scarce so long as there is an abundance of actual value susceptible of representation. It will be hereafter shown, that in all sections of the country, a certain part of the actual value of the property may be so represented by money as to supply an abundant, uniform and good currency, and that a rate of interest may be adopted and maintained, which will reward labor, and promote the public welfare.

CHAPTER VI.

THE NECESSITY OF CREDIT.

To credit is to trust our property, or the reward for our labor, in the hands of others for a limited time. Governments could not exist, nor legislative bodies meet, without credit. The members of Congress trust the Government to pay their travelling expenses, and the nation trusts the Government with funds for that purpose. We continually trust our fellow-men. The laborer who works by the day trusts his employer until evening for his wages. If the employer pay in advance, he trusts the laborer. Daily laborers are supposed to incur little risk by trusting their employers, but in the city of New York they have lost large amounts in this way. The clergyman trusts his parish for his salary; the teacher the parents of the children; colleges their students, etc., etc. Houses could not be rented without credit; the owner credits the tenant with the use of his property; the tenant may injure or destroy it. If it be insured, he trusts the insurance company to indemnify him for loss by fire. If the tenant pay rent in advance, the house may be burned, and he may lose his money. Banks could not exist without credit. The people credit the banks on their bank-notes, and the banks credit the people on their indorsed notes. The people, too, trust the banks with deposits. A very large proportion, at least ninety or ninety-five per cent. of the exchanges of productions, is made on a longer or shorter credit. All merchandise sent by manufacturers to commission merchants in our cities, is trusted in the hands of the latter. A very large proportion of this merchandise is sold on a credit of six or eight months to jobbers, and is then resold by them to retailers on credit, who again sell to consumers mostly on credit. Nearly all our internal improvements are contracted for on a certain time of credit. A considerable proportion of these contracts is paid for by borrowing money on mortgage of the improvements. Even goods sold for cash are usually delivered before payment. Except on an exceedingly limited scale, exchanges of productions could not be made without credit. Neither the General Government nor the State governments could raise money at home or abroad without it. Our country could never have achieved its independence without the money it obtained upon credit.

CHAPTER VII.

A WELL-REGULATED CURRENCY IMPOSSIBLE UNDER PRESENT LAWS.

Our whole banking system is based upon a credit given by law to bank-notes, for which the people furnish the security in their indorsed notes and State bonds. For the legal representative has no value in itself; it rests upon actual capital, the earth and its productions, and not upon the inherent value of its material. It may then be asked, why the State governments cannot bank on the same security, and appropriate the gains to the public benefit, instead of allowing a few individuals to acquire large fortunes by private banking. But bank-notes issued by a State would soon depreciate. The currency must be *national*, and pass equally well in all sections of the country. If a State should make paper money a tender (and this is forbidden by the Constitution), the money, like the money of the banks chartered by the States, must necessarily be redeemed with specie to secure public confidence. But this local redemption would make the money of unequal value in different sections of the Union. Another difficulty would be incurred by a State bank, that unless a few of the largest capitalists were included as stockholders, and the interest of the wealthiest men identified with the bank, it would soon be compelled to suspend payments.

A United States Bank could not regulate the currency. Before the General Government could establish the institution, it would be obliged to consult a few large capitalists to ascertain whether they would take the stock. If the charter were not one which would probably secure an income quite as good as any other investment, they would refuse the stock, and the Government could not establish the bank. If the Government should deem three per cent. a just rate of interest, and should limit the dividends at this rate, the stock would not be taken. But should it allow six per cent. interest, and leave the dividends unlimited, both native and European capitalists would call it a good investment for money, if they could retain sufficient control of the institution.

If under our present laws making all notes redeemable in specie, the General Government should establish a bank, and issue enough paper-money for all business transactions, at a low rate of interest, our large capitalists would array themselves against it by collecting their debts in bank-notes, and demanding specie from the bank. Such a bank, established on a specie basis, could not be sustained a month. The Government and all the producers could not prevent its total failure.

Monetary laws are the most important subjects for legislation. It is the duty of every national government to institute and regulate the medium of exchange; but that this duty has been imperfectly discharged, appears from the fact that where specie is made the only tender in payment of debts, neither the government nor the mass of the people have had or can have, any adequate control over it. Capitalists control the money, and through the money control the Government. The defect of the present monetary laws, further appears from the variations in the rates of interest on Government stocks, perfectly secured at all times, but constantly fluctuating in value. If the Government does not secure a uniform value to money for its own use, how can it be said to regulate the currency of the country.

It is impossible to secure to labor its earnings, under

systems by which the Government and the people depend upon a few capitalists to furnish the medium and standard for the distribution of the productions of labor. In the plan about to be developed, the whole people, through Congress, would hold the power, and fix the rate of interest. They can by a vote put the system in successful operation without consulting capitalists, banks or brokers.

RECAPITULATION.

In the foregoing chapters the following propositions have been considered, and, it is believed, fully sustained.

1. That there is an essential difference between intrinsic value and the value of money.

2. That any material may be made money, by endowing it with the following legal powers, namely, the powers to represent value, to measure value, to accumulate value by interest, and to exchange value.

3. That money which does not represent its full amount of actual value, carries upon its face a false pretence; nothing can in fact be money, that does not represent property.

4. That money, as a measure of value, is controlled by the rate per cent. interest that it bears.

5. That the necessary effects of the present rates of interest, are to accumulate property in large cities, and in the hands of a few capitalists.

6. That the present rates of interest greatly exceed the increase of wealth by natural production, and consequently, call for production beyond the ability of producers to supply.

7. That the rate per cent. interest determines what proportion of products shall be awarded to capital, and what to labor.

8. That in proportion as the rate per cent. on money is increased, the value of property and labor is decreased.

9. That a currency constantly fluctuating in value, by varying rates of interest, is no more suitable as a medium of exchange than an elastic yard-stick is fit for a measure of cloth; that justice requires uniformity of value, and that our present currency is devoid of this quality.

10. That our present banking system rests upon a fictitious basis, is unsafe, and is productive of many and

great injuries; and while it calls upon producers for a large sum of money to pay for the use of its bank-notes, at the legal rate of interest, it assists capitalists, brokers, etc., in monopolizing money, and enables them to extort large sums from merchants, mechanics and other, beyond the legal rate.

11. That the currency, to be of uniform value, must be limited only by the wants of business.

12. That credit is indispensable.

PART II.

A TRUE MONETARY SYSTEM.

CHAPTER I.

THE SECURITY OF A PAPER CURRENCY.

WE now enter upon the most important and yet the simplest part of this subject; namely, the institution of a true monetary system, by which the distribution of wealth can be properly regulated.

It has been proved in our foregoing arguments, that the amount of a currency should be equal to the wants of the people, and that gold and silver, of which the quantity is necessarily limited, are not the proper materials. It remains to be proved that a paper currency can be established, which shall be always adequate in amount, and which can be maintained at a uniform value. The present chapter will offer some considerations of the security and competence of a paper currency, as a medium of exchange.

First, we may notice some of the ways in which paper is now used, and in which a legal power expressed upon it is deemed sufficient security. All titles to land, all loans of money on bond and mortgage or otherwise, the payments for all lands, and for every other species of property on a credit, are secured by paper. These papers must, of course, be made legal liens upon property or they would be worthless, for their value must consist in their control of real property, and not in any worth inherent in their substance. Money, of every description, gold, silver and paper, is created by the laws, and its value consists in its being made by law a public lien upon all property for sale.

The difference between a private obligation, such as a mortgage, or note of an individual, and money, is, that the two former are private liens, one on a specific piece of property, the other on any or all the property of an individual; while money is a public lien on all property for sale, whether that property be owned by individuals or by the Government. Between individuals and the Government, the law secures the fulfilment of contracts by mortgages and other paper instruments. If paper instruments can be made safe representatives of property between two individuals, no good reason appears why paper instruments cannot be made safe representatives of property for any number of individuals. If paper instruments can be made representatives of property for limited periods of time, no good reason is perceived why they cannot be made safe representatives of property when made payable on demand. And if made payable on demand in something capable of producing an immediate income, they are then made competent to fulfil all the uses of money; for money can have no other use than to exchange for property, or to loan for an income.

Governments have falsely assumed that the value of money consists in the inherent worth of the gold, silver and copper materials out of which it has been coined. This is not only palpably a false assumption, but the laws of nations prove it to be so; for in nearly every civilized nation, the governments have authorized paper money (when secured by State and National stocks, bonds and mortgages, and so forth,) to be issued in the form of bank-notes and to circulate as money. England has made paper money a tender in payment of debts; and in other countries, where paper in the form of bank-notes is authorized to be used as money, although it is not a tender, it is generally received as such. Bank-notes are called money, although the laws do not make them a tender for debts. Banks are, however, chartered by law, and, therefore, the bank-notes issued by them are generally considered as money, and answer all its purposes. They are founded, or based on a promise to pay specie on demand. Let us see, however, if they are not practically money, instead of being merely representatives of gold and silver coins. A man exchanges at a bank in New York a hundred dollars in specie for a one hundred dollar bank-note, and takes it to the western country to buy land. The note is thus put in circulation there, is loaned and reloaned on interest, and is used in the purchase of property and products. It is continually active, while the silver for which the bank-note was taken in lieu, lies dead in the vault of the bank, and is neither used to purchase property or products, nor to fulfil contracts, nor to produce an income. The bank-note has performed all, while the specie has performed none of the functions of money. If the former should circulate for any number of years, and should be loaned for an income, and used to purchase property thousands of times, and when it was returned to New York, there should be no specie in the vault of the bank to redeem it, still, every purchase made by the bank-note would be valid, and every mortgage for which it had been received would be a binding lien upon the property of its drawer for the payment of specie both for the principal and the interest. Coins and bank-notes have a legal power to accumulate, not natural to either of them. Both are generally received in tender for debts, so that one is practically as much money as the other. In fact, if either is to be despoiled of its character as money, it must be the specie, for this is mostly deposited in the vaults of the banks, and while so deposited is not practically money; but the bank-notes which perform more than ninety-five hundredths of the exchanges, are really the money of the country, and fulfil all its uses with greater convenience and celerity than could gold and silver. Paper made to represent landed property instead of specie, and endowed with legal power to accumulate, measure, and exchange property would answer every purpose of money, and would be money.

The abundance of paper is not an objection to its use as the material of money, more than to its use for deeds, notes, bonds and mortgages. It would be a better material for money than gold and silver, for these metals are limited in amount, and are troublesome, expensive, and hazardous to remit. If a sufficient gold and silver currency were presented to this nation free of cost, the inconvenience and expense attending the circulation and transmission of the coins, would far overbalance the whole labor and expense to provide and circulate a paper currency.

The question to be settled then, is this; can a currency be formed entirely of paper, which will buy the productions of labor as readily as gold and silver coins—not whether a silver spoon can be made out of a paper dollar, or whether a gold watch-case can be made out of a ten dollar bank bill as well as it could be out of an eagle We do not want money to make utensils and ornaments. We want money for a medium of exchange, to buy such articles as are useful to us, and if it cannot be made of paper so that it will be as good to the man who sells his labor or his products as gold and silver coins, we must not have a paper currency.

CHAPTER II.

THE SAFETY FUND.

SECTION I.

THE FORMATION OF MONEY, AND THE MODE OF ISSUE.

THE Constitution declares, Art. I., Sec. VIII., 5, "That the Congress shall have the power to coin money, regulate the value thereof, and of foreign coin, and fix the standard of weights and measures." Sec. X., I., "No State shall coin money, emit bills of credit, make anything but gold and silver a tender in payment of debts." It is clear that Congress has the Constitutional right to coin money, and regulate its value; to emit bills of credit, and to make anything it chooses a tender in payment of debts. This reserved right makes it the duty of the General Government to provide the money of the nation; and it is, accordingly, bound to make money in quantities adequate to the wants of business, and to institute it in a way which will secure the effectual regulation of its value. The Constitution as plainly calls for the exercise of the Federal power for this purpose, as for the fixing of the standards of weights and measures. Sec. X., I., declares that the States have no right to coin money, emit bills of credit, or make anything but gold and silver a tender in payment of debts. Bank bills are bills of credit, and very hazardous ones too; for millions of them are issued without being representatives of property, and many holders have sustained great losses by their failure. According to the Constitution, the State governments have no right to establish banks, and impose this hazard and loss upon the people; they have infringed the province of the General Government. Having themselves no Constitutional right to issue bills of credit, they can certainly have no power to delegate such right to others.

In the plan we are about to propose for the formation of a National Currency by the General Government, all the money circulated in the United States will be issued by a national institution, and will be a representative of actual property, therefore it can never fail to be a good and safe tender in payment of debts. It will be loaned to individuals in every State, county, and town, at a uniform rate of interest, and hence will be of invariable value throughout the Union. All persons who offer good and permanent security will be at all times supplied with money, and for any term of years during which they will regularly pay the interest. Therefore, no town, county, or State, need be dependent upon any other for money, because each has real property enough to secure many times the amount which it will require. If more than the necessary amount of money be issued, the surplus will be immediately funded, and go out of use without injury. It will be impossible for foreign nations, or any number of banks, or capitalists, to derange the monetary system, either by changing the rate of interest, or by inducing a scarcity or a surplus of money. It will be the duty of the Government to ascertain as nearly as possible what rate of interest will secure to labor and capital their respective rights, and to fix the interest at that rate.

The plan requires the General Government to establish an institution, with one or more branches in each State. This institution may appropriately be called the NATIONAL

SAFETY FUND: first, because the money of this institution will constitute a legal tender of uniform value for the whole people, and will always be safe; second, because the interest being fixed at a just rate it will secure the respective rights of labor and capital; and third, the supply of money being always commensurate with the wants of business, it will effectually protect the nation from financial revulsions.

To make this currency a true representative of property, the Safety Fund must issue its money only in exchange for mortgages secured by double the amount of productive landed estate. The money ought not to be issued on perishable property, nor on the credit of individuals, because such property might be destroyed, or the individuals become bankrupt, when the money would cease to be a representative and become worthless, except for the guarantee of the Government, and the loss would fall upon the nation. The money, then, when put in circulation, will represent and be secured by the first half of productive property, and the interest upon the mortgages will be secured by a portion of the yearly products or income of the property. The Safety Fund will issue its money, bearing no interest, for the mortgages bearing interest. We have shown that money to maintain its value must not only represent property, but must always be capable of being loaned for a uniform income. It is therefore necessary to provide not only for the issue, but also for the funding of the money. No government can regulate the value of money unless it provide means for funding it; this being the only way in which the interest upon it can be kept uniform.

The first of the following obligations will be the money of the institution; the second will be a note bearing interest for the funding of the money:

No. ——   MONEY.   *Dated* ——

$500. $500.

The United States will pay to the bearer five hundred dollars in a Safety Fund Note, on demand, at the Safety Fund Office in the city of ——————

No. ——.   SAFETY FUND NOTE.   *Dated* ——

$500 $500

One year from the first day of May next, or at any time thereafter, the United States will pay to A. B., or order, in the city of —————— *five hundred dollars; and, until such payment is made, will pay interest thereon on the first day of May in each year, at the rate of one per cent. per annum.*

The money will bear no interest, but may always be exchanged for the Safety Fund Notes, which will bear interest. Those who may not wish to purchase property or pay debts with their money, can always loan it to the Institution for a Safety Fund Note, bearing an interest of one per cent. per annum. Therefore the money will always be good; for it will be the legal tender for debts and property, and can always be invested to produce an income.

The money being loaned at one and one-tenth per cent., and the Safety Fund Notes bearing but one per cent., the difference of one-tenth per cent. in the interest will induce owners of money to lend to individuals, and thus prevent continual issuing and funding of money by the Institution.

The Safety Fund Notes are made payable a year after date, to prevent the unnecessary trouble of funding money for short periods. It is not probable that the Institution will issue Notes for a less amount than $500. People having small amounts will seldom wish to fund them. They will loan to individuals or purchase property. If, however, it be deemed desirable to fund small amounts, they may be received, and credited in a small book, as in savings banks, and the interest paid upon these credits as upon Safety Fund Notes.

Having given an outline and brief explanation of the proposed system of currency, we will proceed to show that the money issued by the Safety Fund will possess all the properties, and be capable of performing all the functions of money. We have said in our description of money that it must be a representative of property. The Safety Fund money being based on productive landed estate to double its amount, will be an undoubted representative of property. Second, money must have power to accumulate. The provision made by the Safety Fund for funding the money will secure an income beyond all contingency. Third, it must have power to measure value. The Safety Fund money will not only possess this power equally with coins, but it will possess the additional quality of being a uniform and perfect measure. By establishing a uniform rate of interest, the dollar will be of invariable value, and cannot be made to fluctuate more in the measure of property than the yard-stick in the measure of cloth. Fourth, it must have power to exchange value. Being instituted by the General Government as the legal tender, and its income power established, all persons will be compelled to receive it in exchange for property and labor. We have elsewhere shown that any portable substance possessing these properties will be money. The Safety Fund money will possess all the properties adapted to its use as money that belong to coins, and can be counted and carried with greater convenience, and can be more easily transmitted from one section of the country to another. The effect of its adoption will be to annihilate all difference of exchange between different commercial points, or to reduce it to the merely nominal expense of letter postage.

SECTION II.

THE SECURITY OF THE SAFETY FUND MONEY.

It will be perceived that since the rate of interest on the money will always be uniform, and loans can always be obtained from the Safety Fund on productive property, it will be impossible to induce a financial crisis, and depreciate the value of the property on which the money is issued, so that it would not be good for the interest. Therefore the mortgages will always be ample security for the loans of the Safety Fund; and the money will always be a fair equivalent for property and labor, because it will always truly represent their value. For, if the money can be loaned for a per centage interest which will buy a certain portion of the yearly products of land and labor, the legal value of the principal of the money will be equal to the actual value of so much land as will produce what the interest will purchase. When Branches are established in all the States, every individual can borrow money, at the usual rate of interest, to the amount of half the value of his productive land. Every dollar thus borrowed will be added to the amount in circulation, as much as if it had been imported from a foreign country or coined. The Safety Fund will actually create all its money.

It will require a very small proportion of the property of the country to secure a sufficient currency. The property in Massachusetts, according to the assessed valuation in 1840, averaged $406 50 to each individual. The average wealth in property of our whole population is from three to five hundred dollars. The amount of money needed will not, probably, exceed ten or fifteen dollars for each inhabitant. Therefore, only three or four per cent. of the property of the country will be necessary to secure an ample supply of money. The Government can in this way provide a portable legal value to any extent that may be required. The people can borrow money from the Safety Fund in larger or smaller sums at precisely the same rate of interest.

The mortgages may be drawn payable one year after date, with one and one-tenth per cent. interest; and so long as this interest shall be regularly paid, the principal may remain, in whole or in part, at the option of the mortgagor. So, whenever a mortgagor shall have the means, he can pay off any part of the mortgage, and stop the interest. But he will never be compelled to pay the principal so long as the interest shall be regularly paid.

No aid from large capitalists will be required to establish the Safety Fund, for the money will be made a balance against the landed estate of the people, without a specie basis. It is no more necessary to make money of gold and silver to render it a just balance against property, than to make a mortgage of gold or silver to render it of equal value with a piece of land. The value of the mortgage depends upon its legal power over the land and its products. The Safety Fund money will have a legal representative value which will be capable of purchasing the mortgage, or the land, or the products of the land. The mortgage, or the money as such, can be no more valuable made of gold than of paper. As paper mortgages amply secure individual loans of money, so paper mortgages will secure the money issued by the Safety Fund. If people will readily loan gold and silver coins for paper mortgages on property, they must esteem the paper mortgages as valuable as the coins. A mortgage is a lien upon a specific piece of property. The Safety Fund money will be a general lien upon all property for sale, and a legal tender in payment for all debts. The mortgages given to the Safety Fund will be individual obligations for the payment of money, and will be necessarily local. But the money issued for them will be neither individual nor local. It will be equally good in Maine, New York, Ohio, and Florida. If its owner does not wish to lend it to individuals, he can lend it to any Branch of the Safety Fund at an interest of one per cent.

It has already been stated that it is no more necessary to make money of gold and silver in order to make it good, than to make a bond or note on a silver or gold plate in order to make it good. Still, if the people shall insist upon a mixture of specie in the currency, it can be easily provided. It will only be necessary that the interest to be received and paid by the Safety Fund shall be paid in specie. By loaning money at one and one-tenth per cent., the Fund will always be in receipt of many times the interest in specie that it can be called upon to pay. This will preserve the use of coins as money. It appears evident, however, that the money of the Safety Fund will fulfil all the functions of a public medium of exchange without any admixture of coins.

The Safety Fund money will probably be compared by some to the assignats of France, or to the Continental money issued by the United States during the Revolution. But they are no more alike than a good productive soil and a desert. There is as much difference between the paper assignats issued by France and the paper money to be issued by the Safety Fund, as between two perpetual mortgages, one bearing interest, and the other bearing no interest; the first would be good, the second worthless. If, as heretofore stated, the French Government had secured the payment of the assignats issued to her citizens by mortgages on productive landed estate, not exceeding half its value, and when payment was demanded had funded them with government bonds bearing a yearly interest, they must have continued good. Both the mortgages and the assignats would have been representatives of property, and the yearly productions of the land would have secured the annual interest, and made them safe. The assignats became worthless because they were not representatives of property. If the Government of the United States, instead of issuing the Continental money, had established a Safety Fund, and had lent money for mortgages on productive land worth double the amount of the loan, and had provided notes bearing interest to fund the money, such paper money would have been a representative of property, and invariably good. The Continental money not being a representative of property, of course proved worthless. Had our Government instituted a Safety Fund, it would have had an abundance of money for the transaction of all business; we should have saved the many millions we paid to France for a representative of our own property, and besides, should have prevented the great injury suffered by the country from the scarcity of money and high rates of interest, which then so much retarded business and production.

The objection may arise that if the loans of the Safety Fund be confined to the owners of land, it will place in their hands a great monopolizing power, and instead of diffusing wealth in accordance with the labor performed, will give it to the landholders. But a little reflection will make it evident that the abundant supply of money and the reduction of the rate of interest will be of equal benefit to those who are without property, and depend on their daily labor for their support. The owners of land will obtain loans from the Fund, either to purchase property, or to discharge debts, or to pay for labor; and all the money borrowed for these purposes will go into circulation, and be used by others. The owners of land will not borrow money to keep, for they would lose the interest on it, and be paying interest on their mortgages to the Safety Fund. Every farmer owing money on mortgage of his farm, and paying seven per cent. interest, will probably borrow money from the Safety Fund and pay the debt. The difference between seven and one and one-tenth per cent. on his mortgage will be in favor of the earnings of his own, or others' labor on his farm; the interest will absorb but a comparatively small proportion of the products. The receiver of the payment for the mortgage cannot obtain a higher rate of interest than that charged by the Fund: he must either purchase property with the money, or lend it to individuals at one and one-tenth per cent., or to the Safety Fund at one per cent. interest. If he finds that he can rent out land to others for a term of years so as to secure one and one-tenth, or one and one-quarter per cent. interest, of course he will purchase the land in preference to funding the money; and the laborers who can have the use of land at these low rents, will soon lay up the means to buy farms for themselves.*

SECTION III.

THE RATE OF INTEREST ON THE SAFETY FUND MONEY.

The law granting to all the privilege of lending money at the same rate, has an apparent fairness which is de-

---

* If a laborer who had no property to be represented except his power to labor, could borrow money from the Safety Fund, and his power to labor should fail by sickness or death, the Safety Fund would still be bound to redeem this money with a Safety Fund Note bearing interest, and this loss would fall upon the people. (See Appendix, H.)

ceptive. The fairness depends upon the justice of the rate of interest, and not upon the universality of the grant.

The illustration of the one hundred families clearly shows the accumulative power of money at six per cent. interest, (see Part I., Chap. III., Sec. II.) The same chapter shows this power at various rates, from seven down to one per cent. The Safety Fund can maintain any rate of interest which shall be deemed for the public good If it lend money at six per cent., and fund at the same rate, there will be an abundant supply at a uniform interest in all parts of the country; this currency will therefore be greatly superior to any that has ever been in use. If $300,000,000 be required, and the interest be at six per cent., the Government will gain a revenue of $18,000,000 annually, less the expenses of the Institution. If the Branches be made offices of discount and deposit, and the deposits be reloaned, the gains will probably be doubled, and amount to say $36,000,000. There is hardly a doubt that this latter or a larger sum is annually paid by the producers to the banks for the use of banknotes. It will certainly be more just for the Government to gain this for the general benefit, than to have the banks gain it for their private purposes.

But a rate of interest that will rapidly concentrate the wealth of the nation into the hands of the Government or of individuals, cannot be just. The Government cannot institute money and lend it at six per cent., without giving power to individuals to lend at the same rate, and the loans of the latter will be much greater in amount than those of the Fund, even if its Branches should be made offices of discount and deposit. Besides, as has been already shown, money is a standard, and the rate of interest governs the per centage rent on all property. No way can be devised of establishing a high rate of interest, and doing justice to producers. The evidence adduced in this volume upon the different rates of interest, appears sufficient to prove that one and one-tenth per cent. is as high a rate of interest as money can bear, and secure the rights of producers. Money at this rate will have power to buy property; for in England it has often been lent even at lower rates, after business had been paralyzed by maintaining interest at exorbitantly high rates.

Money is national in its character, and ought therefore to be authorized only by the General Government. The Government should never allow any money to circulate that is not permanently safe and good, and a legal tender in payment of debts. The money should be a just legal equivalent in exchange for labor and property, and at par value in every section of the country. To be thus a fair equivalent of uniform value throughout the country, the rate of interest must be made just and uniform; and it is, therefore, of the first importance to arrive, as nearly as possible, at what would be a just rate per cent. interest. As money is designed for public use, and is not in itself a producing power, we think the interest on the money should not only be sufficient to pay for the necessary material and labor to manufacture the money, but also for the necessary labor of loaning it, as well as for the safe keeping of any money that might remain on hand unused. Whatever rate per cent. interest would be required to defray the necessary expenses of furnishing and issuing a full supply of money for the use of the public, should be the established legal rate of interest, at which all subsequent owners of the money might lend it. The first borrowers of the money would directly pay it over to others to cancel debts, or to pay for property and products. Hence they would seldom be subsequent owners and lenders of the money, because if money should afterward come into their hands, they would be more likely to pay off their own debts, and stop the interest, than to lend the money on interest, and still continue to pay interest on their obligations.

If it should take $500,000,000 of the new currency to supply this nation with money, and the rate of interest should be fixed at one and one-tenth per cent., the income from the Safety Fund would be $5,500,000. If it should take $600,000,000, it would make an income of $6,600,000. At all events, we think this rate of interest would be sufficient to supply the material for making the money, and pay for the labor; as well as to pay the officers and clerks employed in the principal Institution and in the various Branches of the Safety Fund. A just rate of interest would be one that would supply the money and keep the Safety Fund in operation. Thus the Safety Fund would be a self-supporting institution. No good reason can be shown why the interest should be greater than is necessary to furnish the money and keep in operation the means of supplying it.

There is as great a difference in their effects between a well regulated currency with a low rate of interest that will justly distribute productions, and a currency with high and fluctuating rates, as between the fire limited to the domestic hearth, subserving the wants of the household, and the same element exceeding its useful limits, and destroying the house. Steam kept within proper bounds is usefully employed in facilitating production, but increased beyond these, it becomes a powerful agent in destroying life and property. Money with the interest kept within proper limits, will distribute the production rightfully to the producers; but increased interest will deprive them of their rights, and entail upon them poverty and misery

SECTION IV.

ORGANIZATION AND MANAGEMENT OF THE SAFETY FUND.

The Safety Fund may consist of a Principal Institution with Branches. The first may be located at Washington, or some other central town, and the latter wherever convenience may require. The Principal Institution should issue money only to the Branches, and they should be required to make weekly reports to the Principal of their loans, and also of the money returned to be funded. The Principal, at certain times, should report the money in circulation.

For the management of the Principal, one director may be appointed by each State, and one or more by the General Government.

The States may elect the directors of the Branches by Congressional Districts, or otherwise.

The directors should receive salaries for their services, and should not be allowed to borrow money from the Institution, nor be interested in any of its loans. They may hold their offices during good behavior, or until a certain age. All officers and clerks may be required to give bonds, with such securities as may be deemed necessary to secure fidelity and safety.

All money loaned may be paid, in whole or in part, at the option of the borrower after one year, but the interest should be punctually paid.

In case of failure for a certain time to pay the interest, the directors might advertise the property covered by the mortgage, and sell it at auction, giving the debtor timely notice of such advertisement and sale.

Twenty-one different denominations of money will form an ample currency: viz., Three Cents; Four Cents; Five Cents; Ten Cents; Twenty-five Cents; Fifty

Cents; One Dollar; Two Dollars; Three Dollars; Five Dollars; Ten Dollars; Twenty Dollars; Fifty Dollars; One Hundred Dollars; Two Hundred Dollars; Three Hundred Dollars; Five Hundred Dollars; One Thousand Dollars; Two Thousand Dollars; Three Thousand Dollars; Five Thousand Dollars. With these denominations of money any change can be made to a cent.

Our present bank-notes are frequently altered from one denomination to another; as, for instance, by extracting "Two" and inserting "Ten." Against this fraud the money of the Safety Fund may be effectually guarded, by making the size of the paper conform to the denominations. The value of each piece will then be known at a glance by its size, as well as by the engraving. The three cent pieces may be made an inch and a half long and an inch wide; and the size may be increased for each successive higher denomination by adding a quarter of an inch to the width and half an inch to the length. The different denominations may also be of different plates as well as of different sizes.

The people throughout the country will soon become familiar with the money, and there will be little danger of deception by counterfeits.

The paper for the money and Notes may be manufactured by the principal Safety Fund, and farther guarded from counterfeit by water marks, and by the kind and quality of the paper, which should be of the best material for durability.

In preparing the money for circulation no necessity will exist for the signatures of the president and cashier, more than for such signatures on coins. Proper care in regard to the material and making of the paper, and the engraving of the plates, etc., will guard the money against counterfeits more effectually than the quality and coinage of the precious metals can protect coins.

A simple and short form of a mortgage may be provided, so drawn as to save the necessity of a bond, and prevent a multiplicity of papers. With ordinary care in the institution and direction of the Safety Fund, there will be incomparably less danger of frauds than now exists in banks.

The money for the amounts under a dollar will probably be called by the opposers of the Safety Fund, shinplasters, rag-money, a very unsafe currency for laborers, etc., but every one of these small notes will be a representative of its nominal amount of property. They will maintain their relative value to every other piece of money in every section of the country, and will soon be esteemed far preferable to the small silver and copper coins now in use.

SECTION V.

THE PROBABLE AMOUNT OF THE SAFETY FUND MONEY.

The quantity of money used in business is very small compared with the amount of business transacted, for it is only the average balance kept on hand. If a man receive $10,000, keep it one hour, and then pay it out, he uses the money only one hour. A man may be worth half a million of dollars and transact a business of a million a year, and yet his average balance may not exceed five thousand dollars. If he deposits his money in bank, the bank makes an estimate of his balance and lends it to others; so that even this balance is constantly in use.

The amount of money used compared with the contracts fulfilled by it, is not much greater than the number of bushels used compared with the bushels of grain measured by them. The amount which can be kept in active circulation is comparatively small. If the Safety Fund be established, and loan at an interest of one and one-tenth per cent. on all good security, money will circulate rapidly; and if all other money be swept from the country, it is doubtful whether the Safety Fund can keep out a sum exceeding from twelve to fifteen dollars for each inhabitant. Estimate the population of the United States at thirty millions, and $15 to each inhabitant will amount to $450,000,000. Allow this sum to change hands four times a week, and it will cancel $1,800,000,000 of debts each week, and in one year $93,600,000,000. The assessed value of all real and personal property in the United States in 1860, was $16,000,000,000. The $450,000,000 passing four times a week, will in one year pay for nearly six times the assessed value of the whole property of the nation. It is not intended that the Safety Fund and its Branches shall be made offices of discount and deposit. If they should be made such, they would more than double the amount of their loans; but the increase of loans would not augment the amount of money. They would lend the money left on deposit, and thus increase their income, as banks now lend their deposits and gain the interest.*

* With the Safety Fund money, if fifty millions were hoarded and withdrawn from circulation, the amount could be at once supplied; and it would not in the least disturb the regular interest or the value of the money. The Fund would still receive the interest on the fifty millions; and those who hoarded it would lose the interest, and could gain no advantage over others by again laying out the money, because their hoarding would not have made money any less plenty, and when they put it again in use, it would not in the least alter the rate of interest, but would find its way to the Safety Fund, and pay a debt due to the institution, or it would be loaned to the Fund for a Safety Fund Note bearing interest. When money is hoarded it is taken out of use, and it is, therefore, as necessary to supply the amount thus withdrawn as if it did not exist, for it is of no use to the public so long as it is hoarded. The Safety Fund would be as independent of capitalists as of laborers; nor could the Rothschilds with the aid of the Bank of England affect our money or disturb the business of the nation. (See Appendix I.)

CHAPTER III.

THE ADVANTAGES OF THE SAFETY FUND MONEY OVER SPECIE.

The following illustrations will show the different effects of a specie and a paper currency upon the prosperity of countries having materials for the formation of either. Suppose two fertile islands to exist, each containing a silver mine as productive as the average of those now worked. Two parties, of a hundred thousand settlers each, emigrate to these islands, taking with them implements of husbandry, a stock of cattle, merchandise, tools, etc., and provisions for a year, in procuring which they nearly exhaust their money. Arrived at their respective destinations, they locate their lands, etc., and each party begins to make exchanges among its members. The want of money is soon severely felt. The inhabitants of one island determine to have a metal currency, and accordingly prepare to work their silver mine. One-fifth of the whole population, *i. e.*, twenty thousand, are men capable of labor. Three thousand engage in working the mine, and with their families constitute a population of fifteen thousand, who consume the products of others. Suppose each man to earn or make half a dollar a day; total in a year four hundred and fifty thousand dollars. This sum being exchanged by the miners for food, clothing, etc., goes into immediate circulation. It will require nearly three years to supply the money necessary for their internal exchanges, say $12 for each inhabitant, *i. e.*, $1,200,000; and during this period money must be very scarce. The shipment of any specie abroad to pay for goods, will increase the want of money at home. Suppose the population to increase three per cent., that is, three thousand a year, they must continue to mine $36,000 yearly, to maintain the proportion of $12 to each individual.

The inhabitants of the other island determine not to work their silver mine, but to establish a Safety Fund, and lend the paper money as heretofore stated. All have the opportunity to borrow to one-half the value of their productive land. This money costs nothing but the comparatively trifling labor of the paper and engraving. If a surplus be in circulation, its owner can at any time pay off a mortgage to the Fund and stop the interest, or fund the money and receive interest. The exact amount required will always be in circulation, and the interest being regular, the value of the money will be invariable.

The difference between the labor to mine and coin the silver money, and the labor to make and engrave the paper money, will be a clear saving to the island using the paper money; and all this difference of labor can be applied to the production of articles for export. The island using the paper money can export about as great an amount of products as the other island will coin in money. If the latter island require the products of the former, and exchange coins for them, the former island will use the silver money for manufactures, or for export; it cannot need them for money. If the Fund lend at one and one-tenth per cent. interest, the island will always have an abundance of money at a low and uniform rate, so that every branch of industry can be carried on to the best advantage, and the property will be distributed to those whose labor shall earn it. But the business and productive industry of the island using coins will be constantly retarded for want of money, and the high and fluctuating rates of interest will inevitably concentrate the wealth in the hands of a few capitalists, and leave the producers in poverty. The people of the island using the paper currency will be rich, virtuous, and happy, while those using the silver money will be poor, wicked, and miserable, because poverty and avarice will lead to crime. If the two islands, instead of trading with each other, maintain trade with other nations, it must be obvious that the one using the paper money will have a great advantage over the one using the silver money.

Suppose the same number of emigrants to settle on a third island, and borrow their whole currency of a foreign nation, say $1,000,000 in gold, silver, or paper money, at an interest of eight per cent. per annum, payable half yearly. If their imports equal their exports, and they be obliged to issue bonds every six months at eight per cent. to pay the interest, in fifty-three years the island will become indebted to foreign nations $64,000,000; $63,000,000 of which will be interest on the $1,000,000 originally borrowed. The people must lose this amount in consequence of defective legislation. If the emigrants through their government establish a Safety Fund, and provide their own currency, instead of importing it, they will save the whole interest, besides having great advantages by the abundance of money.

Paper money can be as easily made to exceed coins in value, as coins to exceed paper money, because the value of all money is governed by the per centage interest. Let the Safety Fund lend paper money, and fund it with Safety Fund Notes bearing six per cent.; let it lend coins, and fund them with Safety Fund Notes bearing but four per cent., and the paper money will always be the more valuable, and command a premium in exchange for the coins. The paper money will as certainly command a premium above the coins, as a ground rent at six per cent. will command more than one at four per cent. If this nation had a sufficient quantity of specie for a currency, it would still be necessary to have an institution similar to the Safety Fund; for the interest upon it could only be kept regular by the establishment of an institution to make loans at a uniform rate of interest whenever good security was offered, and to fund the specie whenever it was redundant.

A government may obtain an immense power over the property of the people by furnishing a paper currency at six per cent. interest. Suppose our Government to establish a Safety Fund, and make its paper money the only tender in payment of debts. Let the Safety Fund lend an amount equal to say $15 to each inhabitant for a population of 20,000,000, that is, $300,000,000, and money would become plenty. This sum lent on double its amount of landed estate, would cover $600,000,000 worth of property. If the Government should leave the principal outstanding during the regular payment of the interest, it would receive from the interest, after deducting say $1,000,000 for the expenses of the Safety Fund, an annual revenue of $17,000,000. After a year or two let the Fund refuse to make further loans, and yearly collect its net gain of $17,000,000 for ten years, *i. e.*, $170,000,000, and the whole business of the nation must be transacted with the remaining $130,000,000. This would cause a great sacrifice of the mortgaged property and greatly depress the price of other lands and products. In six years more, the Government would collect in $102,000,000 additional interest, thereby reducing the currency to $28,000,000. The interest for two years more would amount to $34,000,000, but only $28,000,000 could be paid, because the whole amount of money would be exhausted. By foreclosing its mortgages, the Government could buy the $600,000,000 worth of property for the $6,000,000 which would still be due. Hence it is evident that the law has power to make paper money control property as effectually as gold and silver coins.

CHAPTER IV.

OBJECTIONS TO THE SAFETY FUND CONSIDERED.

SECTION I.

OBJECTIONS TO A PAPER CURRENCY ON ACCOUNT OF FOREIGN TRADE CONSIDERED.

When the adoption of a paper currency within our own limits is advocated, questions arise concerning the adjustment of our debts with foreign nations, among whom gold and silver are the only legal tender. Great embarrassments are apprehended because our paper money would not be received in payment of debts contracted and payable abroad.

The exports and imports of the United States are nearly equal; probably our whole exports do not amount to more than a twentieth part, or five per cent. of the yearly productions of our labor. Certainly the disposal of five per cent. of our productions is not a sufficient reason for maintaining a metal basis for our currency, which must inevitably affect the market value, and disturb the regular and just distribution among ourselves of ninety-five per cent. of our productions. The chief object of a currency is to effect the internal exchanges of products with facility and justice. Such a one could not impair foreign trade, nor do injustice to other nations. The following illustrations will make it evident that the use of a paper currency at home, instead of disturbing foreign trade would greatly facilitate it. Trade between nations is carried on by individuals, and not by governments. The governments simply make the laws, and fix the standards by which the value, weight and quantity of articles of trade are to be determined, as also the tariffs of duties on imports and exports. Individuals, then, export or import goods as their interests dictate, and receive for them the money in use where the goods are sold. For instance, importers of goods for the New York market, take in payment for their sales the money current in the city. They do this when the banks pay specie. They did the same in 1837, when the banks had suspended specie payments. If they must remit the proceeds of the goods, they buy cotton, or other produce for shipment and sale abroad, or bills of exchange, or specie, as may best subserve their interest. English exporters to New York receive in payment for their goods our current money, and invest the money as they deem most profitable. If we had none but paper money, English exporters to New York would sell their goods for our paper money, buying with the proceeds our products, cotton, flour, or tobacco, or bills of exchange on England, or bullion. Or, they could lend the money here as they now do and purchase products for shipment to England with the interest, or reloan the interest. If our paper money would buy our own calicoes and broadcloths, it certainly would buy English calicoes and broadcloths in our own market. There is no reason why we should provide a currency to pay for the products of foreign labor different from that which pays for home labor.

If we import fifteen millions more than we export, this balance will draw interest against us until we can pay it in specie or products. If State or United States stocks be sent abroad and sold to pay the debt, it is still a form of credit for which we must pay the interest. There is certainly no greater necessity for our Government to provide means for our merchants to pay their debts to foreign merchants, in such cases, than to provide means for southern merchants to pay their debts to eastern merchants, in cases of a partial failure of the cotton crop. When in any year southern merchants buy of eastern merchants more goods than their crops will pay for, the latter must wait for the next crop, meanwhile receiving interest on the amount due. If our Government maintains a currency which a balance of imports over exports demanding a shipment of specie must necessarily derange, and subject debtors to extravagant rates of interest, this legal act must cause greater loss to the people than the failure of the crops which would turn the balance of trade against them. The only embarrassment which could occur in our foreign trade, from the use of paper money, would be delays in payments when the exports should exceed the imports; and the occurrence even of this would be rendered much less probable by the use of paper money, at a low rate of interest, than it is with our banking system, and high rates of interest. The greater facilities afforded to production would yearly save an immense amount of imports; and the difference in the interest account between the United States and England, would save our people many millions of dollars every year.

If we had a sound paper currency, and did not depend on gold and silver, to make our internal exchanges, we could send all our gold and silver coins out of the country to adjust our foreign balances, without deranging our monetary affairs, or enabling foreign or native capitalists to embarrass the exchanges of our products among our selves. If we now have $50,000,000 * of coins, we could ship them, and cancel this amount of our debt to England, by paying our Government and State bonds, and thus save $3,000,000 interest, annually paid to the foreign holders of our bonds, for the use of a representative of our own property. The money, too, on which we pay this interest, goes mostly into the vaults of our banks, and lies there dead, while our bank-notes make the exchanges. It previously lay idle in the vault of the Bank of England, while the notes of that Bank performed the exchanges in England.

But suppose, upon its arrival here, every dollar of the specie should go into active circulation, what service would it render us? It would only assist us to effect our internal exchanges; we should still be obliged to make all our products by our labor, as much as if we had used our own paper money to make our exchanges. If the Bank of England should send $50,000,000 of her bank-notes to the United States, and our laws should make them a tender for debts, they would be no more useful to us than $50,000,000 of our own currency; and we should be compelled to pay to England $3,000,000 worth of our products yearly, in interest. If we sent the bonds of our Government to procure the notes of the Bank of England, or to procure the coins, the property of the United States would secure the money while it remained here. The money would become a representative of our property. Before it could again become a representative of the property of England, we should have to send back the $50,000,000 to England and take up our bonds. As long as the money remained here we should pay to England $3,000,000 yearly, in interest, because the bonds of our Government bear the interest, and not the money. Money is always a dead capital in the hands

---

* Written before the introduction of gold from California—[M. K. P.]

OBJECTIONS CONSIDERED. 299

of the holder. Even after its arrival here, every person who kept it a day, would keep it at the loss of the interest for that day, because money has no power of growth beyond that given by law, which is as impotent for actual production as the picture of a horse is to perform the labor of the horse. We might as well pay to England $3,000,000 yearly for a man to represent us in Congress, as to pay this sum for a representative of our property.

With a just monetary system, we should no more depend upon a foreign nation for money to represent our own property in our own country, than for the air we breathe. When we make our own property the basis of our currency, and furnish all the money we need for the exchange of our own products among ourselves, no foreign nation will have power to affect our money market, and derange the internal exchanges of our products, more than it could induce a scarcity of air, and thus disturb our breathing. No scarcity or abundance of money in foreign nations would affect our monetary system. Gold and silver coins would be imported only to convert into utensils and ornaments, or for re-exportation—these metals could never be needed for money. If a paper currency in this nation were properly instituted, it would become known in England, and it would be a thousand times more likely to be received there than our bank paper. But if it would not pass there at all, many advantages are to be anticipated from its adoption. Bills of exchange, on foreign nations, could be much more easily obtained than at present, because balances, under this system, would probably be in our favor. If our monetary system were such as always to supply the necessary quantity of money at a just and uniform rate of interest, so that production should never be impeded by a scarcity of money or high rates of interest, no one acquainted with the trade and resources of our country can doubt that the amount of our yearly productions would be increased several hundred millions of dollars. The greater the amount of our productions, the greater the amount that we should have to export, and the less we should need to import, and the balance of trade would necessarily be in our favor; and this balance we should be compelled to take in gold and silver, or leave on interest in foreign nations. The foregoing considerations make it evident that no unfavorable results are to be apprehended to our foreign trade from the adoption of a paper currency at home.

SECTION II.

SUNDRY OBJECTIONS—THE EFFECTS OF THE SAFETY FUND ON OUR BANKING INSTITUTIONS, ETC., CONSIDERED.

It may be well to examine a few more of the prominent objections which will be urged against the adoption of the Safety Fund. Our banking institutions will probably complain that its establishment will infringe the chartered rights granted to them by the States. But in instituting the Safety Fund, the General Government will not withdraw their charters, nor pass any law preventing them from banking. Doubtless it has the right to prohibit the issue of such bills of credit as bank-notes; but this will not be necessary. The Government will simply provide a means whereby the people in every section of the country can obtain a fair representative of their productive landed estate, at one and one-tenth per cent. interest, instead of being compelled to procure from banks and individuals an imperfect and unsafe representative of their property, and at six, seven, or eight per cent. interest; as much for the use of a representative as the crops of their land are worth.

It is a frequent remark that legal enactments have no more effect upon the value of money than upon the price of wheat, and that competition in lending money will equitably regulate the rate of interest. By establishing the Safety Fund to lend money at one and one-tenth per cent. to all who offer the required security, and not interfering with the chartered privileges of the banks, we shall ascertain whether legal enactments have any power, and the advocates of regulating the rate of interest by competition among the lenders of money, will also have an opportunity to test the correctness of their opinions.

Banks will object that they do business on a *specie* basis, and the Safety Fund on a *land* basis. It may be difficult to show that the former is better than the latter; for all kinds of money must be as useless without land and products to be exchanged, as yard-sticks with nothing to be measured. It will be fair towards the farmers, mechanics, and merchants, for the Government to institute a paper currency, and equally fair towards the banks; for their bank-notes are no more legally payable in specie than the indorsed and other notes, and even the book accounts of private citizens. If the Safety Fund money will be a safe medium of exchange for products, it will be a just equivalent to pay debts to banks, because the stockholders can buy products or land with it; therefore the issue of a tender based on landed estate cannot do injustice to our banking institutions.

The Safety Fund money being made the legal tender, the banks cannot refuse to receive it in payment of debts. They can easily and safely collect in their dues, withdraw their circulation, and wind up their business without causing a scarcity of money, or any panic in the money market. We shall then have nothing circulating as money which is not a legal tender. If the banks shall still deem their specie more valuable than the paper money of the Safety Fund, and in closing up their business shall not have as much specie to divide among the stockholders as they originally paid in, or if they shall have to pay the whole capital stock in Safety Fund money, still no injustice will be done to them, for the law making paper money a tender in payment of debts, gives to it a value equal to that possessed by gold and silver money regulated at the same rate of interest. While the establishment of the Safety Fund can do no wrong to the banks, it will greatly benefit those engaged in production and distribution.

Believers in the great intrinsic value of gold and silver coins, have nothing to apprehend from the adoption of paper money as a tender in payment of debts, and the reduction of interest. The institution of paper money, and the rejection of coins as a tender, can have no more effect on the intrinsic value of the precious metals, or upon the desire to possess them on account of this value, than the enactment of a law that wheat shall be transported only on horseback will alter the nutritious properties of the wheat, and the desire to use it for food. One would suppose that those who so highly prize gold and silver coins for their intrinsic value, would be strong advocates of paper money; the coins being released from their use as money, the gold and silver would easily and naturally fall into their hands. *

It may be objected that if money be made so plenty, the people will run into extravagant speculations; but a little thought will make it evident that the system will prevent great fluctuations in the price of property, and of course remove the inducements for speculations. †

---

* For thousands who are now compelled to have them to pay debts would not use them; and those who love them for their inherent value, could easily obtain them, and could keep them to look at for a lifetime without injury to others.

† See Appendix, J.

It may be objected that so great an alteration in the medium of exchange and measure of value, will derange and unsettle the value of property, introduce confusion into the various branches of business, and break down all existing relations between money and property. But in substituting a better for a worse, the means to effect the change must be improvements; and every stage, from the commencement to the entire exclusion of the present currency, will be a succession of benefits to the mass of the people. The change will only lessen the power of capital over the future productions of labor. It will deprive no man of the use of his property or money; both will be at his disposal as much as under the present monetary system.

Another objection will be the risk incurred by unfaithfulness in the officers appointed to manage the Institution Every institution must have officers, and a certain amount of power must necessarily be confided to them; consequently a risk of unfaithfulness must be incurred. But other circumstances being equal, the risk is greater or less, in proportion to the action of self-interest; and according to the plan of the Safety Fund, no officer will be allowed to borrow money from the Fund, nor to be interested in any of its loans. Bonds will also be required for the faithful discharge of duty. But, granting there may be risk, yet it will be almost nothing compared with that now incurred under the banking system, where the officers have their own interests to serve in various ways, and especially by increasing the rates of interest and using the funds of the banks for their private advantage.

It may also be objected to the Safety Fund, that it will lessen the incomes of widows and orphans; but there are very few of this class who have incomes. Objectors on this ground will therefore do well to extend their sympathy so as to embrace the nine-tenths whose only means of support is the scanty compensation for their daily and excessive toil, and whose condition, and the reward of whose labor, as well as the earnings of those who have incomes, will be greatly improved by the reduction of the interest on capital. Their sympathies will then lead them to advocate the Safety Fund, unless they are actuated by some other motive than commiseration for the needy.

The greatest difficulty, however, to be apprehended in the introduction of the new currency, will be found in the attachment of the people to ancient laws and customs, sanctioned by the greatest statesmen of the past, and ages of experience ;* but this feeling operates with the

---

* Is the fact that these unjust monetary laws have been in force from the earliest ages, and produced in every civilized nation their natural evil effects, any good reason for the continuance of such laws? Are evils any less evils because they are sanctioned by the laws of ages? On the contrary, do not the evils increase as countries grow older; and do not the wealth and power become more and more centralized, and the laboring classes more and more impoverished until oppression induces civil wars and the overthrow of governments? This has been the experience of nations for ages. There is now in every civilized nation a continual strife between capital and labor. Has there ever been a nation in which the wealth has centralized with more rapidity than during the last ten years in this free Republic? How can we expect to continue this centralizing power and yet ward off its evil effects? Common sense teaches, and experience proves, that like causes produce like effects; and if we persist in giving to money this unjust centralizing power, it will eventually seal the fate of this nation as it has that of other nations in past ages. People do not seem to consider that the laws of right existed before human laws were instituted, but seem to take it for granted that the institution of these monetary laws gives existence to justice and truth; and therefore all men are bound to look upon them with the same awe and submission as if they were founded upon the eternal principles of justice. But justice and truth are prior to all human laws; and these monetary laws are in direct opposition to every act of God's providence, and every just right of man; and are the most egregious national sin that was ever organized, or instituted, because the evil extends as far as these monetary laws extend, corrupting all contracts between man and man, and

same force in other things, and has been found to yield in favor of improvements introduced by the progress of discoveries in the arts and sciences. There needs only undoubted proof that an evil exists, and that a remedy can be applied for its removal, in order to secure the reformation. We have already shown that great evils have arisen from the unjust monetary laws of the past, and to our mind, conclusive proof has been offered to sustain this point. It is now incumbent on objectors to show, for instance, that the inhabitants of cities produce more for the people of the country than the latter produce for the former; that a man by standing on the corner of a street a few hours in a day to lend the legal representative of value to the necessitous at exorbitant rates of interest, produces more of the necessaries of life than a hundred industrious farmers and mechanics; that the yearly use of the present bank-notes in the State of New York is really worth as much to the people as the $4,435,333 worth of products which they are compelled to sell annually to pay the interest; or that one and one-tenth per cent. interest would secure to producers a greater proportion of the products of their labor than they are entitled to receive. If they can prove that the productiveness of land and labor is in proportion to the rate of interest, or that the public good requires that the wealth should be concentrated in a few hands, they will then have shown the superiority of our present monetary system. These are things of which farmers and mechanics and other producers can judge as well as any statesman or lawyer in the country. If scarcity of money and high rates of interest do not affect the market value of

between nation and nation, making the individuals who earn the wealth tributary to those who possess this monetary power; and even making one nation tributary to another that merely furnishes a representative of the wealth.

labor and products, let it be clearly shown to the producing classes. If such questions be evaded, it is but fair to infer that the advocates of existing monetary laws are willing or desirous that the oppression of the producers should be continued, and the people be kept ignorant of the causes of their poverty, instead of having the reward of their labor and their business transactions regulated by a standard which they will perceive to be just, and of which they can understand the operation.

It may be admitted that the theory of the Safety Fund is good, but impracticable at present; it is calculated for some future generation, when men shall have become more intelligent and virtuous. If the same faith shall be held by the generations which are to follow us, it will be difficult to point out at *what* period this desirable reformation will occur, because the evil of our present system will always be in the present, and the good of the plan proposed in the future. We are, however, persuaded that a large majority of the people are aware that their present depressed condition may and should be exchanged for something better, and the Safety Fund will be regarded by them as neither too Utopian nor visionary to be made immediately operative for their benefit. All the objections to the proposed currency, upon the ground that it will lessen the incomes of capitalists who are supported by the labor of others, only serve to show the true working of the Safety Fund system; for its object is to furnish a standard of distribution which will cause men to sustain such mutually just relations as to render it generally necessary for all to render an equivalent in useful labor for the labor received from others.

CHAPTER V.

ADVANTAGES OF THE SAFETY FUND.

The Safety Fund will lend money at a low rate of interest to all applicants furnishing the requisite landed security; hence every town, county, and State, which has the power to perform the necessary labor, can make internal improvements without pledging its property to large cities or to foreign nations to borrow money. A few years since, the high and fluctuating rates of interest so depressed the prices of products, that a number of the States were unable to pay the half-yearly interest due on their bonds; consequently, they fell to a very low price, and many of the holders suffered great losses, while large capitalists were enabled to take advantage of the fall, and to buy the bonds, in some instances, at less than one-fifth of their real value. The canal bonds of the State of Illinois were bought at from sixteen to thirty cents on the dollar. A short time after this, in 1845, the purchasers of these bonds made a negotiation with the State to furnish it with a further sum of money to complete the canal, on condition that a mortgage should be given to them on the canal and adjacent lands, securing the money so advanced, and also securing the par value of the bonds bought at these reduced rates, and the interest. It seemed as if the people thought this money would actually excavate the canal, quarry the stone, and build the locks. But when they had received the money, they were obliged to build the canal by their own labor, and now that it is completed, to collect the tolls for the transportation of their own products, and from all the merchandise passing on the canal, and give this income to the foreign and other holders of the bonds for merely furnishing a representative of Illinois property.

If the Safety Fund had been established, and money had been issued representing the property of the people of Illinois at an interest of six per cent., their property would not have been more encumbered than by being pledged to foreigners at the same rate of interest. The property that secured the loan to foreigners would have been good security to the Fund. The interest on the loan would have been gained by the people of the State, instead of being paid to foreigners. All the interest that Illinois pays to other States or nations, is paid for the use of money, and not for the use of actual capital. If the people of Illinois had had no capital, they could not have borrowed the money; if they had ample capital, they certainly ought to have had the power to obtain a proper representative of it at home, instead of being compelled to go abroad for it. How much greater would have been the prosperity of this State had the Safety Fund been established before she began to make her internal improvements. The necessary money to carry them through without delay could have been obtained from the Fund at one and one-tenth per cent. interest, and no embarrassment from a scarcity of money would have been felt in any department of industry. The improvements would have remained in her own hands, and she would long since have been receiving the advantages of them in tolls and increased facilities of transportation. But under the present monetary system, she has suffered the loss of credit, and to complete her improvements has been compelled to mortgage her canal and canal lands, and the labor of coming generations.

Millions of money are now paid in interest to foreign nations on our Government and State debts. Besides, in all our large seaport towns, many foreign capitalists have agencies or banking houses for drawing bills of exchange, dealing in stocks, discounting notes at enormous rates, etc., and in this way immense fortunes are accumulated from our labor. These capitalists exercise a great influence upon our money market. When our people shall have an ample national currency, at a low and uniform rate of interest, these capitalists and agents will disappear. Money-brokers and stock-jobbers, who now live by fluctuations in the money market, will abandon an occupation no longer profitable.

The value of money being made uniform, all kinds of stocks will maintain a uniform value, determined by the per centage interest which they will yield, and the time they have to run before the payment of the principal. If they bear a higher rate of interest than the legal one, of course they will be above par. All the State stocks which the States have reserved the right to pay before maturity, will be paid with money borrowed at one and one-tenth per cent. Even if the bonds of some of the States have a number of years to run, these States can much more easily pay five, six, or seven per cent. interest per annum upon them during the period, than they can under the present monetary system, because the value of their labor and products will be increased. The same will be true of all private bonds and mortgages having a number of years to run. A few years will extinguish all these old loans, and then there will be a nearly uniform rate of interest on all obligations throughout the nation.

From what was said in the Introduction, it appears that the farmer or planter is very dependent upon the mechanic for his implements of husbandry, for his house, furniture, books, etc., etc. The mechanic is certainly not less dependent on the farmer for the materials of his food and clothing, and these are indispensable to his existence.

There is no such thing as independence among men; they are and must be helps to each other. Although all useful trades and occupations are mutually beneficial and necessary, yet in most nations a jealousy exists between the agricultural and manufacturing interests. But in reality the natural tendency of the prosperity of one is to increase the prosperity of the other. The object of both is to supply themselves and each other with food, clothing, and the other comforts of life. If an ample supply of money were at all times in circulation, at a uniform and sufficiently low rate of interest, both the farmers and the mechanics would find a ready market for their products; and the prices of their products would naturally adjust themselves so that both parties would receive an equitable share of the proceeds of their labor. Each would be justly contributing to the welfare of the other, and each would be benefited by the labor of the other, and would receive an equitable proportion of the products, because the representative power by which the distribution was made, would not be capable by its income of engrossing the products of either party. But so long as the income power is the all-absorbing power which takes the larger portion of what both these parties earn by their labor, a third party that holds this legal power of income, will take without labor the larger share of what both the others produce. While the poverty of producers is supposed to be caused by over production, and the sale of too many products, the evil will be attributed to laws favoring one class of producers to the disadvantage of others. But when the real cause of the oppression, that is, the monopolizing power of money over all the productions of labor is perceived and rectified, the various branches of productive industry will harmonize, and promote one another's welfare.

Some may not understand how the rate of interest on money affects the compensation of labor. Suppose the owner of a small farm is now obliged to work early and late for a mere subsistence. He has little or no means to spare for the education of his children, and in fact cannot give them time to attend school. If this man should be told that the high rate of interest at which money is loaned deprives him and his family of the comforts of life and the means of education, he would very naturally ask: "How can that be? I never borrow money and pay interest, nor do I lend money and receive interest. The payment of a high rate of interest by others does not affect me; it does not diminish my crops. I raise food for my family, and the produce that can spare I sell, and buy such other articles as we need, and the storekeeper does not charge me any interest. I have enough to do to live, without troubling myself about the interest on money." He is indeed aware that many people live with far less labor than he does, and have many more comforts, and this he attributes to their good fortune. He does not grasp the subject sufficiently to perceive that the interest on money is a standard or governing power, which compels him to contribute his proportion of the products required to support all the non-producers in this country, and probably some of the capitalists of Europe. He does not see that a large per cent. is taken from the price of his products by the purchaser, in order to enable the latter to pay his interest and live by the purchase and sale; and that, for the same reason, when he purchases, a large per cent. is added to the price of every article produced by the labor of others. This difference in price must be sufficient to support all who live upon income without labor.

Let the Safety Fund be established, and interest be reduced to one and one-tenth per cent., and after a year or two let inquiry be made of the same farmer about his welfare. He would probably say, "I am doing very well; I am much better off than I was two or three years ago. I send my children to school, and have a good living." Should he be told that his prosperity was owing to a sound currency and low rate of interest, he might say: "I do not borrow any money from the Safety Fund, and I have no money to lend upon interest. I raise corn and potatoes as formerly, and sell them to the same merchants. I do not see how the reduction of the interest on money that other people borrow is any benefit to me." Although he do not perceive the causes of his past privations or of his present comforts, he will be as sensible as any one of the improvements in his condition. If a man suffering intense pain were informed that it was caused by the disorder of a nerve, he might not understand this, nor think so small a cause could occasion such acute suffering. Apply the proper remedy, let the nerve recover its tone, and the pain cease, and he would be conscious of health, although he might not understand how the pain was removed. Whether a man understand the laws relating to his physical system or not, he will suffer if any organ do not perform its duty; and whether laborers understand the constitution of money or not, they must suffer all the consequences of its imperfect or deranged organization.

There will doubtless be a class of objectors to the Safety Fund who will contend that it is by the use of greater talents, and not by the unjust power of money, that a few gain the majority of the wealth in a nation. But it is evident, that if the greater talents of the few are not dependent upon the unjust power of money and the love of gain by its exorbitant rate per cent. interest, that diminishing the power of money and greatly lowering the rate per cent. interest, cannot in the least infringe upon the full and freest use of their greater talents, either for the production or the acquisition of wealth, or for any other just and lawful purpose.

When the natural reward of labor is secured to the laborer, poverty cannot exist in any family whose members are able and willing to work. And those who can so easily provide for their own wants, will cheerfully contribute to the support of the sick and needy. They will be able to supply themselves amply with the comforts of life, and have an abundance of time for intellectual and moral culture. The incentives to vice will be comparatively few. Avarice first arises from the fear of want; to remove want will therefore in a great measure remove this vice, and the unnumbered evils which are its attendants.* It is frequently said that the people must reform, and that not until then may we hope for good laws. Not so: we might as well expect families to grow up virtuous where the parents are cruel, profligate, and vicious, as to expect nations to be virtuous under oppressive laws. Make the laws a standard of right, and their benefits must secure an improvement in the morals of the people.

It is often said that men are naturally lazy, and will not labor unless compelled by an urgent necessity; and it may be objected to the Safety Fund that if laborers are supplied with all the necessaries and comforts of life with far less labor than at present, the effect will be to induce indolence. This opinion is held mainly by men who have accumulated large properties, and by those who have been placed in easy circumstances by their ancestors, and who, under the present system have the power to impose the necessity to labor. This class seem to think it their right, if not their duty, to take all the surplus earnings from laborers, that the latter may be kept at work. If it be true that man is naturally indolent, it will be difficult to show any good reason for compelling the larger part of the race to labor excessively to

---

* See Appendix, K.

keep from starvation, while the greater and better portion of their productions is applied to support a smaller class without labor. There are those, however, who believe that man is naturally industrious. They know that healthy children are continually active, and that when motives of comfort or pleasure are offered, they are ever ready to make great exertions to possess themselves of the desired objects. Hence they believe that if the productions of labor were fairly awarded to the producers, the prospect of the comfort and elevation in store for the industrious, would present sufficient motives to secure all necessary and desirable exertion. This certainly is true unless the natures of the child and the man are radically different. But if, when a child had made great exertions to obtain some desired object, others should by a secret or visible power prevent his receiving three-fourths of his well-earned reward, and the same exertions should be repeatedly followed by the same results, doubtless he would be discouraged from further attempts. If under these circumstances he should become idle, or seek to acquire without labor, it ought not to be attributed to natural indolence, but to the want of a reasonable assurance that his labor would be successful. The situation in which the producing classes of all nations are placed, seems analogous to that of the disappointed child. It has hence become a very common remark that man is naturally indolent. If discouragements were perceived by the minds of children equal to those familiar to the laboring classes, they would be so disheartened in their efforts as apparently to change their natures, and we should then have lazy children. Their efforts also would depend on necessity; and men and children would be found to have the same natures, and to be governed by similar motives.*

* See Appendix, L.

As a further illustration of the foregoing principle, we may notice briefly the policy which our Government should pursue in the sale of the public lands. If a country is to become wealthy, facilities must be afforded to those who perform the labor necessary to make it rich. It is generally admitted that a free people will perform more labor, and make greater production than an equal number of slaves. This seems to prove that those who expect to own and enjoy the proceeds of their labor will produce more than those who are stinted in the necessaries of life by having their products appropriated to the use of others. When large estates are rented, and the landlords take a great share of the earnings of their tenants, the farms are not generally as well cultivated, and the buildings and other improvements are seldom if ever as good as where the farmers are the owners of the soil which they cultivate. The difference is doubtless owing to the hopelessness in one case that even by severe toil they shall materially improve their condition, and to the prospect in the other of enjoying the fruits of their labor. To the former labor is a burden, while the latter cheerfully perform a greater amount. If then our Government desires the improvement of the public lands, encouragement must be offered to those who will purchase and cultivate them. Speculators who buy and sell them at a tenfold profit, and make no improvements on the lands, add nothing to the wealth of the country; but purchasers who go upon the land and improve it by their labor, increase the public wealth. Let then the Government sell the lands to actual settlers only, in parcels not exceeding half a section to any individual. Let a small part of the purchase money be paid down, and let the balance remain on mortgage at one and one-tenth per cent. interest until the occupant is disposed to pay it. In this way the land will at once bring an income to the Government as good as if the whole purchase money were paid and reloaned at the legal rate of interest. The Government will be perfectly safe, and the people will pay for and improve the lands. This will at the same time build up a prosperous and happy people, who will soon add immensely to the wealth of the nation, and who, in improving their own condition, will contribute to the comfort and happiness of others by supplying them with food, and receiving their surplus products in return.

If the laws be such that the people can secure a good living and a handsome surplus without labor, and can earn only a scanty subsistence and no surplus by it, they will seek to exempt themselves from labor. But if the laws be made such that labor will secure to them a good living and a handsome yearly surplus, while without it they can obtain only a poor living and no surplus, people will incline to labor. If interest be reduced to a just rate, almost the entire population of the country will be engaged in some species of productive industry, and the laboring classes will be relieved from the support of a numerous body who now live by their wits—that is, by contriving to obtain the products of others without toil. When money is made a just standard, the injustice of contracts founded upon it will cease, and many laws necessary to support the present unjust standard will disappear.

So long as monetary laws continue a standard that will wrest products from producers, and place and protect them in the hands of non-producers, they will require for their support the aid of the sword and bayonet, because man's natural sense of right revolts against the usurpation and the injustice of such protection. But when monetary laws shall sustain a just standard of value, which will place and protect products in the hands of their producers, they will of course conform to the natural laws of production, which were ordained by a higher than human power. The distribution then being accord ing to justice strife will cease, because a man having his own rights respected and protected, will naturally respect and protect the rights of others. The time is not far distant when this truth will be known and appreciated by all civilized nations, and the mistaken power of legal Might which has such dominion over man, will wither before the meek and peaceable power of Right that exists in the natural laws of a wise and beneficent Creator.

CONCLUSION.

In the previous pages we have discussed the rights of labor and capital for the sole purpose of convincing the public that the rapid increase of capital by per centage, now favored by monetary laws, while it stimulates the enterprise of the few, and naturally and inevitably secures to them great wealth, represses and cripples the enterprise of the great mass of the people, tending to pauperism, crime, and indirectly, but certainly, to the overthrow of the Government, which, disregarding the ratio of the actual increase of property by labor, has given the preference to capital: that justice to labor, while it will secure individual comfort and happiness to all who are able and willing to work, will rapidly develop the highest qualities of our nature, and all the resources of our country, and greatly increase the national wealth; that it will give to civilization an impetus such as the world has never seen, and relieve it from one of its hardest conditions, that of creating desires and necessities which it provides no means to gratify; that it will silence at once and forever the doubt so often felt and spoken, whether the happiness of the mass of men has been promoted by the change from the savage to the civilized state.

It has been shown that labor constitutes the real treasure of a nation, and without claiming for it anything more than its natural rights, we insist that these should be guarded by the most jealous care of government. It has also been shown that under existing monetary laws, labor is not and cannot be properly rewarded. Change is indispensable, and fortunately it can be effected without altering the Constitution of the United States, with out the slightest disturbance to the present institutions of society, or real injury to any one.

It is now for the American people, who have founded their government upon the principles of equality and freedom, to establish the rights of labor, which have been nearly disregarded in all previous time, and only cared for as they have served to minister to the ambition and luxury of courts and nobles. Let the social position of the laborer, to which he is entitled by the ordination of God in the laws of nature, be ascertained and recognized, and poverty, crime, and most other political and social evils, will give place to competency, virtue and happiness.

The facts contained in this volume show plainly that our monetary system favors the rapid concentration of capital in opposition to the rights of labor, and we deem it warrantable to assume, that nearly all who shall carefully examine the subject, will be convinced that our present laws of distribution are continually doing a great wrong to the people.

Nothing more simple than the Safety Fund need be desired, and the more it is considered, the more adequate it will appear to distribute the wealth to those whose labor earns it. This system will as certainly reward labor, as the one now in force has oppressed it. It will infringe no rights of property. The owners of wealth will continue in undisturbed possession. They will be able to lend their money and rent their property as readily at one and one-tenth per cent. as now at six or seven per cent. The dollar received by the rich man in interest or rent will purchase as much as the dollar earned by the laborer; precisely as at the present rates of interest. Landowners will be at liberty to rent their land to tenants, work it themselves, or leave it untilled, according to their own pleasure: the low rate of interest will not prevent it from yielding crops. Capitalists will not be required to favor laborers, nor to give them employment, nor to diminish the hours of toil. Capitalists and laborers will be free to make their own agreements on these points. The Safety Fund contemplates no agrarian distribution. It asks for no distribution of lands nd. property, and for no contributions of money by either the Government or individuals to the support of laborers. Laborers will need no favors. They only require that the Government establish a just standard of value, which will allow them to possess an equitable share of the fruits of their labor.*

Who are those directly interested in the adoption of the Safety Fund? All agriculturists, manufacturers, mechanics, planters, in short, all who wish to earn a support by honest industry. Merchants will do a safe business in exchanging products, and their profits will be moderate and sure. Nine-tenths of our whole population will receive the pecuniary benefit which is justly their due, and the remaining one-tenth will be left in undisturbed possession of their present wealth, and like their fellow-citizens, at liberty to increase it by any useful employment. The desire of capitalists to accumulate is often owing to the wish to leave large fortunes to their children. But if they rightly consider the instability of wealth, they cannot expect all, or even one-fourth of their posterity to remain rich. Will it not be, to reasonable men, a thousand times more consoling to leave such laws as with a moderate amount of labor will secure to their whole posterity the comforts of life and the means of education, than to leave to their children the money and the present monetary laws, which must in a few years compel the larger part to toil incessantly for a scanty subsistence, and deprive them of mental and social culture? Are not just laws a far greater blessing to transmit than any amount of wealth? We believe that many among

* See Appendix, M.

the rich, perceiving the justice and beneficence of this system, will be found among its most ardent supporters.

In all civilized nations much attention is now directed to the enormous evils of society; and thousands, yes, we may say, millions of good and benevolent men are endeavoring to do something for their removal. But there is a great variety of evils, and a corresponding variety of opinions as to the means to be used to accomplish the desired objects; hence reformers split into numerous societies; and one society combats drunkenness, another slavery, another land monopoly and the oppression of labor, another war. These are admitted to be great evils, and all who are truly desirous of their removal are the good men of the age; because they are striving to alleviate the sufferings of mankind, and to improve the moral character and condition of society. Yet their work will only serve partially to modify these evils, and will never eradicate them, because they are working not at the cause but at the effects. To remedy the wrongs they must begin at the foundation which supports them, and make that just and right, and then the evils will be easily removed; as a good house may be easily erected on a good foundation, but on a bad one, the people might always work at the effects produced by it on the work above, and the most that could be done would not prevent its being a rickety, poor building; while the same labor on a good foundation would have built up a splendid edifice. And had the foundation of contracts been just, the labor performed during past ages would not only have provided amply for the physical wants of the race, but would have supplied the best means for their moral and intellectual culture. The root of a tree produces a trunk; the trunk naturally divides itself into branches, which subdivide themselves into thousands of smaller branches and little twigs. All these are supported by the root and trunk. If we girdle one of these little twigs, it will die off above; but will be likely to sprout out below. A large branch cut off will die, and in dying will impart new vigor to the other branches; but killing the root will destroy the tree. So with the evils of society, most of them spring from one root, and they have become a great tree. The trunk divides itself into many branches, which subdivide into many other branches, and little twigs. Girdling this twig, or this or that branch, will never destroy the evil; but kill the root, and then these large, and thousands of smaller branches and twigs will wither, decay and drop off, and the trunk will die. We desire to call the attention of philanthropists of every nation, clime, and sect, to the great, hidden evil which lies at the root and below the surface, that they may combine their strength, and by one joint effort directed at the root, slay the thousand great sins of a nation, so that they will at once begin to wither and decay, like the branches and twigs of a tree killed at the root. If the philanthropists who are now engaged in their works of kindness, and the producing classes who so wrongfully suffer by the present system, would but use their united efforts to have a just currency substituted for the present unjust one, it would be speedily accomplished; and the consequent moral and physical improvement would be without a parallel in the history of man. When any nation shall adopt a just monetary system, the abundant supply of comforts, and the good will, peace and happiness which will ensue, will form such a contrast to the present condition of society as to astonish the world; and all will wonder that the power of money was adequate to the production of so much evil. By the unjust power of money tyrannies have been built up and sustained, and by making it a just standard of value, and an equitable balance against actual production, it will again demolish them, giving to man his rights throughout the civilized world.*

The means necessary to put in operation and sustain the Safety Fund are not confined to the few capitalists who now control the currency, and furnish the Government and the people with money. Our farmers and mechanics alone have sufficient landed estate to secure several times the amount of money necessary for our currency. The only thing required is a law of Congress adopting this system. The passage of this law must be effected by direct petition, and by making the measure a leading question, the people voting only for men who will use their influence in favor of it. Every one, thoroughly convinced of the truth of the positions taken in this book, can do something to diffuse a knowledge of them among his friends and neighbors. The most effectual way to excite interest in the system, and give it prominence, would be to call public meetings and lecture upon the subject. The objects which will be secured by its establishment, are so evidently in accordance with the principles and aims of the Christian religion, that ministers of the Gospel cannot fail to advocate it with the same zeal that they advocate peace, justice, and good-will among men; nor can statesmen who legislate for the well-being of their countrymen, refuse it their support. The public newspapers have

---

* If we could put an end to its unjust use there is no danger of our Government ever becoming a monarchy, the predictions of Europe to the contrary notwithstanding. But should the interest on money be regulated by our Government, at just and equal rates, there would be a Union in this country stronger than any government ever yet established, and, instead of our becoming a monarchy, the governments of Europe would be obliged to adopt our form of government, or very much better their own, for I am persuaded that this oppression of the people who earn the wealth of nations by their industry must, from its severity, cease.—*Currency the Evil and the Remedy.*

great power to awaken the attention of the people, and to disseminate a knowledge of this New Monetary System, and their aid would greatly hasten its adoption. But more than all, let farmers, mechanics, and all men who earn their living by labor, *determine* that Congress shall legislate so as to do them justice.

APPENDIX.

A.—*Page* 65.

A RAILROAD stock that brings in an income of six per cent. per annum is certainly worth only one-half as much as one that brings in twelve per cent. If the income of the one that brings in six per cent. could be let for six per cent. only after it was received, and the one that brings in twelve per cent. could be let at twelve, the stock bringing the latter price would be worth vastly more than double the one that brings but six per cent. per annum. But suppose one of these stocks should bring in one year six per cent., the next eighteen, the next five, the next twenty-four, the next seven, the next four, and the next seventeen per cent., and each year the income uncertain, no one would pretend to say there was a fixed value to this stock, or that it would be a just measure of value, although they now say of the dollar, that it is a dollar all the world over and its value is always the same. They might as justly assert of this railroad stock, that stock is stock all the world over, and always of the same value. But, if the income on this stock were precisely the same, not only every year but every day in each year, and would continue so without fluctuation, other things might vary, but the stock would always be of uniform value. And especially if it were made the standard by which every other species of property were valued, it being the foundation of all value and always producing the same income — stock producing stock as money, at interest produces money, the thing produced being precisely like the thing that produced it, the stock could not possibly vary in value. Suppose a man to have one hundred shares of this stock, which was yearly producing six dollars on each share (amounting to

$600), the interest or dividend ($300) being paid every six months, should the stock and road cease to exist, but the dividend be regularly paid, the non-existence of the road and stock would in no manner affect its value. But let the dividend or interest cease to be paid, and forever cease, and the road continue, the stock would not be worth one cent. Should a farm cease to produce, it would be worthless for agriculture; so, should the interest on money forever cease, I doubt whether any nation, with all the laws it might make, could ever maintain it as a currency. Therefore, money loaned should bear an interest fixed at such rates as never to be oppressive. We might better vary the length of the yard than the interest on money—better allow all the other measures to vary than this, because it measures the value of every species of property, all government expenses, all official salaries, and everything that is sold by the piece, bulk, or quantity. How important is it then that it should be just! A man might as well be allowed to change his neighbor's landmark as to increase the interest on his debtor: he would as much augment the debt, to the injury of his debtor, as he would enlarge his farm to the loss of his neighbor. If the one is just, the other must be so too.

Congress has coined money, but has not determined its value because it has left its use or interest unsettled. It might as well have said that yard-sticks should contain thirty cubic inches and allow them to be made to slide out to any length from two to fifteen feet, and then permit a few people to monopolize them; when buying, to slide out the stick to any length, and when selling, to reduce it two or three feet and call the length of the stick a yard, however long or short it might be. It would no more vary the yard when its length was increased from three to fifteen feet than the dollar is changed when the interest is altered from six per cent. per annum to thirty per cent. or two and a half per cent. a month. (*Currency, the Evil and the Remedy.*)

B.—*Page* 154.

I think none will deny that labor earns the wealth of all nations; yet the laboring classes often suffer for the necessaries of life, and are in distress for the want of employment. For

example: take England, the wealthiest nation in the world, and
contemplate the state of the laborer. Instead of receiving an
equivalent for his labor, he is clothed in rags, lives on scanty,
miserable food, and many times finds great difficulty in keeping
himself from starving. The manufacturer who employs
hundreds of these laborers finds his goods, when manufactured,
sell below their cost, because the interest on money is raised.
He naturally endeavors to lessen his expenses, and, cotton
having fallen, buys his materials a little cheaper. Though he
very much dislikes to reduce the wages of his workmen, and
continues for a time to pay the same price, his losses compel
him to diminish them one-eighth. The manufacturer, still
losing, buys cotton a little lower, and takes another eighth from
the wages of his workmen, which distresses them very much.
Goods fall again, and he is obliged to give the men employment
half the time only at this low price. He would certainly stop
his factory, but he knows the workmen would suffer still more
should he do so; at last his losses compel him to do it; the
laborers are thrown out of employment and cannot get sufficient
food to eat. The manufacturer cannot feed them; for a long
time he has been losing on the goods, his business is stopped,
and he is earning nothing. He feels for his workmen, but
cannot help them; the market is glutted with goods, and they
will not sell. The fault of this change in the price of goods
may not be in the least owing to the manufacturer. It lies beyond all the useful business of the nation—in the money capital.

If the interest of money rise from three per cent. per annum
to four per cent., it is equal to a change or fall in the goods of
twenty-five per cent.; the measure is just one quarter more
than it was. The income of one hundred dollars in a year is
four dollars instead of three, hence a person buying its use has
to pay four dollars where before he paid but three. The *use* is
all the person buys; he rents the money as he would rent any
other property—the money belongs to the party lending or renting out its use, and, at a given period, is to be returned to its
owner, its *use* only being paid for. But if the interest have
risen from three to four dollars, the dollar itself is worth one
hundred thirty-three and a third cents, and as well worth that
as it was before worth one hundred cents. It is the same to the
manufacturer as if he should be compelled when he sells his

goods, to increase the length of his yard-stick to four feet and sell his goods at the same price he did when his yard-stick was but three feet long. He cannot do this unless his workmen will make four yards of cloth at the same rate that they before made three; he must also buy as much cotton now for three dollars as formerly for four, and curtail every other expense in the same proportion, or his business will not be as good as when money was at three per cent. interest. The interest on money continues to rise until it gets to five per cent. per annum; now his yard-stick must be five feet long and his workmen must make five yards of cloth for the same same price they before made three. Where the manufacturer bought a bale of cotton at fifty dollars, he must now pay but thirty and diminish every other expense in proportion. The interest on money still increases to six per cent. per annum, and the use of a dollar having doubled, the dollar itself is just doubled in value. Now his yard-stick must be six feet long and his workmen make two yards of cloth for the same price they before made one: he must buy a bale of cotton for twenty-five instead of fifty dollars, and lessen all other expenses in proportion. Add to this, he is in debt when the change in the interest takes place, although the debt against him is permanent and bears but three per cent. he is obliged to reduce everything in this ratio, $i.\ e.$, buy the cotton, reduce the wages of his workmen, have just as ready sales and collections as formerly, or his interest will be burdensome to him, for it takes just double the quantity that it formerly did to pay the three per cent. interest, and he must sell double the quantity of cloth to obtain the same money. But suppose the property on which the debt is a lien is forced on sale, what will it bring? Certainly if it rented as well as it did before when money was but three per cent. it would not now be worth more than half its former value. Thus the manufacturer is broken up, and every branch of useful business checked, laborers cannot find employment; and all this trouble is attributed to the people who have made the goods and every other useful article: the capital takes nearly all the earnings, allowing the people who have earned the whole wealth of the nation to starve, and this is called "financiering," getting things down to the specie or real value. When this process is over, and the wealth concentrated in the hands of the few, money is offered to the business people at a somewhat reasonable interest; business again goes on for a few years, when the same scene is reacted and the same result produced. . . . .

All laws are made for the government of man. Each nation enacts them for itself, and every citizen within their jurisdiction is bound to obey them. These laws are intended to protect the rights of property, to shield the weak from the strong, allowing no one by oppression or injustice to take property from another without returning an equivalent. Stealing, is appropriating property without the consent of its owner. One who steals is not only bound by law to return the thing stolen, but is also obnoxious to imprisonment.

The laws also protect against gambling. Gambling consists in two or more individuals posting up any sum of money, to which all parties agree, then playing some game, after which, the one who beats takes all the money. This is gambling, because one man takes from others money or property without rendering any equivalent. The others have lost just what the winner has gained, yet it was all done voluntarily, without the slightest necessity for it, so there was no oppression on the part of the winner; the hope of gain prompted each, yet they knew before they played all but one must lose, still each hoped to be the fortunate one. This is fair gambling, but should those who had lost their money discover that the winner had prepared the cards by a private mark on the back of each, and thus had won the game, it would be called *unfair* gambling, and the persons losing would say they had been cheated out of their money.

The laws prohibit these transactions because they are injurious to the parties concerned, their families and the public; corrupting the morals of the community by the pernicious practice of taking from one his property and giving it to another without any equivalent. A gambler is not generally considered a business man. If it were asked in what business such a man is, the answer would be, "None; he is nothing but a gambler." I wish now to speak of other things in the community called business, and ascertain whether the term be more properly applied to them than it is to the gambler. I mean the stockjobbing business. A person buying stock to hold for a time, expects to sell it for a higher price than he pays for it. If it be State stock bearing interest at six per cent. he intends to buy it at such rates that he shall not only receive six per cent. interest, but a profit beside. Let us see whether, if he buys the stock below its par value, others will not lose all he gains. Suppose it to be issued by the State and bear six per cent. interest. Some individual who has taken it at par is compelled, by misfortune, to sell it for fifty per cent. discount, thus losing one half the amount for which he has received no equivalent, while the person buying it has gained precisely what the other has lost, and given nothing for it.

Again, if the State itself be obliged to sell its own bonds bearing the legal interest of the State at twenty, twenty-five or any other per cent., below par value, it loses all the difference between the par value and the amount for which they are sold, and the person buying obtains precisely what the State loses, and this loss must be paid by taxing, directly or indirectly, the citizens of the State. These State stocks bear a certain rate of interest, and both principal and interest are as definite as the pound weight or the yard. The interest is daily going on at a certain rate, and the stock varies from day to day exactly the amount of the accruing interest and no more. But in the stock market one day it is up one, two or three per cent.; the next, down one, two, three, four or five per cent., and then again up. In all these transactions, one party gains precisely what the other loses, as much as if one man should measure the pieces of cloth he bought of another with a yard-stick four feet long, and when he sells measure with one three feet long. He has taken precisely as much cloth from the first man without giving any equivalent, as he has gained from the person to whom he has sold it. The stocks rise and fall daily, because some few individuals combine and run them up by falsely selling to each other without any intention of delivering the stock, or if delivered there is an understanding that it shall be rebought by the person who sold it. This is done to "corner" some other persons who have sold stock on time and have to deliver it within a certain period, which, if they cannot do, they must pay the difference or be disgraced by this very respectable Board of Brokers. In this way, *combining* to run up and run down the stocks, they try to induce innocent people to partake in the same business. It is often the case that sundry individuals combine on certain bank and railroad stocks, and agree not to sell the stocks which they own or control, knowing they have a large majority of that in which they are operators. These same men then go forward and buy, to be delivered in a certain time, a far greater amount of the same stock than there is outstanding, and run it up to double its former price. When the time arrives for it to be delivered, they know it cannot be done unless it is bought directly or indirectly from themselves, and they charge whatever they please for it, or else they take the difference, and the stock is not delivered at all. This is done under pretence that there is some real cause for this great advance, and those unskilled in financial operations are often "cornered," in this way, or in some other quite as unsatisfactory.

Now are these transactions any more fair than a private mark upon the cards before gambling? In all these do not some of the parties lose precisely what the others gain? In all this there has been nothing done to increase the wealth of the nation or the comfort of man; neither has it bettered the morals of any one. No transaction of this kind deserves the name of business; and here let me explain what *business* is.

Take, for instance, a farmer who has an extensive business in wool, and suppose him to have two thousand sheep. He must provide hay and grain to keep them during the winter; he also raises grain to sell. To cultivate so large a farm, he must employ a number of laborers, whom he boards and pays sufficient wages to furnish themselves with good clothing, and enable them at the end of the year to have a handsome surplus. When the wool is ready for market, the farmer sells to the manufacturer for a price which will pay for the labor devoted to the sheep, a reasonable compensation for the use of the part of the farm allotted to them, and a small profit besides. The manufacturer converts the wool into cloth and sends it to a commission merchant in New York to sell, limiting him to such prices as will enable him to pay all his workmen well. The manufacturer also demands a price sufficient to pay himself for his own labor, for the use of his machinery and manufactory, and to insure a small profit. The commission merchant sells these cloths to the wholesale merchant or jobber, and receives his commission, which gives him a good living and a handsome surplus. The jobber again sells the cloths to the country merchant, and receives enough to give him a good living and a reasonable profit. The country merchant sells them to the farmers, mechanics, and various individuals who need them, and they wear them out.

Every one of these persons is making a living and saving a surplus; the people who buy these cloths and wear them out are raising grain, beef, pork, etc., supplying the various manufacturers and mechanics with food, and they also make a good living and some profit. No one has lost what the other has gained, but each and every one of them is gaining. *This* is business: each one is adding to his own comfort, while at the same time he contributes to that of all the others. The same happy result would attend every branch of useful business in our land, if *business* were pursued and not gambling.

If this gambling in stocks and money affected those only who are in that "business," as it is called, the evil would be comparatively small, but it does not stop there. This article, money, is the measure of value of all the productions of the country, and no matter where the farmer, mechanic, laborer, merchant, or any producer may be situated, if he be in debt, the rise of interest from six to twelve per cent. per annum, doubles his debt upon him although he may be paying but six per cent. interest upon it. It will take double the produce to pay six per cent. because it will fall in about that proportion, but at the same time it will take the same labor that it always did to raise a pound of cotton, a bushel of wheat or to make a yard of cloth, and one half the money will pay for it, hence it is doubled in favor of the money capital. To illustrate this, I will suppose: A., who is clear of debt, owns a farm, but it is not as large as he wishes it. B., another farmer, offers for this $4,000, paying $2,000, and giving a bond and mortgage on the farm purchased for the remaining $2,000, payable in instalments of $300 a year, interest at six per cent. He expects, with the assistance of his family, to do all the work on the farm, and thinks he can easily clear $300, as produce commands good prices. A. purchases another farm for $6,000, paying $2,000 in cash, and giving his mortgage for $4,000 at six per cent. interest on the farm purchased. He agrees to pay $500 a year and the interest. He expects to receive $300 a year from B., and to make clear at least $200 besides the interest. But before the year rolls round, the interest on money rises in the Atlantic cities from six to twelve per cent. He sees the newspapers stating the fact, but thinks it has little to do with his farming as he is paying no such interest, his mortgage bearing but six per cent. By the time he gets his crops to market, he finds produce has fallen, and even at lower prices does not sell readily. His neighbor B. does not receive as high a price for his produce as he expected, and is able to pay the interest and $200 only on his mortgage, instead of $300 as he agreed. A, with difficulty makes his interest and $300 beside. He takes the $200 collected from B. and the $200 he has made from his own farm, reduces his mortgage to $3,600, and pays the interest. Still in the Atlantic cities interest continues high, and money has become scarce in the country, the interest rising to twelve per cent., though the farmers are paying but six per cent. interest on the mortgages. When the crops are ready for market, they have fallen one-third from the last year's price: the cost of transporting to the market is the same as formerly, and when expenses are deducted they find they have cleared but half as much money as in the year previous. B. is able to pay his interest and $100 only on the principal. A. can pay the interest on his mortgage and $200. The mortgage is now reduced to $3,400; the person holding it insists upon the amount due being paid and forecloses the mortgage. The farm for which A. paid $6,000 brings but $2,000, and money, by this time, is so scarce that few people have sufficient to purchase it. As A. is pushed, he sues B., and B.'s farm brings but $1,200, leaving B. insolvent and owing $500, which must be paid from his future earnings. When the $1,200 are added to the $2,000 A.'s farm brought, it would still leave A. indebted $200 besides interest and costs. Now what evil have these two farmers done? They and their families have worked hard, and raised from their farms provisions for themselves and a large surplus for the food of others; and who has reaped the fruit of their toil? The moneyed capitalist, and without rendering the slightest equivalent. I appeal to persons in all sections of our country if cases quite as hard as these have not occurred within the limits of their observation. These farmers paid but six per cent. interest, and yet lost, because the measure of value has affected the produce of their farms and tested them by a different measure from the one by which they bought, and therefore they fall short in paying their debts.

For further illustration, suppose the State of New Jersey, during the whole time that the rates of interest were fluctuating in all the other States, had maintained hers at six per cent. and retained all the money that generally circulates in the State, so that any citizen could as easily obtain the money at this rate, as at any period of her existence. Under these circumstances there would have been no complaint of a scarcity of money, and if any one unable to pay his debts had attributed it to usury he would have been called a madman. But look at the facts. The surplus produce of New Jersey, and most of the goods manufactured there find their market in New York and Philadelphia. These productions are tested by the measure of value in these two cities, and they fall off in price from one-third to one-half, while those consumed in the State fall about as much; for the prices at home are governed by the prices in market. This increases the amount of labor to be performed by every debtor to pay his debts, for it requires the same labor as at any previous time to produce a bushel of grain, or any other article, the result of labor.

Farms, manufactured goods, machinery, all fall in price, and this operates against the producers and in favor of the money capital. The citizens of the State may be great sufferers, and many of them entirely broken up, although not one of them has directly paid more than six per cent. interest for money borrowed or previously owed, and not one has been troubled to borrow what he needed for his use. It is as if a planter should agree to deliver, at a given time, a certain number of pounds of cotton, and the man purchasing should put, to balance the cotton, double the weight he formerly did, still calling each a pound. He doubles the pound weight, and the cotton falls short one half. The pound weight tests or measures the weight, but not more than money tests or measures the value. If the value of money be doubled, the debt of every debtor is doubled, and he falls short in payment for the same reason that the cotton falls short in weighing. In weighing cotton, doubling the pound would be considered fraudulent, but doubling the value of money is only "financiering." • • • •

When grain is sold, the size of the bushel with which it shall be measured is not considered a matter of bargain; nor when cotton is sold, the kind of weight that shall be used; but it is taken for granted that these are determined and fixed by law. Were it not thus, there would probably be a street in each of our large cities devoted to the business of changing the weights and measures, especially if a few individuals were allowed by law to engross them, (as the banks, brokers and rich men now engross the money). The one who could increase and shorten the measures most would have the most business. These people would congregate in groups or on the corners of the streets, (as brokers now do,) with their sliding yards, skilfully made, and all sorts of measures with ingenious and false bottoms moved by springs invisible to the common people; and thus the measuring and weighing would be the most difficult thing to accomplish, in the same manner that "financiering" is now the most difficult business in the exchange of property. But it would be impossible to commit so great a fraud in these measures of quantity as is now and has ever been committed in finance by changing the value of the dollar.—*Currency, the Evil and the Remedy.*

C.—*Page* 241.

But again let us look at the money market in the city of New York, say this 24th day of June, 1848. Money is now said to be very plentiful, and is loaned with much difficulty for good security. A rich man may now borrow at from three to four per cent. on good notes not having more than six or eight months to run; yet another, who has not all these advantages, although just as good for all his obligations as the richest, will in the same bank be charged six, or even seven per cent. interest. Even now it is difficult to procure money for a term of years on bond and mortgage at six per cent. interest, and often at seven per cent., because the security is not that on which capitalists wish to loan money. They wish to loan money in such a way that it can at any time be recalled if there is a change in the money market. They hope business will soon start, for when it again prospers they will get seven per cent. interest; and when it is quite flourishing they can, by suddenly calling in their money, get the rates of interest up to twelve, eighteen or twenty-four per cent. per annum. If they do loan on bond and mortgage, they require it to be so secured by the property on which it is loaned that it will be sure to bring enough to pay the bond and mortgage, costs, etc. When the time arrives that money will bring eighteen or twenty-four per cent. per annum, if they buy the property under foreclosure they get it for one-half or one-third its value; hence the difficulty of borrowing money on bond and mortgage; they are not willing to loan on mortgage more than half the present estimated value of property, which is now extremely reduced in value. The man who borrows money at three per cent. and lends it at six makes a hundred per cent. profit, just as much as the man who buys a barrel of flour at three dollars and sells it at six. We might as well make laws which, in their operation, would compel the producing classes that were not rich to pay double price when they bought, and when they sold to the rich to receive but half what they gave: it would not be more certain to operate against the producers and in favor of the capitalists.

I will give an example of the operation of money at the present time. A. being a rich broker in Wall street, finds that, by borrowing ten thousand dollars from a bank for ninety days, there is a good opportunity for him to make money on State stock. He borrows of a bank the ten thousand, at the rate of three and a half per cent. interest per annum, pledging stock for security. The interest on the $10,000 for ninety days is $87 50. B., a Pearl street merchant, needing a discount for $10,000, applies to the same bank the same day, and gets his paper discounted: the bank charges him six per cent. interest; that is $150. C., a mechanic who has just finished a steam engine and boiler, and has taken a note in payment for $10,000, applies to the same bank, which discounts the note for him, charging him seven per cent. interest; that is, $175. Each of the three has bought the use of the same sum of money for ninety days: the money all belongs to the bank and at the end of ninety days must be returned to it. One has paid at the same bank, on the same day, for the use of the same article, $87 50; the next has paid $150; and the third, 175. The bank, we all know, would not have discounted any of these notes unless perfectly satisfied that they were good.

Let us apply the same to merchandise. A. buys of a merchant

a package of goods on three months' credit for $87 50; B. buys the same day of the same merchant a second package exactly like A.'s, and is charged $150 on the same credit; C. the same day buys the third package, and is charged $175. Or, suppose A. needs a barrel of flour; he pays for it $3 50; B. buys the same day and hour another barrel of the same quality, and pays $6; and C. buying another of the same man, is charged $7. A. is richer than B. and B. is richer than C.; and of course the richer the man the cheaper he must buy, and the poorer the man the more he must pay to increase his poverty.

But suppose these three should come to a ferry which they wished to cross, and the ferry-master should say to the rich broker, "Sir, what is your business?" "I am a very rich man; I deal in measures of value, and change these measures as much as it is in my power. I borrow money out of bank for three and sometimes three and a half or four per cent. interest, and I buy good business notes, well indorsed, for six and seven per cent. or even more, as good notes as can be had in New York; and for several years past, when money has been scarce, I have been borrowing money out of bank, paying six or seven per cent. interest; and when I have paid these rates at bank, I have usually received from one to two and sometimes three per cent. a month for the same money that I borrowed at six per cent. a year; and I have made a great deal of money by this, for the merchants have been hard run." "Sir," says the ferry-master, "you may have the use of our boat for twelve and a half cents." Next comes the Pearl street merchant, "And what is your business, sir?" "I am a merchant, but business is very bad, money is scarce with me." "Your fare for the use of the boat to go over the ferry will be twenty-five cents." Next comes the steam-engine maker. "What is your business?" "Why, I am a hard-working man." "Your ferriage, sir." "What is it?" "Why, sir, as you are a hard-working man, I shall charge you thirty-seven and a half cents, sir; our ferry is a great accommodation to the public, and we wish to do all we can to promote industry; step on board the boat and take that seat where there is no cushion; the cushioned seat, sir, is reserved for the gentleman broker." Why not as well pay the difference for the use of the boat to cross the ferry as to pay the difference to bank for the use of money?—*Currency, the Evil and the Remedy.*

D.—*Page* 244.*

To the Editor of the N. Y. Tribune.

Sir: A few months ago this country was enjoying a prosperity unsurpassed in its history. The crops, more abundant than ever before, were sufficient to supply not only our own wants, but to admit of large exportations. Manufacturing establishments and railroads employed a great number of persons. The merchants were conducting their business with as much prudence as at any former period. Houses were being built in the cities and villages, and in the farming districts, and labor was in good demand.

Now affairs are in a very different condition. The business of the merchants is broken up; the manufacturers have suspended their operations; hundreds of thousands of laborers are thrown out of employment and are in danger of starvation; the farmers cannot get their abundant crops to market, and if they could, they would be obliged to sell them at greatly reduced prices. Business stands still.

This great change is rightly said to be owing to the difficulties in finance, to the crisis in the money market. All the money of the nation, bank-notes included, amounts to about five hundred millions of dollars. Probably when the circulation of the banks has been the most expanded the whole currency has never reached six hundred millions. But the productions of labor for the last year are estimated at three billions five hundred millions of dollars—about seven times as much as all the currency of the nation, and these productions or a large proportion of them will change hands through the process of manufacture, and otherwise, from three to eight or ten times before they reach the actual consumers. Now, this comparatively small sum of money must pay for every one of these exchanges, or for every debt contracted in making these exchanges. The same money must also pay all the debts contracted by borrowing money from banks or upon bond and mortgage or otherwise. It must pay for all the lands that are sold by the government and by individuals; for all the bonds issued by railroads, cities, States, and by the United States; for

---

* Published in the "New York Daily Tribune," Nov. 27, 1857.

all the stocks and securities that are sold at private sale, at auction and by the various boards of brokers, and for all the bills of exchange sold from one part of the country to another, as well as for all bills of exchange upon foreign nations. It is evident that this comparatively small sum of money must change hands a great number of times to effect the needful exchanges of this immense amount of property, and that any obstruction to its movement or withdrawal of a portion of it from circulation must seriously embarrass the business of the whole country. The importance of this free circulation of money may perhaps be more fully appreciated when we state that all the money we possess—gold, silver and paper—would not suffice to pay the board of this nation for four months, at $1 per week for each individual.

The city of New York is the financial centre of the country. If the banks in this city keep up their lines of discount so as to supply the business community with money, the banks in all other parts of the country will also discount and supply the people in their neighborhoods. Of course there must be at times, balances greater or less against one part of the country in favor of another, but all these will be easily adjusted, and business will go on prosperously.

In the latter part of August last, the Ohio Life and Trust Company, with a capital of two millions of dollars, suspended payment, with debts against the Company to the amount of six or seven millions of dollars. This failure was the apparent occasion of distrust, and of contraction in bank issues to the amount of some eight millions of dollars in the course of two weeks; and to the 24th of October of about twenty-six millions. This contraction of discounts for the first two weeks only was doubtless a much greater loss to the business men of this city than the entire capital and liabilities of the Ohio Life and Trust Company. The news of this curtailment rushed with lightning speed to all parts of the country, and carried consternation into every city and town where a bank existed; and the banks in this city and throughout the country called upon each other to pay up their balances in specie. Many of the banks in this State were obliged not only to stop discounting, but had to send their State stocks to this city, and sell them at from 15 to 30 per cent. loss to redeem their bank notes and take them out of circulation in order to save themselves from suspension. But this was not the worst of the evil. Merchants, unable to get their notes discounted at bank, were driven into Wall street, and compelled to borrow at exorbitant rates of interest to meet their payments, thus rapidly increasing their indebtedness, and rendering it inevitable that in the end a large proportion of them should be made bankrupt. Many of them paid to usurers for the use of money, one, two, three, four, five and six per cent. a month, and from these rates to a quarter, a half and sometimes one per cent. or more a day, and were compelled to leave double, treble and quadruple securities to obtain the money at all. The banks by curtailing their discounts so that money is not to be had to meet the mercantile engagements, remove the foundation upon which the contracts were based; and the merchants can no more stand up under such an event than a house can stand supported by the air if the foundation be removed from under it. Money is the only thing recognized by our laws as a tender, and all the property of debtors becomes mere collateral security for the payment of money for their obligations. Hence, in a crisis like this, the great wealth of the nation seems to be concentrated in the money.

The banks hold on deposit millions of dollars belonging to the public on which they are paying no interest. If the tables were turned and the public should make the banks pay five per cent. a month on these deposits in advance until they could pay them all off in specie, the banks would soon be as insolvent as the merchants; yet it would be quite as just and more so than for the banks to force this necessity upon the merchants and others. The banks are public institutions, and are authorized by law to furnish the currency. It is a penal offence for individuals to circulate their own notes as money. Labor, bills receivable, goods, wares and merchandise are not money: all of these must be exchanged for money in order to pay debts. The public is entirely dependent upon the banks for this money, and if they do not furnish it, the people must borrow of usurers at rates of interest which are certain to eat up their assets, and in many instances to leave them, after a long life of toil, in absolute poverty.

Our merchants have sold many millions of dollars' worth of their best paper at from three to six per cent. a month discount. From a six months' note for $1,000 take five per cent. a month, and the borrower will get only $700. The discount on the same note at seven per cent. per annum would be $35. In this one transaction this usury increases the borrower's indebtedness $265. If the merchants, manufacturers and mechanics of the city of New York would come out and frankly state, under their own signatures, what rates per cent. interest they have paid for the use of money during the last three months, giving the names of the parties from whom they have borrowed it, and the securities they have pledged to secure the payment of the money borrowed, hundreds, yes, thousands of extortions would be revealed which would greatly astonish the public. Could these transactions be further traced, we think it would be found that a very large amount of the loans of the banks are made to brokers and other usurers, and even to the officers and directors of banks themselves; many of whom would not borrow from bank at all when the street rates of interest were not above seven per cent. per annum. Let us look at the gain a usurer could make on but $100,000. Three months' discount at bank would be $1,750, leaving to his credit $98,250. This sum will buy paper at six per cent. a month to the amount of $119,817 07, and the paper would mature in time to meet his note at bank. Should the usurer renew his note for another three months, he would have $19,817,07 more to invest than he had before, amounting with the $98,250 to $118,067 07. This sum, at six per cent. a month, would buy $143,984 23 worth of notes. Thus the usurer would gain $43,984 23, on six months' investment of $100,000; and this too, without using a dollar of his own money and without having performed any productive labor. The men who sell this paper are indebted $43,984 23 more than they would have been had the banks discounted their notes at the usual rates, instead of driving them to borrow of the usurer. This is the usurer's harvest, when he is reaping what others have sowed and gathering what others have strewed.

How can our merchants pay these exorbitant rates of interest when they sell their goods for a profit of from five to fifteen per cent. at most, averaging probably not more than nine per cent., and then trust them out all over the southern and western States. And this is not all they have to encounter. In consequence of the usurious rates of interest, the exchanges between New York and the South and West are on the average nearly as

much as they made profits on their goods when they sold them. A merchant holding a note due the 1st of November at bank in a western city, may be compelled to wait twenty or thirty days after the note is paid before a bill of exchange can be bought on New York. Interest on money being at from three to six per cent. a month, the buyer of the note would take off the face of it this per centage, in addition to the rate that must be paid for the bill of exchange.

We think we have not overstated the rates of interest that have been paid during this crisis. Things have now reached such a state that usurers have lost nearly all confidence in the ability of debtors to discharge their obligations; for they make close calculations, and readily perceive that the above rates of exchange alone would about eat up all the profits made on goods sold during the last year, even if every debt were promptly paid at maturity. Add to this the depreciation of the goods they have on hand, and it is evident that these must rapidly consume all their former earnings. The indebtedness of the people has doubtless been increased several hundred millions of dollars by this crisis. If business could have taken its usual course the merchants in the city of New York would probably have collected fifty millions of dollars more from the country than they have now been able to do. Had they made these collections and paid debts to this amount, the indebtedness of the people would have been diminished one hundred millions of dollars; for these fifty millions are still owing to the city merchants, and the city merchants owe the fifty millions to others.

Is not the country rapidly sinking, instead of increasing in wealth? We think we shall not overestimate the number, if we say, there will be one million of people thrown out of employment for at least six months by this unnecessary financial crisis. If this million of mechanics and others could be employed at one dollar per day each, their earnings would be six millions a week, and in twenty-six weeks they would enhance the valuation of the country one hundred and fifty-six millions of dollars, which would amount to about as much as one half the banking capital of the whole United States. Those persons who are thrown out of employment must subsist on previous earnings or on the charity of others, so that, instead of being any longer producers, they are compelled to be simply consumers of wealth

All this comes upon us in addition to the diminution of the value of our merchants' assets, railroad assets, and that of all other property in the country. Nor will our grain and cotton crops command the same prices abroad that they would have done if this money crisis had not been brought upon us, hence our debts to foreign nations will be needlessly increased.

The remedy proposed for our financial difficulties is the accumulation of specie; but the people do not want specie; they have never wanted it when bank-notes would pay their debts and make their purchases. We have not a doubt that more than nineteen-twentieths of our debts are paid with paper money; and paper money is, therefore, practically the money of this nation. If the public did not prefer to use it rather than coin, paper money could not be established and made to transact the business. A run for specie has never been made on the banks except when they have been so managed as to throw the business community into the hands of usurers and stock-jobbers—which is only another name for the same class of individuals. Whenever the banks have maintained their lines of discount so as to furnish the community with money, there has been little demand for specie, and the gold and silver coins have, for the most part, lain idle in the vaults of the banks.

When the Ohio Life and Trust Company suspended payment, had the banks in the city of New York discounted every note offered that was considered safe, in less than three weeks, and probably in one week, money would have been as plenty in the city of New York and throughout the country as it has been at any time during the past ten years; and all undoubted securities that were bearing 7 per cent. interest would have commanded money at their par value. The business of the whole nation would doubtless have been as prosperous as it has been at any time during the last ten years. The agricultural productions of the South and West would have been rapidly sent to market, and would have sold at prices that would have remunerated the producer. Now, if they are freely sent into the market they will be sold at ruinous sacrifices. Men will not pay 4 or 5 per cent. a month for money to buy produce unless they feel sure they shall realize a good profit over the 4 or 5 per cent. by the investment.

The banks will tell the people that they could not have gone on safely and discounted all the well-secured paper offered; that the specie in their vaults had been considerably diminished by being drawn for exportation, and was liable to be diminished to a still greater extent. But why, when the specie was called for to subserve its proper uses of paying balances that occurred in trade, should it have been necessary to deprive the people of paper money, for which the security is in State stocks, and not in specie? Several times within the last ten years the banks have sought for and have been glad to discount paper at the rate of five per cent. per annum, even when it had seven and eight months to run; and no good reason has appeared why they were not as in good condition to make money plenty and discount freely in August last as they were at any previous time whatever.

The banks are professedly established for the good of the public, but they are often so conducted as to break down the business of the country and enrich usurers. The capital stock of the banks in all the States of the Union would not exced one-half of that invested in railroads, yet all the railroads are prostrated before the all-absorbing power of the banks. The prostration of business on these railroads, the usurious interest they have paid for money, and the depreciation of their stocks and bonds in market, are doubtless a greater loss to those interested in railroads alone than if they had lost one half of all the banking capital in the Union. Besides this, many of these railroads will doubtless go into the hands of the first and second bond-holders; and thousands of the stock-holders, who have taken the stock hoping to benefit the public, will be turned out of their farms and homesteads, penniless. Is it not strange that these little round pieces of metal and these little pieces of paper in the form of bank-notes, both of which look to be as powerless and harmless as the toys of children, should be clothed with such power as to baffle the minds of the most sagacious men and paralyze the business of the nation?

Now, to show what measures would in reality afford relief to the public, we will state what measures have afforded relief in similar financial crises, both in this country and in England, and the propriety of the immediate application of the remedy will, we think, be apparent to every business man.

In 1834, large contractions were made both by the United

States and the State banks, and for a few weeks there was nearly as great a panic in the money market as there was in August last, and quite a large number of merchants failed. But when the offerings for discount at the banks had become very large, the United States Branch Bank in the City of New York, unexpectedly to the public, discounted every piece of paper offered that was deemed good. The other banks immediately followed this example, and in a very short time the rates of interest went down from two, three and four per cent. a month to five, six and seven per cent. per annum, and business at once revived and went on prosperously.

In 1847 (I quote from memory) there was a great financial crisis in England, the issues of the Bank of England having been limited by the financial bill of Sir Robert Peel, passed in 1844. The rates of interest rose from 3, 4 and 5 per cent. per annum to 1, 2, 3 and even higher rates per month, and thousands of merchants and manufacturers were bankrupted and had to suspend payment. A meeting was called in London, and a committee was appointed to wait on Lord John Russell and request that the Bank of England should extend her discounts so as to make money plenty. Lord John replied that it was contrary to the laws of England to increase the circulation beyond the fourteen millions of pounds sterling secured by government stock; that the issues above this sum must be governed by the amount of bullion in the bank; that he had no authority to exceed this amount, and that the people must take care of their own financial affairs. The committee retired without obtaining any relief. A few days or weeks after, the committee waited again upon Lord John Russell, with a similar request, and met with a similar refusal. But before retiring they remarked that they should break the bank. Lord John Russell asked them if they could do it, and the committee informed him that the gentlemen whom they represented had a much larger amount on deposit than all the bullion in the bank; that they should draw what there was and take their chances for the balance. This strong argument had its effect on the mind of Lord John Russell, for the bank at once began to discount liberally. Money became very plenty at very low rates of interest, and business revived.

In the present crisis, the same means must be used to relieve us from our financial difficulties that ought to have been used to prevent their occurrence. Let the banks in the city of New York discount every piece of paper offered which they consider safe and good, and let them adjust their balances among themselves and with other banks throughout the Union as they have hitherto done when money was plenty. Let them discount paper that has four, five and six months to run as well as short paper. They can do this as well now as they ever could at any previous time. Let them discount thus liberally and the business of the nation will revive; the products of the South and West will find their way to market, and command much better prices both at home and abroad than they possibly can so long as this contraction of bank issues continues. Many of our railroads may yet go on and prosper.

But let the banks continue their present course and they will continue to throw the money into the hands of the usurers, and the usurers will stand between the banks and the business public. Many more of our merchants will be broken, and those who have suspended will be obliged to renew their extensions. There will be hundreds and thousands of starving laborers in our streets, while this year's abundant crops will be stored away in granaries for want of money to get them to market. The property of debtors will be exhausted and thrown into the hands of creditors, and there will be few securities remaining to offer for the loan of money. The usurers will themselves cease to borrow largely at bank, for there will be few left to borrow of them. The banks, then, finding their business falling off, will begin to discount freely, and money will be seeking investment at low rates of interest and the useful business of the nation will gradually revive. Whether business shall revive now, our manufacturers resume their operations, our laborers be employed; or whether the present condition of the money market shall continue until the country is completely prostrate, and the wealth of the nation, for the greater part, accumulated in the hands of the usurers, is at the option of the banks in the city of New York.

EDWARD KELLOGG.

Brooklyn, Nov. 13th, 1857.

E.—*Page* 245.

When we read of our ancestors in ages long past carving out of wood some strange and grotesque image, and then falling down in adoration before it, as though it had some mysterious power by which the heavens and earth were brought forth and sustained in their orbits; and to which the nations of the earth were bound to offer up not only the choicest fruits of their labor, but also their own lives and those of their children in order to appease this deity, and that even kings and the chief rulers of nations bowed down in worship before the power of a wooden or brazen god, we look back with astonishment at the ignorance and superstition that prevailed, and congratulate ourselves that these have disappeared in the sunshine of an enlightened age. But the time is not distant when people will look back on this gold-ridden age with as much wonder at our ignorance, and at the superstition that now attaches to the power and worth of the gold, as we do at the power and worth which our ancestors gave or attached to the wooden god. Their wooden gods had as much power to create and sustain the world, as the gold has to nourish the human body, or bring out and sustain the virtues of the human mind. We sacrifice the choicest fruits of our labor upon the altar of this golden god. We sacrifice to it in wars and tumults the property and lives of our own citizens, and those of the men, women, and children of neighboring nations. Even the rulers of nations must bow down before the " almighty dollar." If these golden images are hidden in vaults under the earth, and the rulers want to carry on wars, they must make sacrifices of the fruits of the labor of future generations, that they may be brought forth to sustain the slaughter. If these mighty coins should move off, and cease to be seen in our land, we should have to bow down our heads in the dust, and clothe ourselves in sackcloth and ashes until they were returned to us; the laboring poor would die of hunger in the streets of our cities, and desolation and gloom would spread over the country. But how does it happen that these gold and silver dollars could cause all this? Is it because the metals have any more sustenance for man than the carved images which ruled over our fathers? Have we not as much made and formed these gold and silver images with our hands as they did the images that they carved out for themselves with their hands? Has the gold or silver a single more element for human support than their carved images; and if they have, are the inherent qualities of these metals any more used while they form a currency than the inherent qualities of the wood when it was formed into an image and daubed over with pitch and paint? Or would the earth cease to bring forth her increase because the gold and silver had absented themselves from the land, more than if these carved images should have been removed from the land of our fathers? No doubt the removal of the images would have been thought a great calamity, but not more so than the removal of the gold and silver money in our day; and they would have had as much reason for their distress as we should for ours. The removal now of a few tons of gold and silver coins from our country to a foreign one, or even from one part of our country to another, causes great agitation and consternation; but the time is not far distant when the removal of a few tons of these metals will have no more influence upon the happiness and welfare of the people than the removal of a few hundred tons of iron or lead.—*MSS.*

F.—*Page* 247.

The most fundamental and important truths in relation to the nature of money, have always been so covered up by the technicalities of law as completely to deceive the people respecting its true character, although they have always known and felt that there was something wrong in its power. Writers upon political economy as well as the public in general, have taken it for granted that the laws of nations were right in founding the value of money in the innate value of the gold and silver metals out of which it was coined: hence the conclusions at which they must all arrive, are just as false as the premises upon which they start. And political economists may continue to write and the public may continue to argue upon these premises for centuries to come, and be just as far from the truth as when money was instituted upon this basis. Notwithstanding this mystification about money, its true character and power are very simple, and need only to be clearly and fairly stated to meet the approval of the common mind; and then the public must know that the present centralizing power of money is as gross an imposition upon the common sense of man, as it is upon the common rights of labor and property. For if the material of neither gold, silver nor paper money can in itself be used as food, clothing or shelter, then certainly the scarcity or abundance of money, or the scarcity or abundance of the materials of money, ought never in the least to interfere with a general and full supply of all the necessaries of life. For these necessaries of life are evidently the product of labor, and not the product of money. Yet the present power of money is such that the people are compelled first to work for money, and then to depend upon the power of money to supply the necessaries of life. Thus the power of money is first, and the power of labor is second. The money commands the labor instead of labor commanding the money. This is exactly reversing the true order of things, for it is making a dead centralizing power to rule and tyrannize over the living, productive power, whereas the productive ought always to command the unproductive power. If any writers upon political economy, or any financiers, have discovered the true nature, power and use of money, they have not made such discovery manifest to the understanding of the public. For the laws of nations as well as the newspapers and other publications of the day, are still carrying forward and enforcing the idea that money is a productive, living power. Yet the power of money is entirely a dead power, and totally unproductive notwithstanding its legal, accumulative powers.—*MSS.*

G.—*Page* 253.

Let me illustrate the effects of "free trade" in the use or interest on money loaned—a plan which is advocated by many people in our cities, and doubtless by many in the country. They say, Make merchandise of money, let the man who will give the most for its use borrow the money, and allow no laws to interfere between the parties contracting—if A. has money and B. wants it, let B. buy its use as cheap as he can from A., and, if he is not suited with the price A. demands for it, let him borrow of some other person: he is not obliged to take A.'s money any more than he is compelled to buy A.'s potatoes; has not a man a right to do what he will with his own? A captain of a ship at sea might see on fire near him another ship, full of people, and say to the passengers and crew of the burning vessel, "If you will give me all your possessions in money, goods and chattels, I will take you on my ship: but, if you do not wish to comply with my terms, I shall not take you on board; this ship is mine, and I have a right to do what I will with my own. I shall not urge you to come on my vessel on the terms I propose; you had no business to place yourselves in such a situation; it is your own fault, not mine; therefore if you do come it is because I like to help people out of difficulties. My *humanity* prompts me to make this offer." Do you not think the passengers and all would accede to the terms, and be glad to get on board of the ship of this humane man? If this benevolent captain had secretly, by the aid of ship-brokers, set the vessel on fire with a slow match, and then happened to be near and proposed these terms to those in distress, he would be in principle much like our modern usurers, who hoard the public measure of value when they very well know that it is impossible for the public —either individuals, States, or the United States—to fulfil their contracts without the money, and they can make any terms they please with those in distress. The captain of the ship would have about as much good feeling for the passengers and crew of the burning vessel, as these men have who hold the money to extort the last farthing from the producers.

Suppose a surveyor owns his chain to measure land, and, when appointed by government a public measurer of land, should say to one needing his service, "The chain is mine, and I will stretch it out to double its legal length if you will give me so much for measuring;" to another, "I will contract so much if you will pay me for it; the chain is mine, and have I not a right to use it as I please? Who has any right to dictate to me what I shall do with my property?" Now, the length of the chain being altered one-third, does not more effectually alter the quantity of land measured, than adding one-third to the interest on money alters every contract based on money, and the public measurers would have as good right to use their chains in this way as a man loaning money has to alter the interest on the money. No matter in whose hands money may be, it is a definite thing, and the only public measure and base of value of everything in all nations.

Free trade in the use in loaning money is as certain to prove destructive to the debtor's property as a free right, because you own your knife, to plunge it into your neighbor's breast would be certain to endanger his life. We are as much in duty bound to protect our citizens by law from these depredations upon their property, as we are to protect them by law against the assassin's knife. For many a man who through a long life has been able to support his family comfortably, has not been able to bear up under these sudden and unexpected robberies, generally called misfortunes, and aberration of mind or death has been the consequence, and he has left his family to the cold charities of the world.

H.—*Page* 282.

If the Safety Fund should lend its money at six per cent. interest, and Richard Roe should borrow $1,000 on mortgage of his farm that rents for $120 a year, every year he would have to pay to the Safety Fund $60 interest or one half the rent of his farm. The $1,000 in money would represent the first half of the value of the farm; and Richard Roe would have to lose all the second half before the Safety Fund could lose any portion of the half on which it had lent him the money. The Safety Fund money being always the representative of the first half of the value of productive property the second half of the value must entirely sink before the first half could be at all deteriorated.

The lower the interest on the Safety Fund money, the greater would be the certainty of its perfect security and goodness. For, if Richard Roe should borrow from the Fund the $1,000 at six per. cent. interest yearly, in less than twelve years he would have to pay over to the Safety Fund in interest a sum equal to the principal that he borrowed; that is, one half the entire value of his farm. But suppose the interest should be fixed at one and one tenth-per cent. per annum, and he should borrow the $1,000 at this rate on mortgage of his farm, he would have but $11 a year to pay instead of $60, and it would be above sixty years before he would have to pay back to the Safety Fund in interest a sum equal to the principal borrowed, that is, one half of the value of his farm.

If the per centage interest be regular, the producer cannot be made to pay a sum in rent or interest equal to the principal in any shorter time whether you call a given lump of gold or a certain farm worth $100 or $1,000. If John Doe owns this lump of gold or this farm, and rent either to Richard Roe at ten per cent. per annum without compounding the interest, in ten years the latter must pay a sum in interest equal to the principal borrowed. If the lump of gold or the farm were called worth only $100, and were rented at the same rate of ten per cent., Richard Roe would still pay back in ten years a sum in interest equal to the principal borrowed. But if he borrowed the same lump of gold or the same farm at one per cent. without compounding the interest, it would be a hundred years before he would have to pay to John Doe a sum in interest equal to the principal.

The interest on money is the standard, and the rents of all property must conform to its governing power. Although this principle has been repeatedly stated, as it is important that it should be clearly understood in connection with the Safety Fund, we will offer another simple illustration. Suppose John Doe's farm, in consequence of the reduction of interest on the establishment of the Safety Fund, to rise in value from $2,000 to $10,000, and the Fund to lend him on mortgage of it $5,000 at one and one-tenth per cent. interest. The yearly interest on the $5,000 would be but $55, and before John Doe must return to the Safety Fund a sum in interest equal to the principal borrowed, the same number of years would elapse as if the farm had not risen in price in consequence of the reduction of the rate of interest. John Doe need not pay to the Fund a sum in interest equal to one-half the value of his farm in less than sixty years, but if the interest were at six per cent., he would have to pay a sum in interest equal to the principal borrowed in less than twelve years. It must be borne in mind that the value is in John Doe's farm and not in the money: the money merely represents the value of the farm. The interest that accrues on the money borrowed is a representative of production, but it is not production. The production is made by labor upon the farm; the interest that accrues upon the money is an arbitrary, legal, balancing power against a certain part of the products of the farm. The money merely helps the people to exchange one commodity for another; and the rate of interest decides what proportion of the products of labor shall be awarded to those who perform the labor and what proportion shall go to those who receive the income without labor.—*MSS.*

I.—*Page* 289.

I will examine a little further the operations of money upon our commerce and foreign trade. In order to explain, I will suppose a case: It is known to our government and citizens that very many wealthy houses of Europe have agents or bankers in our large commercial cities. The Rothschilds, Barings, and many others of this class wield an immense capital, and are able to raise almost any sum of money which can be advantageously invested. The very purpose for which these houses are established here is to make money by buying stocks, advancing on securities and drawing bills of exchange on foreign nations, etc. The general business of these bankers is dealing in money, not in merchandise; they may make advances on cotton, but this is not dealing in cotton—it is simply holding the pledge of cotton as collateral security for the payment of money loaned. These houses are in the habit of drawing bills of exchange on England, Germany, France and other countries, for large sums, and it is in their power at any time to derange our whole monetary system and disturb our domestic trade throughout the country. Thus they could make great profit, but it would be by robbing us of our just rights; and the consequent fluctuations would put it in the power of creditors throughout the nation to take undue advantage of debtors. I will merely state the case, and I think no business man can fail to see the practicability of such an operation. These bankers in the different Atlantic cities have wealth and credit sufficient to draw bills of exchange on England, France and Germany, dispose of and get the money for them in the course of one or two months to the amount of five, six, seven or more millions of dollars, as our foreign trade amounts to about one hundred millions a year, which are paid by bills of exchange; thus the drafts to pay this sum would average over eight millions a month, and when the largest amount is required to be remitted, it would be an easy matter for these bankers, through their agents, to sell in two months seven or eight millions of exchange on the various countries before mentioned. Several houses have agents in a number of our Atlantic cities and whether they sold bills of exchange on England or France at New York, New Orleans, Baltimore, Philadelphia or Boston, they could easily concentrate all the funds in New York, and as the money came in for the bills of exchange sold, they could draw the amount from the New York banks in specie, and ship it to England or any other country to meet the drafts. The drafts being drawn as usual, payable sixty days after sight, they would have sixty days to prepare and ship the specie to meet the drafts at maturity. If they have the credit to draw and sell the drafts, all these operations could take place with little or no capital. If even three or four millions in specie in the course of one or two months were drawn from the New York banks, it would curtail their discounts and probably raise the rates of interest in Wall street to one, one and a half or more per cent. a month. Should it be attempted to draw suddenly seven or eight millions, no doubt a suspension of specie payment by the banks throughout the Union would be the result; exchange on England would rise to fifteen or twenty per cent. above par, and a general scarcity of money would ensue; cotton would fall to half its former price, and as it fell in our market it would also fall in England; exchange on England being very high, the cotton at greatly reduced prices would be hurried forward to pay debts in England, and we should be compelled to send double the quantity of cotton or any other product to pay our debt abroad (or again to import the same amount of specie) that we should if our currency had not been deranged. Thus we should be robbed of nearly one half of our products without receiving for them the slightest equivalent; and the debtors in our own country, by the rise of interest and the scarcity of money, would be obliged to give double the labor or property to meet their engagements at home. The exchanges would be deranged throughout the country, the banks would curtail their discounts, and distress and ruin ensue. Such operations as these, impairing the ability of producers and consumers to buy, by causing a fall in the price of cotton and other products, would in turn destroy the market for goods manufactured, and cause goods and labor to fall in England, and the laboring poor would be impoverished there; the capital or wealth of both nations would be concentrated in the hands of a few without rendering the least equivalent to those who earned it. Now, to what would all these troubles be attributed, and to what have like revulsions been always attributed? Why, to over-production, over-trading, too much credit, etc. These disasters are laid at the door of the honest producer and trader, while the real cause is either concealed, or at all events is not understood. . . . .

Suppose one hundred of the richest men in the city of New York should agree to draw specie from the banks and hold it themselves for a given time—say one, two, or three months— keeping the engagement to themselves, so that the public would be unacquainted with their intentions: less than eighty-five thousand dollars for each individual would draw every dollar of specie from every bank in the State, and some of these men could easily furnish several times the sum allotted to each. All who would make these drafts are the actual owners of the money they would draw from the banks; and as they owe no one, they could keep it as long as they pleased, whether one, two, or three months or longer. I presume no one acquainted in New York would doubt the ability of one hundred of our citizens to command this money without being indebted to any one for a dollar; but should this be questioned, it would only be necessary to add a few to the number to accomplish it. Should this be done, every bank in the city must stop specie payment; and this would probably cause a run on the banks in all the Atlantic cities, and another suspension throughout the United States would be the consequence. This would at once occasion a great scarcity of money, and would reduce property much below its present price; then suppose the men who held this specie should denounce banks and State stock, saying all this kind of paper is worth next to nothing, and that all sorts of property ought to be sold for specie, as there is certainly no dependence to be placed in banks. Let these men still hold the specie, and not buy a dollar's worth of property themselves for six months—I ask what would property bring, provided a mortgage, or one hundred mortgages, were foreclosed in New York, and the property sold for specie? If a bank should be sued, and it held State stock as collateral security, and should sell it for specie, what would the stores, houses, and State stock bring in specie? Who would have the specie to buy them? The property would not sell for more than a quarter of its present estimated value;

yet these men have a right by law to do all this, and the State Government and the United States Government would be utterly powerless in the matter, and could not help themselves nor the citizens. These hundred men would hold nearly all the legal tender of the State, and the citizens are bound by law to pay their debts in this tender, which it would be impossible for them to procure; they could no more pay them than the children of Israel could make brick without straw; they could neither get the money from abroad nor at home: credit would be entirely prostrated and the laborer beg from door to door. Yet such are our laws on this all-important subject: our citizens are absolutely legally robbed by their own neighbors and before their own eyes, but have no power to prevent it.

It will be said that these hundred men would lose the interest on their money, and therefore there would be no inducement to this; but I answer specie would bring a much greater premium than all the loss of interest, or they could buy good bonds and mortgages at an enormous sacrifice, or property for less than half its value. If they chose, before they made the run on the banks, they could sell State or bank stock, to be delivered at a certain time within three or six months, and calculate with a moral certainty that the stock would fall in price so that they could take the difference without buying the stock at all; and if they should buy it, they could have it delivered the same day, and draw the money they pay for the stock from the persons to whom they sold, without encroaching on one dollar of the specie drawn from the banks. These hundred men by this means would doubtless more than double their money. The public have nothing to guard them against this but the tender consciences of these men, and the people who have within a few years past paid to them from one to four per cent. a month for the interest or the use of money, with every pledge which the parties could possibly give to secure the safe return of the money, can pretty well judge as to the conscientious scruples of our most wealthy moneyed men in the city.

When hard times begin, the merchants, who are the first to feel the pressure, look about to see what expenses they can avoid. They dismiss some of their clerks and cut down the salaries of others; for their families they procure houses of which the rent is low, or else get their landlords to reduce the rent of those they occupy, and the same with stores. The clerks find a cheaper place to board, or reduce the price at their present places. The manufacturers dismiss some of their hands, and cut down the wages of those whom they continue to employ, and all mechanics do the same. Cotton falls in price, and those producing it must buy fewer goods and pay less for the production of the cotton. All articles for food fall in price, and of course the farmers raising them must pay less for the labor they employ, and buy less clothing for their families, and all those who work for them must do the same; hence people consume more of articles produced with little labor and less of those which require more. Many without employment are unable to buy even the cheapest food and clothing at these low rates, and all lands, tenements, everything in the country produced by labor, falls in price. When this occurs, it is said that it makes no difference if you receive low wages, you buy all those things at a proportionably low rate, so one thing balances another. They do not even consider that all these things are in the same end of the scale, and bear the same way; they do not perceive that little devil—money—in the other end of the scale, and his imps (the usurers) laughing in their sleeves at the folly of the producers, and saying, "With six cents we can now weigh in this balance as much as we did before with twelve, eighteen, or twenty-five. However divisible this labor may be, whether large or small, from a penny to the sale of the Exchange in New York for over eight hundred thousand dollars, we are so divisible that we can at all times fix an exact balance, and by a sort of magic can expand ten or twenty cents to a dollar, and again contract to ten or fifteen cents. I and my imps never want a balance for all or any of the bounties of Providence: I can by my imps draw myself up into a nut-shell, and I and my possessors as much balance all these things when so drawn up as when I by them expand over the world. When I through them expand, the people think less of me; when I by them contract myself, I draw the nation with me, government and all; they feel my power, and reverence my authority, and they are as much compelled to bow before me as the people of Babylon were to the golden image set up by Nebuchadnezzar."—*Currency, the Evil and the Remedy.*

J.—*Page* 302

Again, in regard to the amount of currency which would be required for the business of the nation, I think it would be less than has generally been in circulation. The currency being at par in every section of the country, no delay in procuring drafts for remittance, or any holding on for higher rates of interest, money would circulate with great rapidity, and consequently for the same amount of business a less quantity would be necessary; and, as to wild speculation, there would be less danger from that than there ever has been in any country. The great speculations which make so much noise, in building-lots, houses, lands, etc., would never very materially interfere with the general business of the nation; the business of a few individuals might be broken up where they bought on credit and agreed to pay for property a larger sum than they could make the property pay interest on; but this would never interrupt the general prosperity of a people. We never hear of hard times in any country except when the interest on money advances; the first complaint is always of a scarcity of money, want of what is necessary to do business; not only a scarcity of money to pay for building-lots, but a scarcity for all business purposes. From great abundance, we are suddenly in great want, and the rates of interest have increased double, treble or quadruple. One now borrows money at six per cent. interest at bank because he is among the favored; another pays in the same street the same day twelve per cent., another twenty-four, and another, who is "cornered," thirty-six; the last buys the use of the same article, in the same street, on the same day, and pays six times as much as the first; he does this from necessity. Why is not one person obliged to pay on the same day in the same market, for a barrel of flour or a bushel of potatoes, six times as much as another individual who may happen to be in better credit or greater favor? Is there not as great a risk in selling these articles as in lending money? Do people give better security when they buy merchandise than when they borrow money? What would be said of a grocer who made as much difference in the price of a pound of sugar or a quart of molasses, charging those who were in the greatest need the most exorbitant prices? Those who can buy almost any quantity of goods at the usual market prices in their own names without giving any security, pay these enormous prices for money. Goods, wares and merchandise, which are the products of labor, we trust out on a single name, without requiring any security for the payment of the debt. We do not expect the persons buying these goods to be impoverished by the purchase; if we anticipated any such result, we should certainly demand security, as we should know we were injuring our customers. But, as a general thing, we should not sell to them at all, for if it were usual for people to lose by the purchase of goods, wares or merchandise, or any property whatever, the product of labor; none of these things would be sold without security, and all confidence between individuals would be lost. Society could scarcely exist in this state; it would indeed be in a wretched condition. We may discourse about a cash system without credit as much as we please, but it is an impossibility; it never did and never can exist.

Why is it necessary that in lending money it should be hedged about with so many securities, and these securities so often suffer by it? The only reason which can be assigned for it is that people are compelled to pay more for the use of money than the use of money is worth. If this were not the case, to loan money would not be hazardous. All the debts contracted by the purchase of goods, wares and merchandise, are payable in money as much as debts contracted by borrowing money. Why should not a debt be as sacred where a shoemaker has bought his leather and given his note or paid the money on it, and spent his labor in making the shoes, as a debt for money loaned? May not a man as well lose his money as his labor and leather, when he depends upon these for his bread, as much as the other does upon his money for his subsistence? I believe more than nine-tenths, and probably more than ninety-nine hundredths, of these debts in both cases are lost in consequence of unjust laws in the monetary system. The interest on money in all countries is far higher than the producers can afford to pay, and not only so but interest has never been regulated in any nation. Money being the base of all contracts, the change in the rates of interest, and the monopoly of money change the base of every contract in the nation after the contract is made, and then the producing classes are blamed for over-production and extravagance, while those who have done the evil are esteemed for their wisdom and prudence.

There are few people who contract debts without intending to pay them, and no one except a thief at heart would do it unless compelled to it by actual want. But thousands, by expecting to obtain work and being disappointed in this, become discouraged and broken down by the hardships they endure. These men are to be pitied instead of being blamed, as they now are by the community—they need encouragement instead of condemnation and imprisonment; no man should seek for employment and be unable to get it.

Until there is a radical change in the monetary system, these evils must and will continue as certainly as cause will produce effect. No remedy which does not strike at the root of the evil can remove it, and the power to do this is in the hands of the nation.

The sudden scarcity of money does not depend on the showers of the heavens or on an abundant crop, but upon the will of a few moneyed men, Wall street brokers and petty banks, who determine when it shall be scarce and when plenty, and when the rate of interest shall be high or low. When they have, by sudden curtailment, after a prosperous season of business, concentrated in their hands a large portion of the earnings of the people, it is for their interest again to lend money at low rates of interest, that the people may earn more property to be again taken from them by the same unjust means.—*Currency, the Evil and the Remedy.*

K.—*Page* 313.

The avarice that pervades the civilized world has been ingrafted upon society by the too great power of money. In most countries it has made production by labor degrading to the child whose necessity compels him to perform it. The skill to gain by lending money, and by taking advantage of others in bargaining, has been, and is taken as evidence of superior talent, until, by example and precept, avarice has been instilled into the minds of children. It has grown with their growth and strengthened with their strength until it has corrupted the very foundations of society. The per centage incomes on bank, railroad, State, and other stocks, and the rates at which money can be borrowed and lent, are the great leading topics of a business community. The topics are not, How shall we contrive to produce by our labor the greatest supply of all the necessaries of life for the general good? but, on the contrary, How shall we contrive to get the largest possible per centage income with the least possible production on our part? This state of society is directly at variance with such a one as a just monetary system would naturally induce. It is as much opposed to the natural rights of society as falsehood is to truth; and no continuance of competition in production or distribution, under the present monetary laws, will be any more likely to remedy the evils of this debasing system, than competition in falsehood would be likely to produce and sustain truth. We must begin improvement by doing away the great gain by unrighteous per centage interest on money; and then the wealth will naturally be widely distributed among those who do the most for the good of man, instead of being gathered by a few, who thus become the great oppressors of the human family.—*MSS.*

L.—*Page* 314.

As the present monetary laws have adjusted society, what prospect is there before a young man starting in life? Is there any reasonable encouragement for him to produce the means of subsistence as God has ordained—that is, by his daily labor? If he sells only his own labor, or the articles which his own daily labor will produce, without any other traffic, trade, or speculation by which he may gain undue advantage from the labor of others, he is doomed to the severest toil for his whole life, especially if he marries and maintains a family. Should he be disabled for a season by sickness or other misfortune, or in a money crisis happen to be thrown out of work, then he and his family are compelled to be solicitors of public or private charity, or else they must suffer for the want of food, clothing, and shelter. Thousands in the cities of New York and Brooklyn are now (on this fifteenth day of February, 1855) in this sad predicament. Yet these evils and sufferings are very often attributed to the mysterious workings of the laws of God, while they are ev dently owing to the mysterious magical workings of the monetary laws of man; and are as much in opposition to the righteous laws of God as the acts of an individual who commits arson or murder, and are as much more aggravated in their character, and effects upon the welfare of the public, as a national transgression is greater than an individual one.

Mr. R. W. Emerson, in one of his lectures, speaks of judges or governments acting in their official capacity as the brains of the nation. If the brains of this nation cannot make laws that will govern the dollar, then the dollar is greater than the government brains that made it; for if two great powers meet in competition with each other, the greater will rule the lesser power; and in this, as well as in other civilized nations, the dollar is the greater power, and rules the brains. Governments both theoretically and practically admit, that they have not brains enough to govern the use of the dollar, and so they bow down in submission to the gold and silver idols which they have set up; and by and through the use of these idols the nation is governed in opposition to every just law of God and man. The dollar not only governs the brains of the nation, but it also comes into competition with the physical and muscular powers of the laboring classes; and though their brains direct how they shall perform their manual labor in production, yet all the machinery brought into use, and all the labor that man can perform, have no power at all to stand in competition with the centralizing power of money.

What does the Government of the State of New York say in relation to this important matter? It says that borrowed money is worth seven per cent. interest per annum, which means just this: that the producing classes are bound by law first to support themselves, and in addition to this, that they shall by their labor, every ten years and three months, make all the improvements that have been made in this State from its first settlement down to the present day, and also produce all the machinery, goods, wares and merchandise which are now on hand, or which they may use in making these improvements, and give all these improvements to the capitalists who now own the property, for the ten years and three months' rent of this property. If all the inhabitants of the State were now to engage in active production, it is doubtful whether they could support themselves, and make all the improvements that now exist in this State even in fifty years: for the inhabitants of this State have been at work nearly two hundred and fifty years to produce these improvements; yet the monetary laws of this State require those who are engaged in production and distribution to perform all this in ten years and three months. The laws require of the laboring classes that which they cannot possibly perform, and then cast censure upon them for not performing impossibilities. These remarks upon the centralizing power of money are no fictions, but are truths susceptible of the clearest mathematical demonstration, and under such impositions upon the producing classes, is it any wonder that people should seek for some profession, or engage in traffic, trade, and speculation, or almost any other calling, rather than that of productive labor?—*MSS.*

M.—*Page* 320.

The rights of property in a nation cannot be protected except by general laws; for it would be impossible for the Government to see that every individual in making his bargains with others got the exact value of what he sold, and that the purchaser got the exact worth of his money. The Government could not fix a price for the daily labor of each individual, and compel others to employ him at this price, unless it should also compel others to buy the products of labor at remunerating prices. It is utterly impracticable for the Government to have a supervision over the individual agreements in the nation, and superintend the business transactions of the public. All that it can or ought to do in this important matter, is to make such general laws for the government of the property as will naturally tend to effect its equitable distribution. Money holds a legal position in regard to other things which gives to it a controlling power. It is the legal standard by which all values are determined, and the medium by and through which the exchange of all valuable things is effected. It is by and through the power of money that the individual rights of property in every nation are awarded and protected. The laws sustain the money in its position and protect its power while it is performing its functions in making the distribution of wealth. The laws protect the rights of property by enforcing the fulfilment of agreements, so that each shall receive what the power of the money has distributed to him as his share of the wealth. Hence the protection of the rights of property must depend entirely upon the just power of the money; if the power of the money be unjust, it will be certain to make an unjust distribution of the property, and the laws will protect the unjust distribution, for they must support the power of the money and enforce the fulfilment of individual agreements made in conformity with its legal standard power, otherwise they would be totally inconsistent in themselves.

Governments establish and sustain money, and make it the basis upon which individual agreements must be founded, and then leave individuals free to make their own agreements one with another, in exchanging their land, labor and commodities. This is the way in which all civilized nations protect the legal rights of property; and there is no other practicable way in which they can be protected. There is an exception to this in countries where the laws recognize a privileged class, and landed property held by this class is protected by special laws, and is not liable to be sold to pay their debts. By thus exempting their property from execution, it is not under the controlling power of money, but all the other property in the country is governed by this power.

Money holds a legal position as totally different from that held by labor and property as the position held by the helm of a ship is different from that held by the ship and its cargo. It is its position that gives to the helm the power to govern and direct the destiny of the ship; and it is the legal position of money that gives to it the power to govern the value of all property, and control the distribution of wealth." If the helm were removed from the ship's stern and placed in the hold, it would be as powerless to control the direction of the ship as any other part of the cargo; and the ship and cargo, helm and all, would be at the mercy of the winds and waves. If all the gold and silver coins in the Sub-Treasury and banks were made into plate for private use, they would be as powerless to govern the value of property and the distribution of wealth as the helm of the ship when stowed in the hold to direct the course of the vessel. They would both have lost their position to govern. The money might be recoined, and it would be restored to its former position and power; and the helm might be again attached to the stern of the ship, and thus be restored to its former position and power. The helm of a ship made of wood, iron, and copper is better and more convenient for use than it would be if it were made of solid gold; and money when made of paper is far more convenient for use than when it is made of gold and silver. If the National Government will institute good paper money, and by making it the legal tender, place it in its true position, it will save an immense amount of labor, besides being a far safer currency for public use. When the Government shall institute paper money secured by landed estate, and then found its value upon a just rate per cent. interest instead of upon its material, and shall make it a tender in payment of debts, it will rightly govern the value and distribution of property, for it will be sure to distribute the wealth according to the earnings o labor; whereas it is now sure to help a few to monopolize the wealth that the many produce by their labor. If the money be thus instituted, and a rate per cent. interest be established sufficient only to pay the expense of furnishing it, the money will form a just foundation upon which to build contracts.

We are aware that the financiers of this and other nations will tell the public, and endeavor to persuade the governments that this is impossible—that since it never has been done, it never can be done. They will be just as positive in relation to this all-important matter as kings and despots are that they have a divine right to reign, and that a democratic or republican government is a trespass against Divine authority, and never will be permitted to stand except for a brief period of time. To fix and maintain a right rate per cent. interest for the use of money is striking at the very root of despotic power; and the producing public must expect to have it called impracticable, and to have a strong opposition to its adoption. Yet we do know that it is as practicable for the Government to supply the necessary quantity of money that shall be permanently safe, and regulate the rate per cent. interest as to fix and regulate the length of the yard. The Government can do this so effectually that any person can as readily tell what the rate of interest will be in every part of this nation for five or ten years to come as to tell what will be the length of the yard. Money is as much a standard of value as the yard is of length, and it should and can be so instituted and governed that any one may as readily tell the value of money as the length of the yard.—*MSS.*

"𝔈𝔢 𝔰𝔥𝔞𝔩𝔩 𝔫𝔬𝔱 𝔣𝔞𝔦𝔩 𝔫𝔬𝔯 𝔟𝔢 𝔡𝔦𝔰𝔠𝔬𝔲𝔯𝔞𝔤𝔢𝔡, 𝔱𝔦𝔩𝔩 𝔥𝔢 𝔥𝔞𝔳𝔢 𝔰𝔢𝔱 𝔧𝔲𝔡𝔤𝔪𝔢𝔫𝔱 𝔦𝔫 𝔱𝔥𝔢 𝔢𝔞𝔯𝔱𝔥."

INDEX.

A.

Agreements. Of capitalists with laborers, 28. Freedom of, fails to secure just reward of labor, 28. Foundation of, unsound, 29. Freedom of, limited by standard of value, 29. Unjust, 29. The rate of interest ought not to be a subject of, 65. Fair appearance of, but false foundation, 88, 151. With just rate of interest, just rents fixed upon in voluntary, 134, note. Voluntary, no test of justice, 161, 167 166. Gambling, void, 164, 329. Mutual, cannot make gambling just, 165. With just money, will award just share of production, 165. Made by use of the power of money without its material substance, 257. Money, the basis upon which, must be founded, 364.

Avarice, how generated, 360.

B.

Banks. Receive their charters by legal enactments, 193. How they resemble and how differ from manufacturing companies, 195. How established, 196. What constitutes capital of, 197, 198. Securities partly furnished by the borrowers of money, 197. Principle upon which their contracts with the people are made, 199. Capital of, under General Banking Law of the State of New York, 200. Failures of, during six or seven years, 201. Deposits in, ought to be as secure as the bank-notes circulated, 203. Chartered with a professed specie capital, average of specie held by, 205. Specie capital of, how made up, 206. Discounts made by, in New York, 207. Expenditures of, 210. Their contractions of loans said to be judicious, 210. Relative position of, toward the people reversed, 212, 213. Gains of, by deposits, 218, 219. Power of, in regard to discounts, 220. Operations of, illustrated in management of discounts, 220, 221, 222, 223. Profits of, from fluctuations in value of money, 237. Can easily raise rate of interest, 238. In instituting new monetary system need not interfere with charters of, 300. Safety Fund money competent to pay debts to, 301. Institution of Safety Fund will do no injustice to, 302. Risks greater with present, than under Safety Fund system, 303.

Bank-notes. As valuable to purchase property as coins, 55, 271. Value of, in legal authority, 55. Not merchandise, 195. Security for, furnished by the public, 196, 210. While interest is kept low, State bonds good security for redemption of, but no longer, 202. Labor of producing them small, 211, 222. Amount paid by the people for the use of, 211. Balancing power of, 217, 218. Not a legal tender, 271. Practically money, 271, 272. Bills of credit issued without constitutional right, 194, 274, 300.

Bank of England. Basis of, 215. Indorsed notes secure the bank notes of, 215. Issues of, 215, 216. Gains of, by rise of interest unfairly taken from people, 216. Weekly reports of, show that notes of, are secured by indorsed notes, and not by bullion, 217.

Borrowers. States paying high rates are most frequently, 183. Effects in Wisconsin of high interest on, 183, 184. Only the use of principal bought by, 227, 327.

Bullion. Why value of, is equal to that of coins, 55. Pretence that it is real wealth, 216. Amount of, compared with deposits in Bank of England, 217. Issues of Bank of England above £14,000,000, governed by, 345.

Business. What it is, 331, 332. What exchanges must be made by money to carry on, 338.

C.

Capital. Money not, 70, 125. Easy to make money to represent the value of, 125. Oppression of labor by, at present rates of interest, 80, 86, 91, 92, 95, 100, 106, 112, 114, 138, 151, 152, 174. Why money appears to be, 231.

Capital of Banks. Furnished partly by stockholders and partly by the bor

367

368   INDEX.

rowers of money, 196, 197. Under General Banking Law of the State of New York, 200. Security of, by whom furnished, 202, 207, 208. So-called specie, 205. How the, is made up, 205, 206. Proportion of the, furnished in specie by stockholders of banks in the State of New York, 209.
Cities. Consumers of wealth, 20, 99. Atlantic cities supposed to be cut off from country, 21. Majority of people in, poor, 21. How the wealth of nations accumulates in large cities, 97, 98, 99. Present rates of interest gather wealth in cities, 100, 101, 102. Table of accumulation, 102, 103, 104. Different result to, at one per cent., 105, 106. Loans of the city of New York to the country, 107. Accumulate wealth without earning it, 108. Disproportion of wealth of the State owned by the city of New York compared with its population, 108, 109. How to estimate disproportion, 110. Disproportion of wealth owned by the city of Boston, as compared with the State, 120, 121.
Coins. Increase in amount no improvement in means of distribution, 38. Of base metal could be made good money by law, 78. Are the material of money, not its power, 168. With good paper money at home could ship, to pay foreign balances, 298.
Commodities. Exchange of, indispensable, 31. Standard of value needed to exchange, 34. Money not a commodity, 69, 73, 74. Commodities not currency, 75.
Constitution of the United States. Powers of Congress in respect of money, 273. States debarred from exercising powers of Congress respecting money, 273. No change needed in, in order to establish just monetary system, 318.
Contracts. Could not be made without money, 34. Gambling, void in law, 34, 164. Varying and unjust on an unjust foundation, 35. Change with rate of interest, 36, 350, 327, 328, 332, 333, 350. Public standard or foundation unjust, 151, 174, 304, note. Which ought to be restricted and which left free, 164. Principle upon which, made between the banks and the people, 199. In large cities mostly paid by checks on banks, 219. Fulfilment of, between individuals and the government secured by paper instruments, 270. Money, how constituted to form a just foundation of, 365.
Credit. Definition of, 261. Extent of, 261. Necessity of, 262, 359. Banking system based upon, 263. State and United States stocks, a form of, 297.
Currency. Amount of, required, 254, 260, 285. Effects on a nation of a gold and silver, 254, 255, 290, 291. Must be national, 263. United States Bank could not regulate the, 263, 264. Security of a paper, 269. Character of, proposed, 274. How to make paper, a true representative of value, 275. Proportion of property required to secure a sufficient paper, 278. Mixture of specie in, 280. Different effects of a good and bad, 285. Borrowed of foreign nations, 292. Power of a paper, 293. Chief object of a, 295. Paper, will facilitate, not hinder foreign trade, 296. An easily deranged, a greater loss to the people than the failure of crops, 297.

D.

Debts. Definition of, 45. Money tender for, 45, 200. To absentees at six per cent. would impoverish the nation, 99, 100. Increase of national and state, shown at various rates of interest, 122, 123, 124. Of Southern and Western States, 124. Of nations and individuals, how caused, 134, 135, 292. Increased by a rise of interest, 155, 167, 202, 243. Require more labor and property to pay, 163. National debt of England increases depression of labor, 190, 244. Reduction of interest on English national debt would benefit producers, 191, 192, 244. Founded upon and paid in money, 196, 359. Legally payable in specie, 198. Curtailments of bank discounts increase, 239, 240. Under new monetary system, adjustment of, with foreign nations, 295.
Dependence, mutual, of all men, 31, 32, 33, 309, 310.
Discounts. Process of extending and contracting bank, 220, 221, 222, 223, 225. Of post-notes of Delaware and Hudson Canal Bank, 226, 227. Made by capitalists from 1836 to 1840, 228. Table of, at various rates, 235. Effects of refusal of, by banks, 238. Curtailment of, not a violation of law, 239.
Distribution. No agrarian proposed, 40, 320. Just standard will regulate, 40, 320. Unjust, owing to one cause, 246. Power of money opposed to just, 248. Money must be abundant to make just, 248. New monetary system will furnish just standard of, 306. Of wealth made by money under protection of law, 363, 364, 365.
Dollar. Most important measure, 58. Measures value every time it passes, 58. Value of, determined by rate of interest, 61. Value of, rises and falls with rate of interest, 64, 163, 327. Doubled in value, 64. Value of, not due to labor to mine and coin silver for it, 75. Measures more or less value according to rate of interest, 156. Human law cannot make naturally productive, 172. Greater than the government brains

INDEX. 369

that made it, 362. Machinery and labor cannot compete with, 362. How it varies in value, 325.

E.

Evils. Cannot alter past, 39. Of money national, 39, 2.8. Legislative, 81, 248. Second evil needed to modify first evil of bad monetary laws, 174. Must choose between two, 229. Popular way of accounting for, 247. Not diminished by their long continuance, 304, note. Many will disappear under just monetary system, 319. Root of most of present, 321, 322.
Exchange. Of commodities indispensable, 31, 32, 33. Medium of, necessary, 33, 125. Of commodities augmented by machinery, 37. Distinction between medium of, and articles of actual value, 68. Rates of, increased by a rise of interest, 236, 341, 342. Rate of, on Philadelphia, 13 per cent., 237, note. With good paper currency at home, bills of, could be more easily obtained, 299.

G.

Gambling. Compared with stock jobbing, 329, 330, 331. In stocks and money, how it affects producers, 332, 333.
Gold. Not used as material of money, must have been like other articles of trade, 72. Possesses no peculiar excellence, 72. Difference between use as utensils and as money, 72, 73. Of little intrinsic value, 77. Images of, innate value attributed to them, 245. With good paper currency would not be needed as money, 299. Institution of good paper money cannot affect intrinsic value of, 302. Superstitions worship of, 347, 348.
Government. Protects rights of property, 18, 329, 363, 364. Of United States supposed to confer all possible benefits, 27. Provides schools, 27. Established to protect interests of governed, 30. Ought to furnish money in the various States to represent value of their own property, 124. Determines what proportion of earnings of labor shall be paid for the use of capital, 152, 79. Directed by money-lenders, 169. English, intervene in collection of taxes, concealing cause of oppression, 191. General, reserves right to coin money and emit bills of credit, 194. State, has established banks, 194. Financial power instituted by, 242, note. Cannot institute a good currency on a specie basis, 263, 264. Present monetary laws tend to overthrow of, 318. Has left the value of money unsettled, 326. Just monetary system will sustain and preserve, 328, note. Cannot supervise individual agreements, 363. Must make general laws, 363. Establishes and sustains money to make and govern distribution of wealth, 364, 365.

I.

Income. Of English securities holder, how collected, 190. Money gathers an, whenever it is lent, and for longer or shorter periods, 240. Value of stocks varies with yearly, 325, 326, 330.
Innovation. Every improvement an, 38.
Interest. Valuable because can be exchanged for actual value, 44. Determines length of time in which borrower shall double lump of gold, 60. Does not grow on money or obligations, 61, 149, 171. Determines value of the dollar, 61. Can be established by frequent transfers of money to take the income of many pieces of property, 63, 64, 183. Must be kept uniform, that the money may be of uniform value, 64. Bentham's theory of, 65. Rate of, determines relative proportion of earnings paid to capital and labor, 80, 266. Governing power of distribution, 80, 266. Results to laborers of various rates of, 81. At seven per cent., 81, 83, 84, 87. At three per cent., 82, 83, 189, 190. At six per cent., 82, 91, 92, 94. At one per cent., 85, 88, 89, 93, 94, 144, 145. Results to borrowers of various rates, 86, 89, 90. Extent of operation of, 91. Establishes rent of property, 91, 145, 147, 170. Individuals cannot withdraw from law of, 95, 96, 165. Present rates of, gather the wealth in cities, 100, 266. Power of, invisible, but draws things visible to itself, 106, note, 168. Received by city of New York on loans to country, 107. Increase of value demanded by present legal rates compared with the increase of assessed valuations of the States of New York and Massachusetts, 111, 112, 113, 114, 115, 116, 117, 118, 119. At two and a half per cent. too high, 114. Doubling of principal at various rates of, 121, 122, 176. Accumulation of, on State and National debts, 122, 123, 308, 309. At seven per cent. accumulates property more rapidly than labor can earn it, 126. Table, 127, 128, 129, 130. Accumulation at one per cent., table, 130, 131, 132, 133. Two per cent. too high a rate, table, 135, 136, 137, 138, 189. Reduced would benefit producers whether prices should rise or fall in consequence of reduction, 139. Table of, at one per cent. and labor at $6 per day, 139, 140, 141, 142. How high and fluctuating rates of, affect producers, 142, 143, 307, 308.

When rates increase, property falls in price, 154, 155, 266. As interest increases, rents diminish, 157, 158. Value of money rises in direct proportion to increase of, while value of property and rents fall, 158, 159. Relative proportion of, to the principal doubled when rate of, rises to double, 159. Value of, at twelve per cent. four times greater than at six per cent, 160. Value of money increases in geometrical proportion to rate of, 160. Not the lender's money, but the borrower's obligation that bears, 169, 298. Means to pay, must be gained from property, 170, 171. A yearly tax levied on producers, 174. Reduced, will benefit laborers, 174. An essential power of money, 175. How to estimate the just rate of, 176, 177, 284. Should pay for labor to institute and circulate the money, 178, 284. Lowering of rate of, a benefit to producers whether property rise or fall, or remain at present prices, 178, 179, 180. Lowering of rate of, a benefit to trade, 181, 182. Low rate of, would not drive specie from the country, 182, 183. High in new countries, and centralizes property rapidly, 186, 187. Too high in old countries, 187, 188. Paid by the people on their indorsed notes given to the banks, 197. High rates increase indebtedness, 202. By whom paid on securities of banking capital under General Banking Law of the State of New York, 202, 203. Amount of, paid by the public to banks in State of Connecticut, 204, 205. Amount of, paid by people of State of New York on bank notes beyond professed specie capital, 211, 212. Payment of exorbitant rates of, accounts for commercial revulsions, 225. Rate of, paid on post notes of Delaware and Hudson Canal Bank in 1837, 226, 227. Differing rates of, in different sections of the country, 231, 232, 233, 234. Rates of, paid in New York in 1854, note, 240, 241. High rate of, cannot enable a too small sum of money to discharge debts, 259, 260. Under new monetary system money obtained at a low rate of, 307. Increase in, compared to increase in length of yardstick, 328.

L.

Labor. The producer of wealth, 19. Moderate amount produces good supply of comforts for man, 20, 247, note. Present labor indispensable, 24. Efforts to secure it a better reward, 30. Powerless to discharge debts, 48, 156. Present monetary laws opposed to the reward of, 96, 151, 318, 319, 361, 362, 363. Must produce what is gained by financiers, 172. Under just monetary system equivalent in useful, must be rendered for labor of others, 306. New monetary system will reward, 319, 320.

Laboring classes. Their poverty not due to their ignorance or extravagance, 23. Results if those unemployed in financial revulsions could have been set at work, 26. Ought not to need public schools for their children, 27, note. Make their own bargains, 28. No chance of securing their rights by combinations of labor, 80, 86, 99, 106, note, 152. At two per cent. interest they must double the capital of the nation in thirty-four and a half years, 138. Land-owners not their greatest oppressors, 147. When prices of products are low, laborers suffer, 163. Impossible for them to pay four or five per cent. interest and have comforts of life, 173. High rates of interest cause of their poverty, 190. Pay income of English bondholders, 190, 191. How to eradicate oppression of, 191. Do not cause financial revulsions, 242, 243, note. Prosperity increased by liberal loans by the banks, 243. Their condition in England when interest rises, 327.

Land. Has no natural monopolizing power, 148. Monopoly of, not so injurious as high rates of interest, 149, 150. How tenants of, are affected by high rates of interest, 150, 151. Land-owners of England not more oppressive than money-lenders, 190, 191. Policy to be pursued in the sale of public, 315, 316.

Laws. Fundamental, 17. Monetary, most important, 17, 18, 34, 264. Extremes of wealth and poverty in nations in proportion to the age of their monetary, 20. Make producers dependent on capitalists, 29. Cannot withdraw labor and products from influence of, 30. Must not interfere with freedom of contracts, 31. If monetary laws are evil, the contracts made in accordance with them must partake of the evil, 34, 165, 167. Prohibit gambling contracts, 34, 164, 329. Just monetary, more important than inventions, 38. Antiquity does not prove excellence, 39. Must institute and fix value of money to make it a tender, 45. Aim in regulating value of money, 45. Give money its properties, 45. Powers created by, 46. Immaterial; principles, not substances, 52. Profess to establish value of money in its material, but fail, 53. Monetary, enacted on false principle, 75, 169, 246, 247. Collection of property in few hands due to monetary, 86. Subsequent laws can do little to modify evil of false basis of fundamental, 174. Require performance of impossibilities, 214. Making gold and silver a tender adapted to build up monarchies. 215. How to ascertain whether they affect the value of money, 301. Benefits of just, 316, 317, 320. Better leave to children just, than wealth, 320. Rights of property must be protected by general, 363. Money sustained by, while making the distribution of wealth, 363.

Lien. On property what, 43. Money a public, 43, 50. Money superior to mortgages and judgments, 43. Money a lien on property, 43, 50, 270. Notes of hand liens on property, 43, 50, 270. Lien engraven on silver plate not more valuable than paper instrument, 66, 67.

M.

Machines, labor-saving, have not relieved producers, 37.

Material. Of money cannot be equal in value to the property and products which it exchanges, 46. Legal power of, superior to natural value, 50. Value of money not dependent on, 50. Gold or silver material of money used for spoons no longer money, 51. Yardstick of elastic, 64. Of money a legalized agent, 71. Natural powers of, do not make it money, 71. Quantity and quality of, do not fix value of money, 79.

Measure, of value changeable, its effects, 333, 334.

Measures, definition of, 56. Determined by law, 57, 65. Money a measure of value, 57. Not invariable, fraudulent, 57. Dollar most important of, 58. Money measures property as often as it passes, 58. Distinction between measures of value and articles of value, 58. Measure of value passes to seller, 59. Divisible, 59, 69. Farmers, etc., do not inquire whether enough can be had to weigh and measure quantity of products, 66, note. Material of, indifferent, 71. Any other, may better vary than the dollar, 326, 335.

Money. Gold and silver, not a substitute for other productions, 19. A tender for articles of trade, 34. Value and prices of products estimated by, 34. Variations in value of, illustrated by Government bonds, 35. Nature of, not understood by political economists, 36. Nor by laborers, 230. Power of, legal, 43, 259. National medium of exchange, 45. A public tender, 45, 48, 231. Definition of, 46. Properties or powers of, 46. Material of, 46. Must have legal power to represent value, 48, 177, 266. Held in lieu of property, 48. Only legal tender, 48. Determines value of labor and property, 48. Negotiable power of, 50. Legal power superior to natural value of material, 50, 256. Cannot be used as actual value, 50, 51, 63. Power of, not material, but legal, 52, 53, 55, 168, 256, 259. Worth of, not in material, but in legal representative value, 53. Of paper, can fulfil functions of coins because both are representatives, 54, 55. Measures value, 57. Individuals prohibited from making and issuing, 58. Governments reserve right to coin, 58. Accumulates value by interest, 60. Not a producer of value, 60, 149, 183, 349. Valuable in proportion to its rate of interest, 61, 177, 266. Worthless if it lose power to draw good interest, 62. Illustrated by Continental money, 62. How Continental, could have been made good, 63, 281. Capable of measuring its own value frequently, 63. Value not fixed nor regulated by weight and kind of metal, 66, 177. Must be parted with to make valuable, 67, or useful, 68, 69, 170. Exchanges property, 68. Legal, not actual equivalent for property, 69, 76. Not real capital, 70, 125, 308. Not invested in property, but passes on, 70, note. Value of, does not inhere in precious metals, 73. Not a commodity, 74. Labor to procure, does not make value of, 75. Legal standard of value, 79, 230, 231. Power of, unavoidable, 91, 152, 165. Legal power of, most influential of all earthly powers, 167, 168. Strictly speaking, always dead, 170, 171, 298, 349. Not susceptible of being improved by labor, 171. Ought to be a legal tender, 177. Worthless if it does not represent intrinsic value, 177. Why scarce in Wisconsin, when plenty in New York, 184. Rates at which lent in Wall street, when discounts are contracted, 223. Speculations in, their effect on producers, 228, 332, 333. Must be abundant to make just distribution, 248. Power of, unjust and oppressive, 248. Amount of, should be limited only by wants of trade, 254. Bad results of limited amount of, shown in miniature nation, 254, 255. Power of, omnipresent: used in the absence of the material substance, 257, 258, 259. Certain amount of, required to fulfil business engagements, 259, 338, 339. Amount of, required in business small compared with transactions, 288. Power of, commands labor, 349. People buy or rent only the use of, 327. Operations in, their effect on commerce and foreign trade, 353, 354. A little devil, 357. With unjust power, will make an unjust distribution of wealth, 364. Legal position of, 364. Description of, which will rightly govern distribution, 365.

Money-market. Would be none if money were rightly instituted and regulated, 230. Can be affected by two or three wealthy individuals, 256.

372 INDEX.

Condition of, in June, 1843, and various operations in, 335, 336, 337.

Mortgage. Rights given by a, 43. Holder of a, must cancel if money is tendered, 43. On what, value of a, depends, 43. Increased value as to property when interest rises, but lessened as to money, 155.

N.

National Safety Fund. Why new institution for issuing money so named, 275. How the money of, should be issued, 275. Security of money of, 275, 278, 279, 351. Means of funding money of, must be provided, 275. Form of MONEY of, 276. Form of SAFETY FUND NOTE of, 276. Money of, will bear no interest, but can be exchanged for interest-bearing Safety Fund notes, 276. Rate of interest on money and notes of, 276, 351, 352. Money of, will perform all the functions of money, 277. Money of, more convenient than coins, 277, 278. Small proportion of property required to secure sufficient currency, 278. Amount probably needed, 279, 288, 289, 358. Rate of interest uniform on all loans, 279. Mortgage securities of, may remain outstanding so long as interest is regularly paid, 279. Purchasing power of money of, 279. Money of, not local nor individual, 280. Mixture of specie with money of, can be easily provided, 280. Mixture of specie with money of, not needed, 280. Money of, essentially different from Continental money or assignats of France, 280. How the Continental money and the assignats of France could have been made good, 63, 281. Money of, will have no monopolizing power, 281, 282. Why money of, should be founded on permanent property, 282, note. Rate of interest at six per cent. on loans of, too high, 283, 293. Just rate of interest on loans of, 284. Income from loans of, 285. Principal institution and branches of, 286. Directors and officers of, 286. Payment of loans of money of, and interest on mortgages given to, to be enforced, 286. Denominations of money of, 286, 287. Protection from counterfeits of money and notes of, 287. Fractional money of, will maintain its relative value, 288. Hoarding of money of could not disturb circulation, 289, note. Advantages of, over silver money illustrated in small nation, 290, 291, 292. Money of, can be made to exceed coins in value, 292, 293. With money of, should not depend on other nations for loans, 299. No injustice done to banks or individuals by institution of, 300, 301, 302. What risk of unfaithfulness in management of, 303. What objection to, on account of decrease of incomes, 303, 304. What objection to, on account of custom, 304, 305. What advantage from, to States in making internal improvements, 308. What advantage from uniform value of money of, 309. With money of, harmony of industries, 310. Establishment of, will benefit laborer who neither borrows nor lends, 311, 312. Will not prevent the use of talents, 312. Will promote benevolence, 313. Will not make men indolent, 313, 314. Will not infringe rights of property, 319. Means to put in operation and sustain, 323.

New Jersey, State of, how affected by high rates of interest in New York and Philadelphia, 334.

Note. Dependence of legal value of, on actual value of property of drawer, 49, 69. Trifling labor to provide note, 49, 69. Not payable in products, but in money, 49, 69. Value increased as to property when interest rises, but lessened as to money, 155. Offerings of notes for discount greatly increased when there is a scarcity of money, 225. Discounts off well-indorsed notes, from 1836 to 1840, 228.

P.

Paper. Power delegated to, 49. Becomes a representative of value, 49. Value added to its inherent qualities, 49. Legal value of, depends on actual value, 49. Power of attorney does not increase inherent power of, 49. Worthless without property, 50. Papers securing English national debt, laws could annul value of, 67. Paper need not be abandoned for making obligations, because more exists than is needed, 77, 272. Money of, representing specie should have a specie dollar for every dollar of, 200. Currency of, can be established of adequate amount and uniform value, 269. Titles to land, loans of money, and other credits secured by legal instruments on, 269, 270. Endowed with requisite legal powers can fulfil uses of money, 270, 272. In form of bank-notes now circulates as money, 271. Abundance of, not an objection to its use as the material of money, 272.

Prices. Fall when interest rises, 154. Low, injurious to producers, 161. Illustration of, 161, 162. Why low for labor in England, France, and Germany, where interest is low, and high in United States where interest is high, 185, 186, 187. Low, where money is scarce, 255, 256. Fluctuations in, lessened by institution of new monetary system, 301.

Production. Active when the wealthy few lend money liberally, 168. Large, gives better reward to labor than half-production at double price, 163. Laws of, not altered by laws establishing income power, 173. Will have just reward with low interest on non-producing capital, 175. Would increase if interest were reduced, 184. Facility in, no reason for maintaining high rate of interest, 189. No increased, made by changing market value of stocks, 223, note. Facilities to, afforded by good paper currency, 297, 300.

Products. Accumulate in hands of nonproducers, 20. Injustice of present distribution, 24. Apparent overstock of, during financial revulsions, 25. Best sent to cities, 28, 99. Yearly, applied to two purposes, paying interest and rent on capital, and paying for labor, 80. Accumulation of, at six per cent. interest, illustrated, 93, 94. Accumulation of, at one per cent., illustrated, 94. How increased rates of interest affect producers and distributers of, 145. Planter, 145. Manufacturer, 146 Merchant, 146. Have no natural monopolizing power, 148. Market value of, decreases with rise of interest, 155. Good market for, when labor is at a high price, 163. Plenty of money would not destroy their value, 163. Of hatter and shoemaker must be exchanged, 165. Required for rent of land lessened by lowering rate of interest, 181. Have no legal value, nor power over money, 231. Low prices of, from scarcity of money, 256.

Property. The product of labor, 19. Must have use of, to preserve life, 25. No change in ownership from regulation of money, 40. Cannot discharge debts except with creditor's consent, 45. Real value in, 46. Powerless to discharge debts, 48. Power of attorney conveys control of, 40. Difference between money and, 63. Money of little real value compared with, 76. Money invested in, accumulates as if lent on interest, 108. Erroneous idea that a large property can be accumulated by one man's labor, 130. Monopolizing power of, artificial, 148. Means of concentration of, 151. Price of, falls when interest rises, 154, 155. Legal rights of, at variance with actual justice, 165. Accumulates rapidly in few hands in United States, 188. Has no power over money, 257.

R.

Rent. How soon, paid in property at seven per cent., doubles property in hands of owner, 81, 83, 87. At three per cent., 82. At six per cent., 82. At one per cent., 85, 88. Accumulations by, result of law of interest, 86. Must conform to standard, 88, 153. Determined by rate of interest, 145, 170, 171. Rising to double the land will sell for double, 159.

Representative. Of value necessary in division and distribution of products, 33. Money and obligations represent actual value, 44. Powers of a, 46, 47. Power of a, specific, 47. Power of attorney makes a man representative of property, 49. Silver dollar and paper dollar both, 54. Representative of property ought to be furnished to applicants in their own States, 124. An obligation for the payment of money a private, 155. Of value, can be made where there is actual value, 260. With true monetary system the people not compelled to have unsafe and imperfect, 300.

Revulsions. In trade every few years, 25. Over-production and over-trading supposed cause of, 26, 242, note. Real cause in power governing distribution, 27. Progress of, illustrated, 222, 223, 224, 225. Neither labor nor products can prevent, 256. Safety Fund money will protect from, 275. Due not to employer or employed, but to false institution of money, 327. How one can be easily brought about, 355, 356.

Revulsion of 1857. Discounts made by banks in city of New York control supply of money throughout the country, 339. Contraction, following on suspension of Ohio Life and Trust Company, 339. Consequent payment of usury by debtors, 340. Banks force payment of usury on the people, 340. Rates of usury paid, 341. Gains of usurers, 341. Profits of merchants compared with rates of interest and exchange, 341, 342. Increase of indebtedness, 342. Unemployed laborers, 342. Loss of production, 342. Depreciation in price of property, 343. Accumulation of specie proposed as a remedy, 343. Specie not wanted, 343. How the crisis could have been avoided, 343. Professions of the banks, 343, 544. Their power to prostrate business, 344. Why have these bits of metal and paper such power? 344. Measures that afforded relief in the United States in 1834, 344, 345; and in England in 1847, 245. Same means must be used to relieve that ought to have been used to prevent, 346. The power lies with the banks in the city of New York, 346.

S.

Silver. Made into spoon does not make a money spoon, 52. Mere metal not a tender, 52. Silver dollar fulfils the uses of money no better than paper dollar, illustrated, 54. Dollar of, cannot make twelve or two valuable representatives of itself, 200.

Specie. Capital of banks has little basis of, 198. Bank-notes payable on demand in, 198. Law does not furnish them with, to pay their debts, and redeem their bank-notes, 198. Paper money cannot represent, unless there be a dollar in, for every paper dollar, 200. Banks could not pay liabilities in, 202. Amount of, held by the banks in the State of Connecticut, table, 204, 205. Amount of, held by Connecticut banks a fraction more than four per cent. of their loans, 205. Bank capital of, how made up, 205, 206. Banks have enough to redeem only one-fifth of their capital stock, 209. Could never have paid, in, for a week, 211. Not enough of, in existence to fulfil requirements made by law, 214. With basis of, impossible to establish a good currency, 263, 264. Lying in vault, performs no function of money, 271, 298. Borrowed of other nations, assists only in making our own exchanges, 298. Basis of, not better than land, 301.

Stocks. Cause of rise and fall of, 330, 331.

Supply and demand. Agreements according to, 28. Do not regulate value of money, 61. Do not make rate of interest uniform nor just, 166.

T.

Tender. Law making money a tender imparts life to metals, 60. No money should circulate which is not a, 177. The tender for debts traded in by banks, 222. Nothing but money a, 246.

Trade. Not carried on by governments, 296. Foreign, greatly facilitated by use of paper currency at home, 296. Under just monetary system balance of, in favor of United States, 300.

True monetary system. Its proposed operation and objects, 274.

U.

Usury. Rates of, published in newspapers, 241. Laws against, petitions to abolish, 249. Reasons given for abolishing laws against, 249, 250. Reasons for retaining laws against, 249, 250, 251, 252. Power of, to monopolize wealth, 250.

V.

Value. Definition of, 41. Of property, how estimated, 41. Kinds of value, 42. Definition of actual value, 42. Definition of legal value, 42. Distinction between the two kinds of, illustrated, 42. Of labor and property controlled by money, 48. Actual and legal, of note compared, 49. Of estate represented by owner, 49. Of lands, goods, etc., not dependent on legislation, 51. Of money, not in material, 59. Of money, depends on its legal powers, 50, 53, 55, 61, 64, 66, 78, 266. Money, legal standard of, 79, 258. How to affix true value to money, 177. Of money, standard governing market value of stocks, 224, note. Of stocks made uniform by uniform value of money, 309. Just standard of, will conform to natural laws of production, 184, 316.

W.

Wealth. Not distributed according to usefulness of owner, 20, 245. Accumulates in cities, 20. Respective amounts flowing to city and country opposed to just reciprocity, 21. Disproportion of, owned by few in city of New York, 21. In United States, 22. How to estimate disproportion of, 22. Unfair distribution of, how caused, 31. Present possessors of, not worse than others, 39. How accumulated in cities, 97. Where it shall be centralized, determined by money-lenders, 168. Money supposed to be, but not really wealth, 172. Centralizes, according to rate of interest, 168. Of nations, not in the vaults of banks, 245.

www.ingramcontent.com/pod-product-compliance
Lightning Source LLC
Chambersburg PA
CBHW030345230426
43664CB00007BB/543